Network+ Test Success

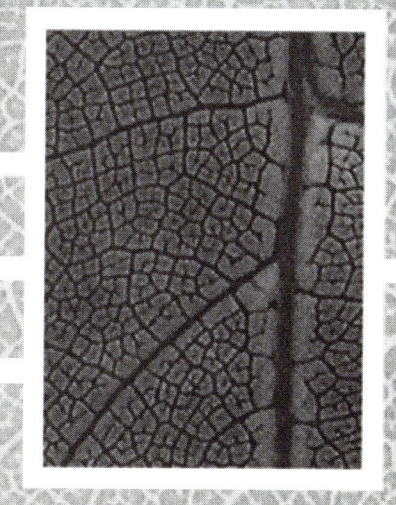

Network+™ Test Success™

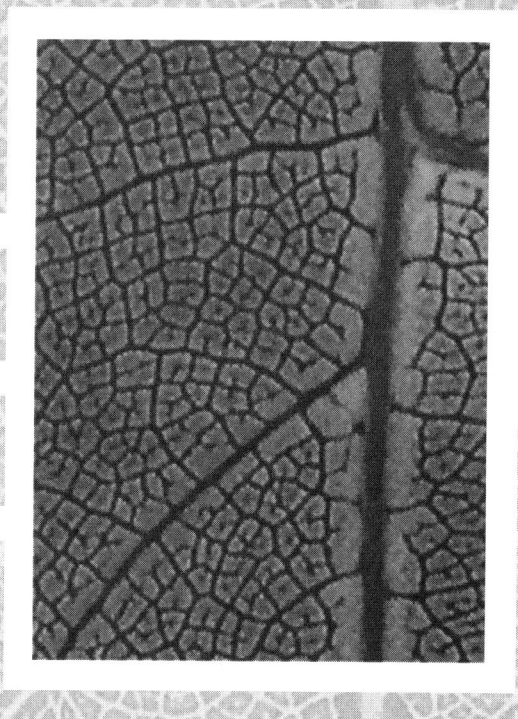

David Groth
Matthew Perkins

San Francisco • Paris • Düsseldorf • Soest • London

Associate Publisher: Guy Hart-Davis
Contracts and Licensing Manager: Kristine O'Callaghan
Acquisitions Editor: Neil Edde
Developmental Editor: Linda Lee
Editors: Kathy Simpson, Marilyn Smith
Project Editor: Malka Geffen
Technical Editor: Donald Fuller
Book Designer: Bill Gibson
Graphic Illustrators: Tony Jonick, Jerry Williams
Electronic Publishing Specialist: Adrian Woolhouse
Project Team Leader: Teresa Trego
Proofreader: Susan Berge
Indexer: Nancy Guenther
Cover Designer: Archer Design
Cover Illustrator/Photographer: FPG International

SYBEX, Network Press, and the Network Press logo are registered trademarks of SYBEX Inc.

Test Success is a trademark of SYBEX Inc.

Screen reproductions produced with Collage Complete.

Collage Complete is a trademark of Inner Media Inc.

TRADEMARKS: SYBEX has attempted throughout this book to distinguish proprietary trademarks from descriptive terms by following the capitalization style used by the manufacturer.

The author and publisher have made their best efforts to prepare this book, and the content is based upon final release software whenever possible. Portions of the manuscript may be based upon pre-release versions supplied by software manufacturer(s). The author and the publisher make no representation or warranties of any kind with regard to the completeness or accuracy of the contents herein and accept no liability of any kind including but not limited to performance, merchantability, fitness for any particular purpose, or any losses or damages of any kind caused or alleged to be caused directly or indirectly from this book.

Copyright ©1999 SYBEX Inc., 1151 Marina Village Parkway, Alameda, CA 94501. World rights reserved. No part of this publication may be stored in a retrieval system, transmitted, or reproduced in any way, including but not limited to photocopy, photograph, magnetic or other record, without the prior agreement and written permission of the publisher.

Library of Congress Card Number: 99-62577
ISBN: 0-7821-2548-4

Manufactured in the United States of America

10 9 8 7 6 5 4 3 2 1

This book is dedicated to my little naches. May you be happy and healthy.
—*David Groth*

I would like to dedicate this book to my loving wife Joy Marie Story-Perkins, who stood by my side throughout, and to my brother Nicholas Rock Perkins — always remember to smile and look at the bright side of life.
—*Matthew Perkins*

Acknowledgments

It takes many people to put a book together; this book is no exception. First, I would like to thank my co-author (and now brother-in-law) Matt Perkins. He wrote most of this book and should be proud of his accomplishments. Matt is system a engineer for Ikon Solutions in Phoenix, Arizona, and is well on his way to becoming one of that company's top system engineers.

Thanks also to my technical editor, Don Fuller, who checked this book for technical accuracy. Don is a senior technical instructor at New Horizons Computer Learning Center of Long Island. He has more than 20 years' experience in the computer industry and maintains the following certifications: A+, MCP, MCT, MCSE, MCSE + I, CNA, and CCNA.

This book would not have existed if not for the developmental editor at Sybex, Linda Lee. Thank you for putting up with all my phone calls and neurotic e-mails! Additionally, thanks to Malka Geffen and Kathy Simpson for turning my first drafts into a cohesive, useful test-success guide and exam-preparation tool.

I would also like to acknowledge my wife, family, and friends. My wife, Linda, tirelessly wrote and edited the Glossary, as well as kept me on the right track. She was a real trouper, because she did all that work while she was pregnant and sometimes sick. Thank you to my family members and friends who understood when I couldn't go out because I had to work on the book. I really appreciate your understanding.

Finally, thank you, the reader, for purchasing this book. I know that it contains all the information you need to pass the test. If you have questions about Network+ or this book, feel free to e-mail me at dgroth@corpcomm.net, and I can forward requests to the other author, if necessary. The other authors and I worked very hard on this book to make it the best Network+ study guide available, and I hope you feel that it is.

Contents at a Glance

Introduction   *xv*

Unit 1	Network Fundamentals	1
Unit 2	The Physical Layer	49
Unit 3	The Data Link Layer	67
Unit 4	The Network Layer	79
Unit 5	The Transport Layer	89
Unit 6	TCP/IP Fundamentals	101
Unit 7	TCP/IP Suite: Utilities	131
Unit 8	Remote Connectivity	149
Unit 9	Security	169
Unit 10	Implementing a Network Installation	183
Unit 11	The Change-Control System	209
Unit 12	Maintaining and Supporting the Network	247
Unit 13	Identifying, Assessing, and Responding to Problems	265
Unit 14	Troubleshooting the Network	277
Unit 15	Final Exam	319
Appendix	Study Questions and Sample Tests Answers	341
Glossary		389

Index   *431*

Table of Contents

Introduction   *xv*

Unit 1		**Network Fundamentals**	**1**
		Basic Network Structure	5
		Physical Topologies	5
		Network Hierarchy	9
		Major Network Operating Systems	10
		Novell NetWare	10
		Microsoft Windows NT	10
		Unix	11
		Major Protocols	12
		IPX/SPX	12
		TCP/IP	12
		NetBEUI	13
		Fault Tolerance and High Availability	13
		Mirroring	14
		Striping	14
		Duplexing	16
		Tape Backup	17
		Volumes	18
		The OSI Model	19
		Networking Media and Connectors	21
		Media Options	21
		Distance and Speed	24
		Connector Types	24
		Networking Elements	27
		Duplex Communications	28
		Network Categories	28
		Computer Roles on a Network	28
		Common Connection Devices	30
		Bandwidth	30
		Gateway	31

Unit 2		**The Physical Layer**	**49**
		Troubleshooting on the Physical Layer	51
		Network Interface Card Configuration	51
		Network Interface Card Diagnostics	53
		Understanding Networking Components	54
		Hubs	55
		Switching Hubs	56
		Multistation Access Units (MAUs)	57
		Repeaters	57
		Transceivers	57
Unit 3		**The Data Link Layer**	**67**
		Bridges	69
		The IEEE 802 Standards	70
		802.2	70
		802.3	70
		802.4	71
		802.5	71
		MAC Addresses	72
Unit 4		**The Network Layer**	**79**
		Routing	81
		Routers	81
		Brouters	81
		Routable Protocols	82
		Route Selection	83
		Default Gateways	84
		Subnetworks	84
Unit 5		**The Transport Layer**	**89**
		Transport Options	91
		Connection-Oriented Transmissions	91
		Connectionless Transmissions	92
		Name Resolution	92
		Service-Requester-Initiated	93
		Service-Provider-Initiated	93

Unit 6 — TCP/IP Fundamentals — 101

- TCP/IP Fundamentals — 103
  - IP Default Gateways — 104
  - Windows TCP/IP Concepts — 104
  - Individual TCP/IP Protocols — 106
  - Domain Server Hierarchies — 108
- TCP/IP Addressing — 110
  - Network Address Classes — 110
  - Port Numbering — 111
- TCP/IP Configuration Concepts — 112
  - IP Proxy — 113
  - Workstation TCP/IP Configuration Parameters — 113

Unit 7 — TCP/IP Suite: Utilities — 131

- ARP — 133
- NBTSTAT — 134
- NETSTAT — 135
- FTP — 135
- Ping — 136
- ipconfig/winipcfg — 137
- tracert — 138
- Telnet — 139

Unit 8 — Remote Connectivity — 149

- Remote-Connectivity Concepts — 151
  - Point to Point Protocol (PPP) — 151
  - Serial Line Internet Protocol (SLIP) — 152
  - Point to Point Tunneling Protocol (PPTP) — 153
  - Integrated Services Digital Network (ISDN) — 154
  - Public Switched Telephone Network (PSTN) — 156
- Dial-Up Networking — 157
  - Remote-Connection Requirements — 157
  - Modem-Configuration Parameters — 157

Unit 9		**Security**	**169**
		Network Security Models	171
		User-Level Security	172
		Share-Level Security	172
		Passwords	172
		Encryption	173
		Firewalls	174
Unit 10		**Implementing a Network Installation**	**183**
		Network Preinstallation	185
		Accounts	185
		Passwords	186
		IP Addresses	187
		IP Configuration	187
		Relevant Standard Operating Procedures (SOPs)	187
		Protocols	188
		Environmental Factors Affecting Computer Networks	188
		Room Conditions	188
		Device Location	190
		Computer Equipment	190
		Error Messages	191
		Network Elements	191
		Peripheral Ports	191
		External SCSI Connectors	192
		Network Components	193
		UTP Cable Installation Issues	196
Unit 11		**The Change-Control System**	**209**
		Documenting a Workstation Baseline	214
		Returning a System to Its Original State	215
		Performing Workstation Backups	216
		Tape Backup	217
		Other Removable Backup Media	218
		Folder Replication	219

Removing Unnecessary Software Components		221
Understanding Local Changes That Cause Adverse Network Effects		222
Version Conflicts		222
Overwritten DLLs		223
Local-Resource Use		224
Performing Drive Mapping		224
Drive Mapping in Windows 95/98 and NT		224
Drive Mapping in NetWare		225
Mapping Drives in Unix		226
Capturing Printer Ports		226
Capturing a Printer Port in Windows 95/98 and NT		227
Capturing a Printer Port in NetWare		227
Capturing a Printer Port in Unix		228
Verifying Network and Critical-Application Functionality		228
Verifying Equipment Functionality		229
Using Permissions for Administration		229
Understanding Network-Administration Concepts		230
Login Accounts		231
Administrative Utilities		231
Profiles		232
Rights		232
Policies and Procedures		232
Unit 12	**Maintaining and Supporting the Network**	**247**
Support Documentation		249
Patches		250
Fixes		250
Upgrades		250
Network-Maintenance Issues		251
Network Backup		251
Network Patches and Fixes		256
Antivirus Procedures		256
Unit 13	**Identifying, Assessing, and Responding to Problems**	**265**
Determining the Nature of an Apparent Network Problem		267
Information Transfer		268

	User Training (Handholding)	268
	Technical Service	269
	Prioritizing Multiple Network Problems	269

Unit 14 Troubleshooting the Network 277

Identifying the Problem	281
Determining Whether the Problem Exists Across the Network	282
Determining Whether the Problem Is a Workstation, Workgroup, LAN, or WAN	282
Determining Whether the Problem Is Consistent or Replicable	283
Troubleshooting a Network Problem Systematically	283
Identify the Issue	284
Re-Create the Problem	284
Isolate the Cause	285
Formulate a Correction	285
Implement the Correction	286
Test the Solution	286
Document the Problem and Solution	286
Give Feedback	287
Determining Whether the Problem Is the Operator or the System	287
Recognizing Physical and Logical Trouble Indicators	287
Checking Link Lights	288
Checking Power Lights	288
Checking Error Logs and Displays	289
Running Performance Monitors	290
Using Common Network Troubleshooting Resources	290
Knowledge Bases on the World Wide Web	291
Telephone Technical Support	291
Vendor Support CDs	291
Determining the Most Likely Cause of a Problem	292
Recognizing Abnormal Physical Conditions	292
Isolating Patch-Cable Faults	293
Checking Server Status	293

	Identifying Configuration Problems	294
	Checking for Viruses	295
	Validating User Accounts	296
	Verifying Login Procedures	296
	Running Appropriate Diagnostics	296
	Using Common Network Tools	297
	Crossover Cable	297
	Hardware Loopback	298
	Tone Generator and Tone Locator	299
	Selecting the Appropriate Troubleshooting Tools	300
Unit 15	**Final Exam**	**319**
Appendix	**Study Questions and Sample Tests Answers**	**341**
	Unit 1 Answers	342
	Unit 2 Answers	348
	Unit 3 Answers	351
	Unit 4 Answers	352
	Unit 5 Answers	354
	Unit 6 Answers	356
	Unit 7 Answers	360
	Unit 8 Answers	362
	Unit 9 Answers	364
	Unit 10 Answers	366
	Unit 11 Answers	369
	Unit 12 Answers	374
	Unit 13 Answers	376
	Unit 14 Answers	378
	Unit 15 Answers	383
Glossary		**389**
Index		*431*

Introduction

One of the greatest challenges facing corporate America today is finding people who are qualified to manage corporate computer networks. Almost every company uses computers, and almost all companies connect their computers by using networks.

Toward that end, many companies that produce network products have developed certifications to test people on their knowledge of those products. The problem was that until now, no certification track tested a person's general knowledge of networking. The Computer Technology Industry Association (developer of the general hardware certification, A+) developed the Network+ certification for people who have 18 to 24 months of networking experience.

Why should you become Network+ certified? The main benefits are that you will have greater earning potential and that an Network+ certification carries with it industry recognition. Certification can be your key to a new job, a higher salary—or both.

So what's stopping you? If you don't know what to expect from the tests or are worried that you might not pass it, this book is for you.

Your Key to Passing the Network+ Exam

This book gives you the key to passing the Network+ exam. Inside, you'll find *all* the information that's relevant to this exam, including hundreds of practice questions, all designed to make sure that when you take the real exam, you'll be ready for even the most specific questions.

Understand the Exam Objectives

To help you prepare for certification exams, CompTIA provides a list of exam objectives for each test. This book is structured according to the objectives for the Network+ exam, which measure your understanding of basic network components, as well as your understanding of how to design, administer, and troubleshoot many vendors' networks.

The more than 400 study questions bolster your knowledge of the information that is relevant to each objective and of the exam itself. You learn exactly what you need to know without wasting time on background material or detailed explanations.

This book prepares you for the exam in the shortest amount of time possible—although to be ready for the real world, you need to study the subject in much greater depth and get a good deal of hands-on practice.

Get Ready for the Real Thing

More than 200 sample test questions prepare you for the test-taking experience. These multiple-choice questions resemble actual exam questions—and some are even more difficult than those on the exam. If you can pass the Sample Tests at the end of each unit and the Final Exam at the end of the book, you'll know that you're ready.

Is This Book for You?

This book is intended for people who have 18 to 24 months of networking experience and is especially well-suited for people in the following categories:

- Students who are using courseware or taking a course to prepare for the exam, and who need to supplement their study material with test-based practice questions.

- Network engineers who have worked with the product but want to make sure that there are no gaps in their knowledge.

- Anyone who has studied for the exam—by using self-study guides, by participating in computer-based training, by taking classes, or by getting on-the-job experience—and wants to make sure that this preparation is adequate.

Understanding Network+ Certification

To become Network+ certified, you must pass only the Network+ exam.

> **TIP** For the most up-to-date certification information, visit CompTIA's Web site at http://www.comptia.org.

Preparing for the Network+ Exam

To prepare for the Network+ certification exam, you should try to work with networks as much as possible. In addition, you can learn about the products and exams through a variety of resources, including the following:

Instructor-led courses

Online training   This option is useful for people who cannot find any courses in their area or who do not have the time to attend classes.

Publications   If you prefer to use a book to help you prepare for the Network+ test, you can choose among a wide variety of publications. These publications range from complete study guides (such as the Network Press *Network+ Study Guide*, which cover the Network+ exam in more detail) to test-preparedness books like this one.

After you complete your courses, training, or study guides, you'll find *Network+ Test Success* to be an excellent resource for making sure that you are prepared for the test. This book will help you discover whether you've got the exam covered or still need to fill in some holes.

> For more Network+ information, point your browser to the Sybex Web site, where you'll find certification information and descriptions of other quality titles in the Network Press line of Network+ related books. Go to http://www.sybex.com.

Scheduling and Taking an Exam

When you think that you are ready to take an exam, call Prometric Testing Centers at (800) 755-EXAM (755-3926). The company will tell you where to find the closest testing center. Before you call, however, get out your credit card, because each exam costs $185. (If you've used this book to prepare yourself thoroughly, chances are that you'll have to shell out that $185 only once.)

> The fee for the exam stated here is current at the time this book was published. Also, if you are a member of CompTIA, you will get a discount.

You can schedule the exam for a time that is convenient for you. The exams are downloaded from Prometric to the testing center; you show up at your scheduled time and take the exam on a computer.

When you complete the exam, you will know right away whether you passed or not. At the end of the exam, you receive a score report, listing the six areas in which you were tested and telling you how you performed. If you pass the exam, you don't need to do anything else—Prometric uploads the test results to CompTIA. If you don't pass, you can pay another $185 to schedule the exam again. But at least you will know from the score report the areas where you performed poorly, so you can study the pertinent information more carefully.

Test-Taking Hints

If you know what to expect, your chances of passing the exam will be much greater. The following sections provide some tips that can help you achieve success.

Get There Early and Be Prepared   Right before the exam is your last chance to review. Bring your copy of *Network+ Test Success*, and review any areas about which you feel unsure. If you need a drink of water or a visit to the restroom, take the time before the exam. When your exam starts, it will not be paused for these needs.

When you arrive for your exam, you will be asked to present two forms of identification. You will also be asked to sign a piece of paper, verifying that you understand the testing rules (the rule that says you will not cheat on the exam, for example).

Before you start the exam, you will have the opportunity to take a practice exam. This exam is not related to Network+; it is offered simply to give you a feel for the exam-taking process.

What You Can and Can't Take in with You   These exams are closed-book exams. The only thing that you can take in is scratch paper provided by the testing center. Use this paper as much as possible to diagram the questions. (Many times, diagramming questions helps make the answer clear.) You will have to give this paper back to the test administrator at the end of the exam.

Many testing centers are very strict about what you can take into the testing room. Some centers will not even allow you to bring in items such as zipped-up purses. If you feel tempted to take in any outside material, be aware that many testing centers use monitoring devices, such as video and audio equipment (so don't swear, even if you are alone in the room).

Prometric Testing Centers takes the test-taking process and test validation very seriously.

Test Approach   As you take the test, if you know the answer to a question, fill it in and move on. If you're not sure of the answer, make your best guess and then mark the question, so that you can return and answer it after you have answered the ones that you know.

At the end of the exam, you can review the questions. Depending on the amount of time remaining, you can review all of the questions, or you can review only the questions that you were unsure about. I always like to double-check all my answers, just in case I misread any of the questions on the first pass. (Sometimes, half of the battle is trying to figure out exactly what a question means.) I often find that a related question provides a clue about a question that I was unsure of.

Be sure to answer all questions. Unanswered questions are scored as incorrect and are counted against you. Also, make sure that you keep an eye on the remaining time, so that you can pace yourself accordingly.

If you do not pass the exam, note everything that you can remember while the exam is still fresh in your mind, to help you prepare for your next try. Although the next exam will not be exactly the same, the questions will be similar, and you won't want to make the same mistakes again.

When You Become Certified

When you become Network+ certified, CompTIA provides some items to prove that you are Network+ certified:

- A Network+ lapel pin to show the world that you are Network+ certified
- A Network+ logo and use guidelines (you can put the Network+ logo on your business cards, for example)
- A Network+ certificate, suitable for framing

How to Use This Book

This book is designed to help you prepare for the Network+ exam. It reviews all the objectives and relevant test-taking information, and offers you a chance to test your knowledge through study questions and sample tests.

The units in this book correspond to the CompTIA objective groupings. Unit 15 is a Final Exam, which contains test questions that pertain to all the preceding units.

For each unit, do the following things:

1. Review the exam-objectives list at the beginning of the unit. (You may want to check the CompTIA Web site at http://www.comptia.org to make sure that the objectives haven't changed since the book was published.)

2. Read the reference material that follows the objectives list. This section helps you brush up on the information that you need to know for the exam.

3. Review your knowledge in the Study Questions section. **This section consists of straightforward questions that test your knowledge of the topic. Answers to Study Questions are listed in Appendix A at the back of the book.**

4. When you feel sure of your knowledge of the area, take the Sample Test. The Sample Test's content and style match those of the real exam. Set yourself a time limit, based on the number of questions: A general rule is that you should be able to answer 20 questions in 30 minutes. When you've finished, check your answers in Appendix A in the back of the book. If you answer at least 85 percent of the questions correctly within the time limit (the first time you take the Sample Test), you're in good shape. To really prepare, you should note the questions that you miss and be able to score 95 percent to 100 percent correctly on subsequent tries.

5. When you successfully complete Units 1–14, you're ready for the Final Exam in Unit 15. Allow yourself 90 minutes to complete that test, which features 76 questions. If you answer 85 percent of the questions correctly on the first try, you're well prepared. If not, review your knowledge of the areas that you struggled with; then take the test again.

6. Just before you take the test, scan the reference material at the beginning of each unit to refresh your memory.

At this point, you are well on your way to becoming certified. Good luck!

UNIT 1

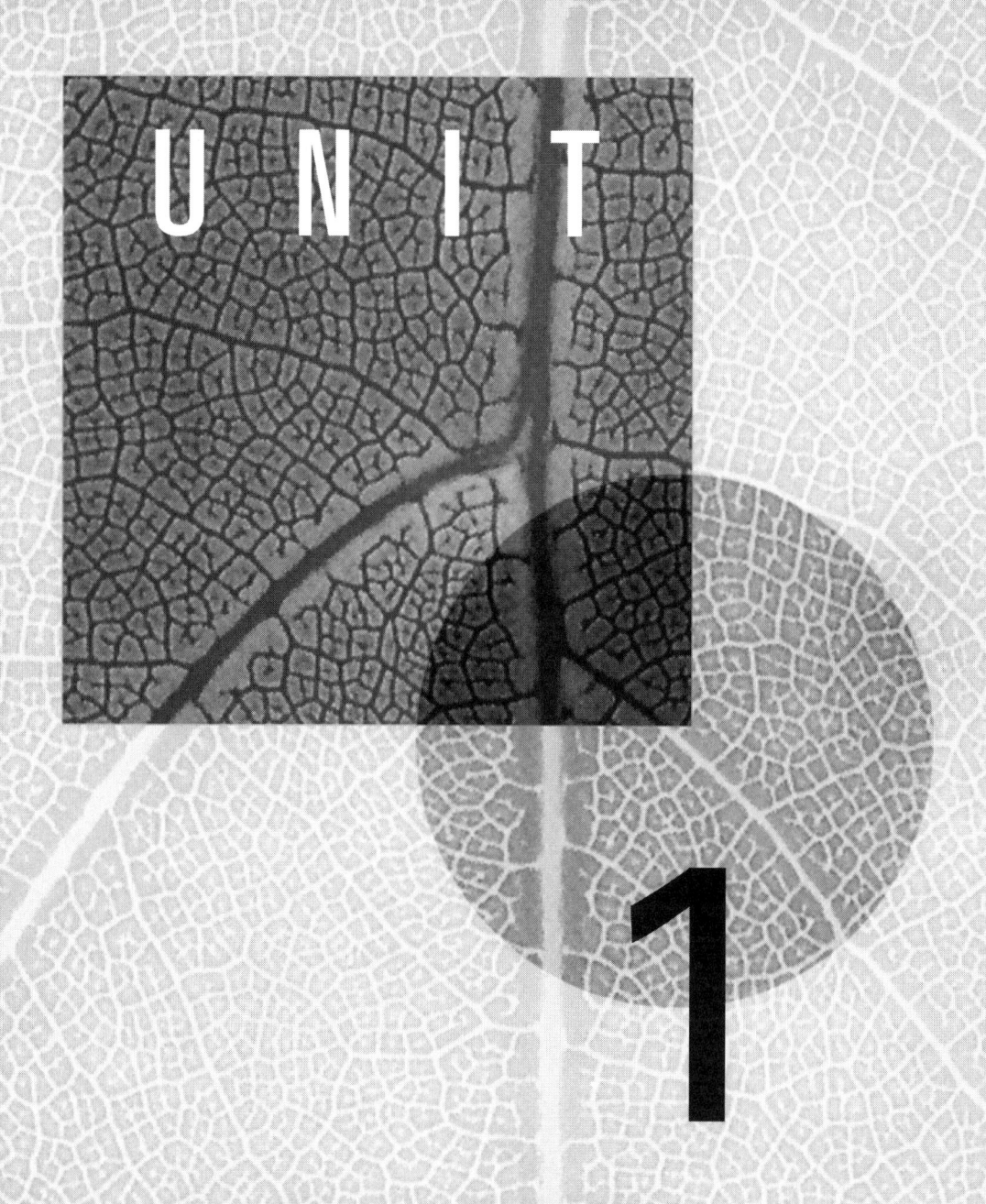

Network Fundamentals

Test Objectives: Basic Knowledge

- **Demonstrate understanding of basic network structure, including:**
  - The characteristics of star, bus, mesh, and ring topologies, and their advantages and disadvantages
  - The characteristics of segments and backbones

- **Identify the following:**
  - The major network operating systems, including Microsoft Windows NT, Novell NetWare, and Unix
  - The clients that best serve specific network operating systems and their resources
  - The directory services of the major network operating systems

- **Associate IPX, IP, and NetBEUI with their functions.**

- **Define the following terms, and explain how each relates to fault tolerance or high availability:**
  - Mirroring
  - Striping (with and without parity)
  - Duplexing
  - Volumes
  - Tape backup

- **Define the layers of the OSI model, and identify the protocols, services, and functions that pertain to each layer.**

- **Recognize and describe the following characteristics of networking media and connectors:**
  - The advantages and disadvantages of coax, Cat 3, Cat 5, fiber optic, UTP, and STP, and the conditions under which they are appropriate
  - The length and speed of 10Base2, 10BaseT, and 100BaseT
  - The length and speed of 10Base5, 100BaseVG (AnyLAN), 100BaseTX
  - The visual appearance of RJ 45 and BNC, and how they are crimped

- **Identify the basic attributes, purpose, and function of the following network elements:**
  - Full- and half-duplexing
  - WAN and LAN
  - Server, workstation, and host
  - Cable, NIC, and router
  - Broadband and baseband
  - Gateway, both as a default IP router and as a method to connect dissimilar systems or protocols

Note: Exam objectives are subject to change at any time without notice and at CompTIA's sole discretion. Please visit CompTIA's Web site (www.comptia.org) for the most current exam-objectives listing.

This unit introduces some network fundamentals, including physical topology, network operating systems, protocols, fault tolerance, high data availability, the OSI model, network media, and network elements.

Basic Network Structure

Networks are complex entities, made up of many components that must work together to accomplish the job of moving data from computer to computer. Before discussing all the detailed components of a network, this unit addresses physical topologies and the differences between backbones and segments. These two topics govern the way that a network is physically designed.

Physical Topologies

Physical topology is a key component of a network. The choice of topology can affect a network's fault tolerance, its speeds, and its capacity for growth. Ring, bus, star, and mesh are a few of the design choices for a network's physical topology. Although these topologies can exist independently, they can also coexist, as shown in Figure 1.1. Multiple star topologies can be connected by a bus topology, for example.

Ring Topology

A network designed with a *ring topology* consists of devices connected in circular fashion. The signal travels in one direction and is strengthened as it passes through each of the devices in the ring, which act as signal repeaters. Figure 1.2 shows a ring-topology design. Each device within the ring is connected to two other devices. One device creates the incoming signal, and the

FIGURE 1.1

Mixed physical topologies

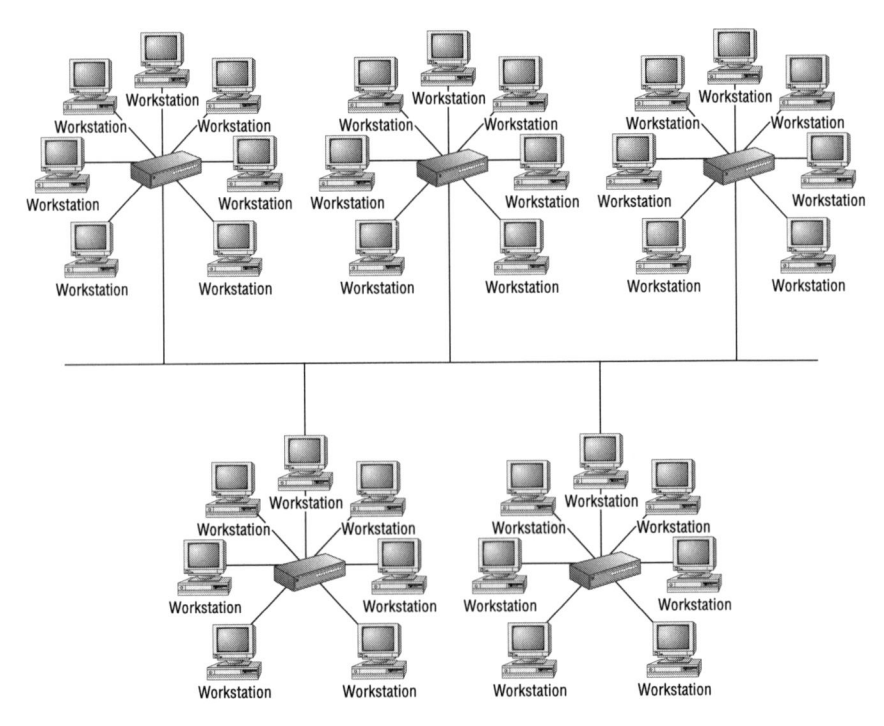

other generates an outgoing signal. This design uses more cable, because the signal must be returned to the first device, thereby creating the ring. This is how ring topology differs physically from bus topology.

FIGURE 1.2

Ring topology

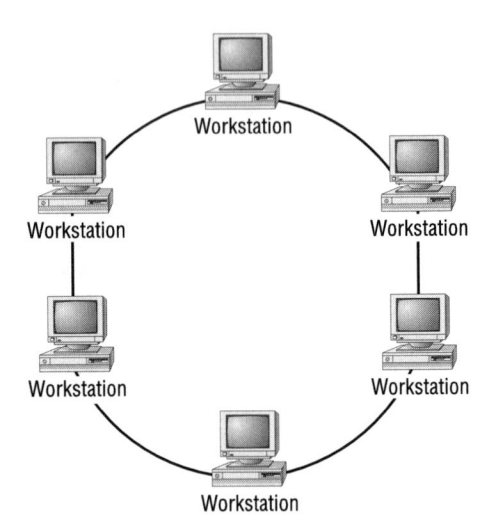

Bus Topology

Bus topology, shown in Figure 1.3, requires the smallest amount of cable compared with the other topologies. Each device is connected to the next in a chain. The first and last devices in the chain are each connected to a terminator (resistor) rather than to another device. Bus topology provides the least redundancy, because each device relies on the preceding device to pass along the signal. A failure in a cable brings down the entire chain.

FIGURE 1.3
Bus topology

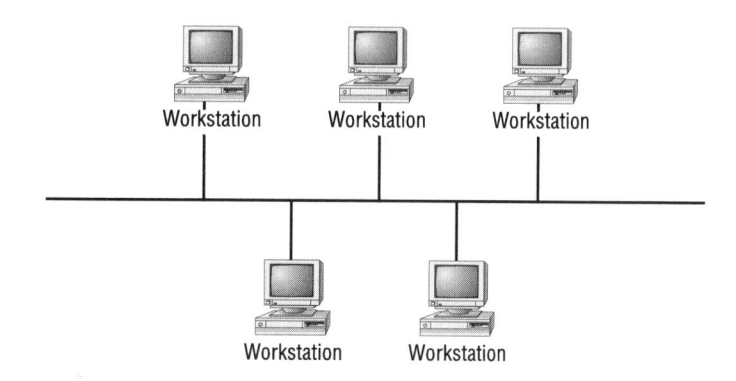

Star Topology

In a star topology, each device accesses the network through a dedicated cable extending from a central point (see Figure 1.4). Hubs, switches, and routers are some of the devices that can be implemented at the center of a star topology.

> **NOTE** The star topology is sometimes known as a hub-spoke.

A star topology creates the most redundancy for the price, because each device relies on its own dedicated cable for connection. Star topology requires a great deal of cabling (although not as much as the mesh topology), because each device has a dedicated connection to the network. A failure in the cable connected to the hub affects only one node. (A *node* is any device connected to the cable that can communicate with the system, such as a workstation, a hub, a repeater, or a server). The remainder of the network is still operational.

FIGURE 1.4

Star topology

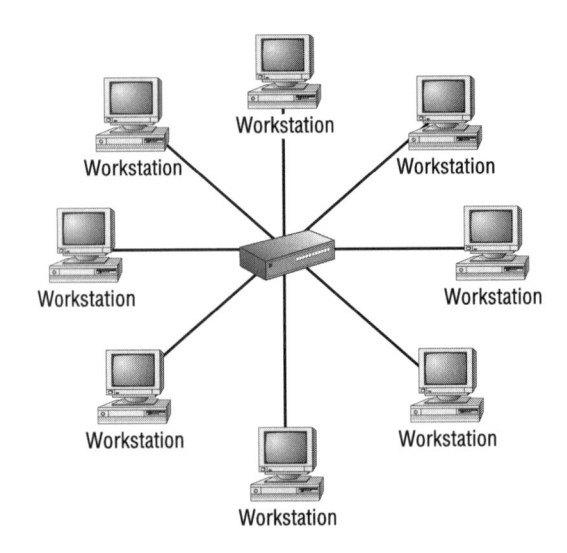

Mesh Topology

Mesh topology exists when every device on a network is directly cabled to another, as shown in Figure 1.5. Of all the topologies discussed in this unit, mesh topology provides the most redundancy and requires the most cabling. This type of topology is complicated to troubleshoot, because so many cables are used to connect devices. In addition, mesh topology is very hard to install and to maintain. If one cable fails, all nodes continue operating.

FIGURE 1.5

Mesh topology

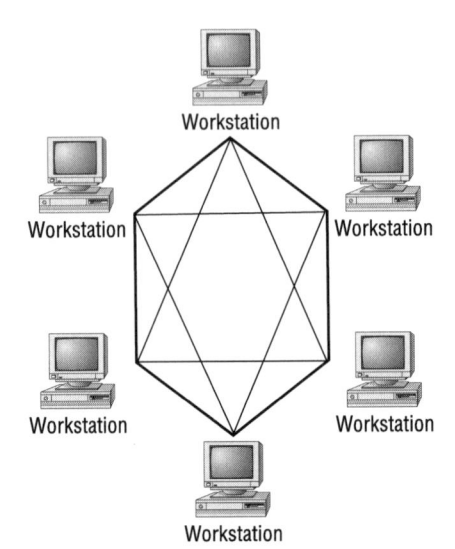

Network Hierarchy

Physical topologies and networking technologies have physical limitations in terms of the length of the cable and the number of nodes that can be supported. For this reason, networks are commonly divided into backbones and segments. Figure 1.6 shows a sample network and identifies the backbone and segments. Refer to this figure when necessary as the unit discusses backbones and segments.

FIGURE 1.6

Backbone and segments on a sample network

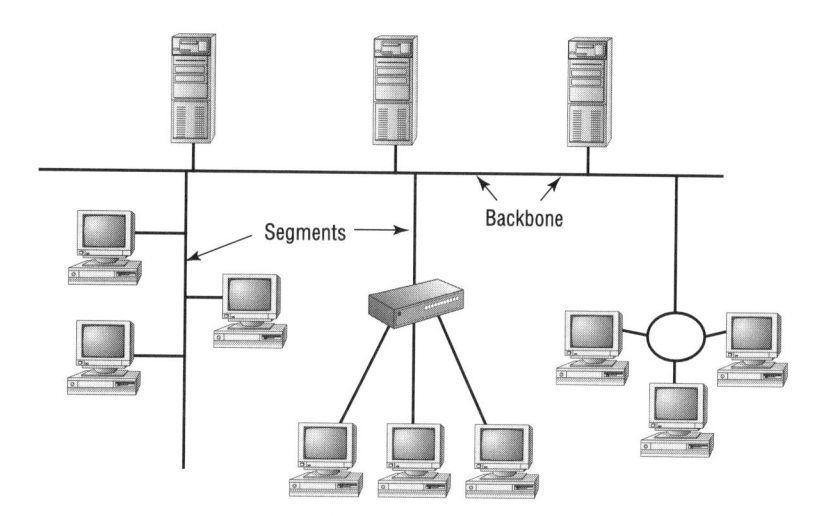

Backbone

A *backbone*—the part of the network to which all segments and servers connect—provides the structure for any network and is considered to be the main part of any network. A backbone usually uses a high-speed communications technology of some kind that can travel long distances (such as FDDI, 100 Base FX or 10Base 5). All servers and all network segments typically connect directly to the backbone, so that segments connected to the backbone are only one segment away from any server on that backbone. The fact that all segments are very close to the servers makes the network very efficient. In Figure 1.6, the three servers and three segments connect to the backbone.

Segments

Segment is a general term for any short cabled section of the network that is not part of the backbone. Just as servers connect to the backbone, workstations connect to segments. Segments are connected to the backbone to give the workstations on them access to the rest of the network. Figure 1.6 shows three segments.

Major Network Operating Systems

Many types of network operating systems (NOSes) are available, each of which has different client and directory services. The most common network operating systems are Novell's NetWare, Microsoft's Windows NT, and Unix.

Novell NetWare

NetWare is a 32-bit network operating system. IPX, which is discussed later in this unit, is the default protocol for NetWare 4.x. NetWare uses NetWare Loadable Modules (NLMs) as applications on the server. NetWare 4 and later versions use NDS (Network Directory Service), which is based on X.500, as the management tool. NDS can allow multiple networks and their devices to be managed from one location.

The NetWare 4.x server console is a nongraphical interface. This version of the network operating system is managed mainly from a workstation, but NetWare 4.x and later can be managed from a graphical user interface on a workstation running the proper client software. Many clients are available for this NOS, but the most popular are the Windows 9*x* and NT clients. Both Microsoft and Novell have their own clients for NetWare, but to get the fullest NDS administration functionality on 9*x* and NT clients, you must use the Novell Client for Windows 95 or the Novell Client for Windows NT.

Microsoft Windows NT

Windows NT (New Technology) is available in different functional configurations, the three most common of which are Server, Workstation, and Terminal Server.

> **NOTE:** The Network+ exam tests you primarily on the NT Workstation configuration.

All the different configurations use true multitasking, which other Windows products lack. Windows NT has the following features:

- Is a 32-bit NOS
- Runs on the New Technology File System (NTFS)
- Uses the New Technology Directory Services (NTDS) as its directory-services database
- Supports folder and file security when used with NTFS
- Supports the Distributed File System, which allows Windows NT to store files on multiple machines even though the files are accessed as though they reside on a single machine
- Can be managed from the console or from a remote workstation

Windows NT has clients for DOS, Windows 9*x*, and NT (Server and Workstation). Because Microsoft designed and sells all these OSes (as well as the Server OS), it supplies clients for all three OSes and includes them with Windows NT and 9*x*.

Unix

Unix is a 32-bit, multitasking network operating system. TCP/IP is the default protocol for a Unix operating system. Unix comes in many versions; some of the most popular are Linux, Irix, and Solaris. Unix is often used for high-end graphical workstations and Internet content servers. Linux is a freely distributed, up and coming, Unix-based operating system that contains most of the features of the true Unix system.

No clients are available specifically for Unix, but many vendors design client-side tools for Unix. You must choose the tool that best serves your interests.

Major Protocols

Many protocols are used in networked environments. Each protocol has its own strong points. Before deciding on a protocol, you should review them all and identify the best one for your environment. IPX, TCP/IP, and NetBEUI are three protocols that are commonly used today.

IPX/SPX

The *IPX* protocol is a portion of the *IPX/SPX* (Internetwork Packet Exchange/Sequenced Packet Exchange) protocol stack. The IPX portion of the stack sends data to a specific destination and redirects data to the correct location within the operating system or network operating system. The SPX portion of the stack confirms successful delivery to the specific destination, checks for packet corruption, and checks for correct destination. IPX/SPX was developed by Novell for use by NetWare, but many other network operating systems have adapted it (including Windows NT).

TCP/IP

The *TCP/IP* (Transmission Control Protocol/Internet Protocol) protocol stack is a suite of networking protocols primarily used for communication on the Internet. TCP/IP, which is the default protocol for the Internet, has received significant NOS support in the past four years.

TCP/IP uses a unique address made up of four 3-digit octets and a subnet mask. In the address 121.152.153.112, for example, 255.255.255.0 is the subnet mask. Each octet is an 8-bit unit, also known as a *byte*. Each device on a TCP/IP network requires a unique address. The address can be assigned statically, via a dedicated unique number, or the address can be assigned dynamically by a DHCP or BOOT P server. When configured dynamically, each time the device boots and connects to the network, the NOS assigns an address from a pool of available IP addresses.

NetBEUI

The *NetBEUI* (NetBIOS Extended User Interface) protocol is an implementation and upper-level portion of the NetBIOS (Network Basic Input/Output System) protocol. NetBEUI is a basic protocol used almost exclusively by Microsoft Windows products including Microsoft Windows for Workgroups and Windows NT. The protocol does not travel between separate LANs and cannot be routed, but it works within a single segment of a LAN.

Fault Tolerance and High Availability

Fault tolerance, disaster recovery, and high availability are key components of a successful network. *Fault tolerance* is the capability of a network or network component to recover from an error condition by itself. *Disaster recovery* is the process that a network administrator follows to recover from a disastrous network failure. *High availability* is a category of fault tolerance that, upon implementation, ensures that a network resource will be available 99 percent to 100 percent of the time (so that you won't have to perform disaster recovery).

To create fault tolerance, a network administrator might implement disk mirroring, disk striping, disk duplexing, or a tape backup system, all of which are methods of creating disk fault tolerance. To achieve high availability, it is important to use volumes, which are ways of organizing disk space into logical chunks. One standard for drive fault tolerance is *RAID*, which stands for Redundant Array of Inexpensive (or Independent) Drives. RAID consists of six levels, 0 to 5; level 0 offers the least fault tolerance, and level 5 offers the most. Additional, higher levels have been created for proprietary companies and have not been adopted as standards.

> **NOTE** High availability is provided through a combination of the methods mentioned in this section.

Mirroring

Mirroring (also known as RAID 1) creates an exact duplicate of all data that resides on a drive. A server with six drives, for example, would actively use only three drives; the second set of drives would be an exact copy of the first. To create more fault tolerance, the entire server can be mirrored, as shown in Figure 1.7.

FIGURE 1.7 Drive mirroring

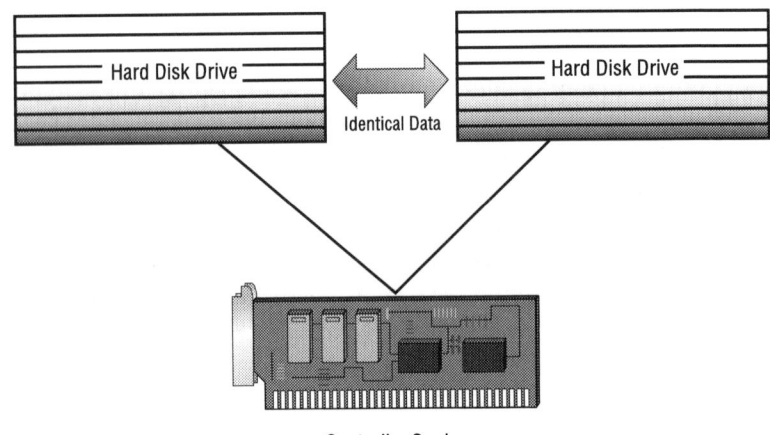

Striping

Striping is another method of achieving fault tolerance. The two main types of striping are parity and nonparity. *Parity* is a mathematical method of ensuring data integrity. *Nonparity* striping is known as RAID 0. The data is striped across multiple drives. If a drive fails, you lose all data. Disk striping provides the fastest access to data but provides no fault tolerance. Disk striping with parity (RAID Levels 3 and 5) provides very fast read access to

Fault Tolerance and High Availability

data but slower write access, due to the generation of parity information. Disk striping with parity produces fault tolerance. RAID 3 and RAID 5 take advantage of parity striping in different ways. RAID 3 uses one physical disk to hold all parity information (as shown in Figure 1.8)—information about how, where, and what has been striped along the other physical drives in the server. If a data disk goes down, it can be rebuilt from the parity information on the parity disk. If the parity disk goes down, the data is lost.

FIGURE 1.8

Striping with parity (RAID 3)

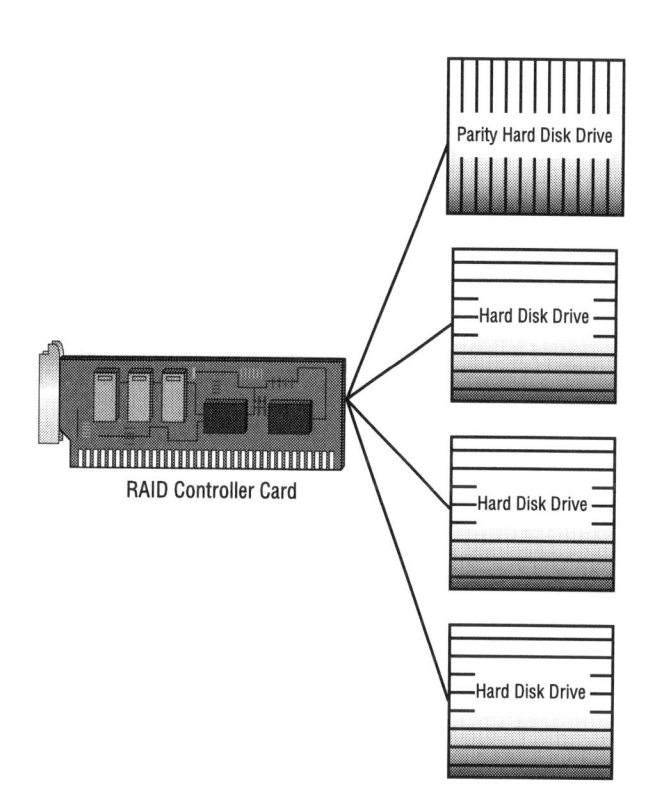

RAID 5 places a portion of the parity information on each drive, ensuring that the data can be recovered in the event of any single disk failure. RAID 5 produces the highest level of software-based fault tolerance. Figure 1.9 shows how a RAID controller places parity information and data on each drive in a RAID 5 configuration. RAID 5 requires a minimum of three data drives in an array.

FIGURE 1.9

Striping with parity (RAID 5)

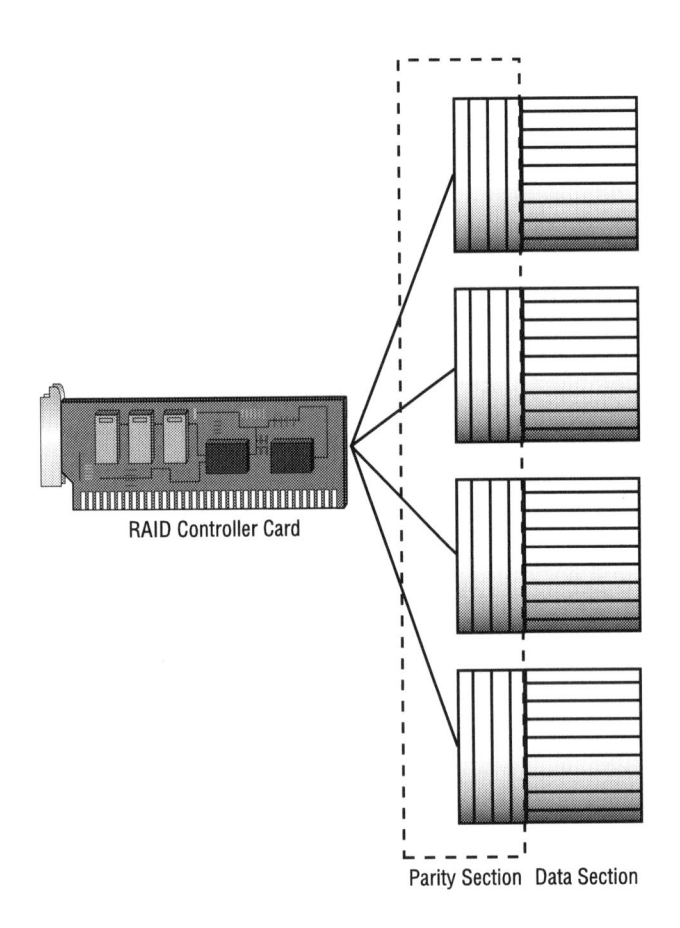

RAID Controller Card

Parity Section   Data Section

Duplexing

Disk duplexing is similar to mirroring, except that the mirrored hard drives are attached to separate disk controller cards, adding another level of redundancy. Duplexing, as depicted in Figure 1.10, also improves drive access time, because the system splits the workload between drives.

Fault Tolerance and High Availability 17

FIGURE 1.10
Drive duplexing

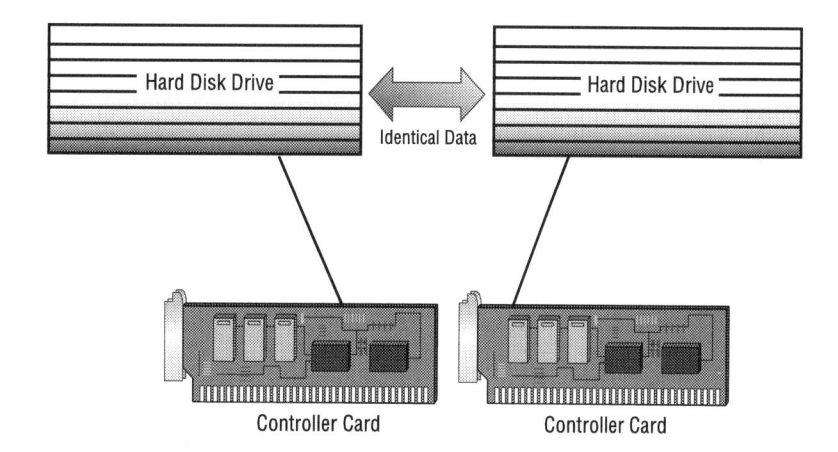

> Although duplexing improves the drive access time, it taxes the server's processor, because it works with twice the normal number of requests.

Tape Backup

One of the most important aspects of disaster recovery is the tape backup system. When all else fails, the tape backup system may be your last line of defense. You can use many strategies for backups; some of those strategies are listed in Table 1.1.

TABLE 1.1: Backup strategies

Backup Strategy	Description	Example
Full	Backs up all data on volumes or workstations that are defined within a backup session.	On Monday, a backup is performed to back up all data on all volumes; on Tuesday, a backup is performed to back up all data on all volumes.

TABLE 1.1: Backup strategies *(continued)*

Backup Strategy	Description	Example
Differential	Backs up any data that has changed since the last full backup.	A full backup is performed on Monday. On Tuesday, a backup is performed to back up data that has changed since Monday. On Wednesday, another backup is performed to back up data that has changed since Monday.
Incremental	Performs a full backup on a periodic basis and backs up data that has changed since the last backup.	A full backup is performed on Monday. On Tuesday, a backup is performed to back up data that has changed since Monday. On Wednesday, a backup is performed to back up data that has changed since Tuesday.

After you choose and implement a tape backup strategy, you must be sure to conduct ongoing tests. You must test the tapes and the restoration of files from those tapes to ensure the integrity of the backup. The backup procedure may evolve as a network expands.

Volumes

The task of creating high availability of data is assisted by the use of volumes. A *volume* is a logical drive that can span multiple physical drives. Volumes can contain either data or system information, but not both. Figure 1.11 depicts four physical drives. The top section of the figure shows two volumes configured with two physical drives each. The bottom section of the figure shows one volume configured with 2.5 physical drives and the other volume configured with 1.5 physical drives.

FIGURE 1.11
Volumes

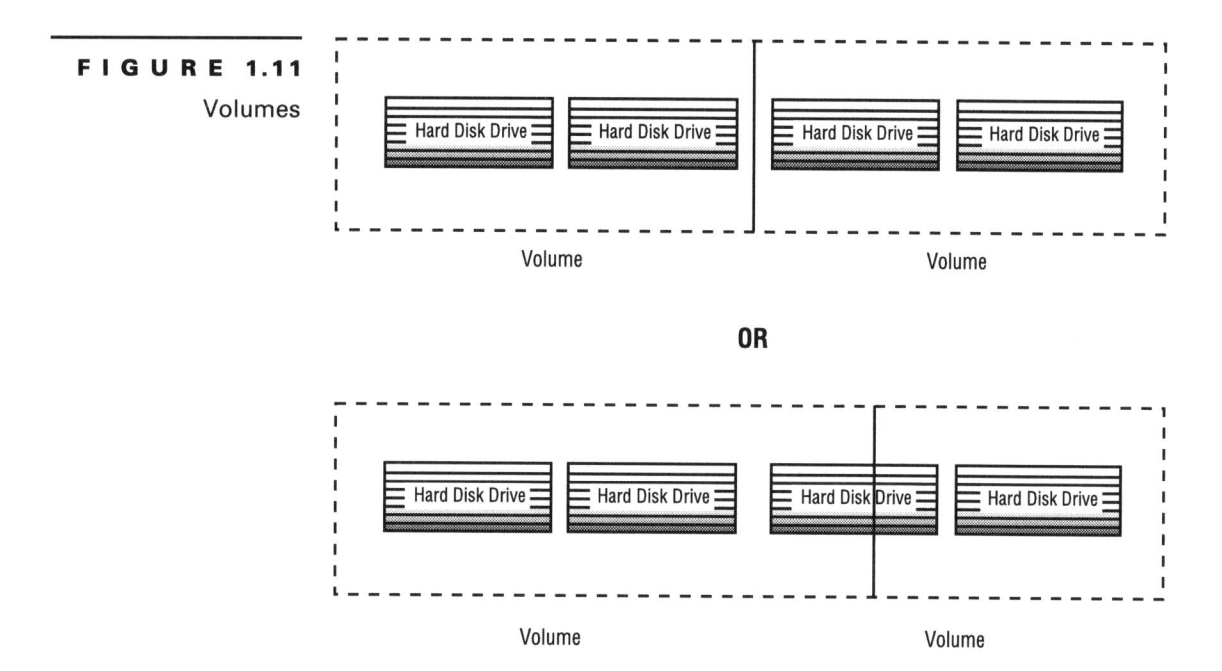

The OSI Model

The Open System Interconnection (OSI) model was built to create a standard for protocol generation and operation that describes the functional aspects of each layer (portion) of the protocol. This model also allows diverse vendors' products to be described by this standard model. The OSI model consists of seven layers: Physical, Data Link, Network, Transport, Session, Presentation, and Application. This model is most commonly compared with a layer cake, as shown in Figure 1.12. Each layer of the cake is stacked on the next.

Table 1.2 describes the layers of the OSI model, listing the functions and common protocols (or implementations) available at each layer.

FIGURE 1.12

The OSI-model cake

Layer 7 — Application Layer
Layer 6 — Presentation Layer
Layer 5 — Session Layer
Layer 4 — Transport Layer
Layer 3 — Network Layer
Layer 2 — Data Link Layer
Layer 1 — Physical Layer

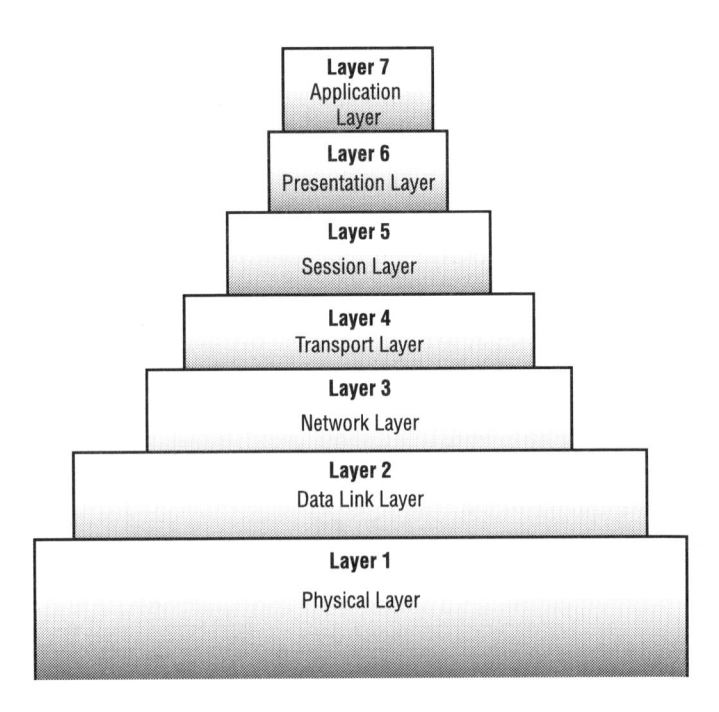

TABLE 1.2: OSI-model layers, protocols, and functions

Layer	Functions	Common Protocols/Implementations
Physical	Serves as the physical aspect of the network, including the connections, the media, and the conversion of upper-layer data into electrical impulses.	Twisted-pair, coax, AUI, network interface card
Data Link	Creates, transmits, and checks data packets. The Data Link layer also provides services for the Network layer and uses the Physical layer to transmit and receive data.	MAC Addressing, Ethernet, Token Ring
Network	Establishes and maintains logical connections, finds a route between source and destination nodes, and determines addresses.	IPX, IP
Transport	Provides mechanisms for reliable end-to-end communications and performs flow control.	TCP, UDP, NetBEUI, SPX

TABLE 1.2: OSI-model layers, protocols, and functions *(continued)*

Layer	Functions	Common Protocols/ Implementations
Session	Synchronizes and sequences the dialogue and packets in a connection. The Session layer also ensures that the connection is maintained until the transmission is complete.	NCP, Telnet
Presentation	Controls the way that data is represented to the Application layer. The Presentation layer is responsible for character-set translation, encryption, and compression and decompression.	SMB, NCP, EBCDIC, ASCII
Application	Defines the various network services that are provided to network clients.	FTP, HTTP, NCP

Networking Media and Connectors

Aside from the other components discussed so far in this unit, the nuts and bolts of the network are the media and the connectors. The network medium is the physical pathway (typically, a cable of some sort) on which the network signals travel. The most common type of network medium is a network cable (also called a *bounded medium*). The network connectors are placed on the end of some network media to facilitate the physical connections between the network devices. This section discusses a few of the most popular network media and connectors that you will find on networks today.

Media Options

Within the world of networking, many types of bounded media are used, including coaxial, twisted pair, and fiber optics. Each type has multiple subtypes, each with its own speed allowance, maximum length, and appearance.

Coaxial (Coax) Cable

Coaxial (coax, for short) cable uses a core conductor that is insulated and surrounded by a braided or solid foil aluminum shield. This type of cable looks similar to the television cable that enters your house.

WARNING A television coaxial cable and a data coaxial cable are not the same; don't try to interchange them.

Because it is shielded, coax cable is fairly resistant to crosstalk and electromagnetic interference (EMI), but it is expensive and more difficult to work with than other types of cable media. The connector for a coaxial cable is called a BNC, which is discussed later in this unit. As shown in Figure 1.13, a coaxial cable consists of a jacket, an outer conductor, an insulator, and a center conductor.

FIGURE 1.13
Coaxial cable

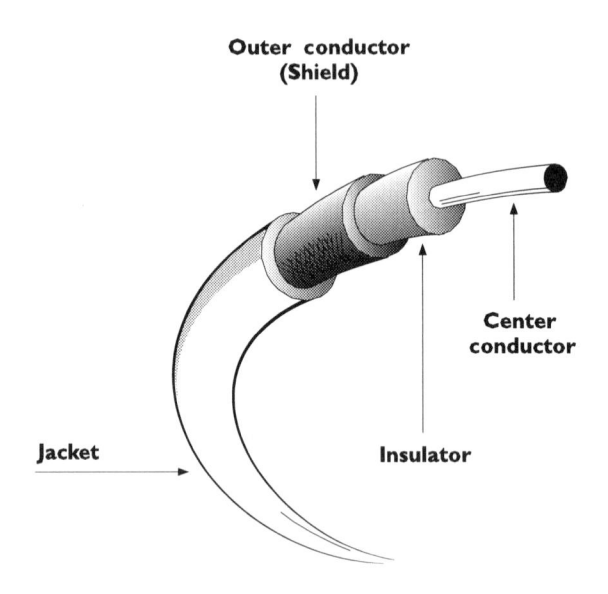

Fiber Optics

Fiber-optic cable uses a strand of glass or plastic, rather than copper, for the core of a cable. A layer of plastic and then a layer of either gel or wire shields the core. Fiber-optic cable allows the network signal to travel a greater distance and is completely resistant to any type of electrical interference. A fiber-optic cable contains two or more strands. Figure 1.14 depicts fiber-optic cabling.

FIGURE 1.14

Fiber-optic cable

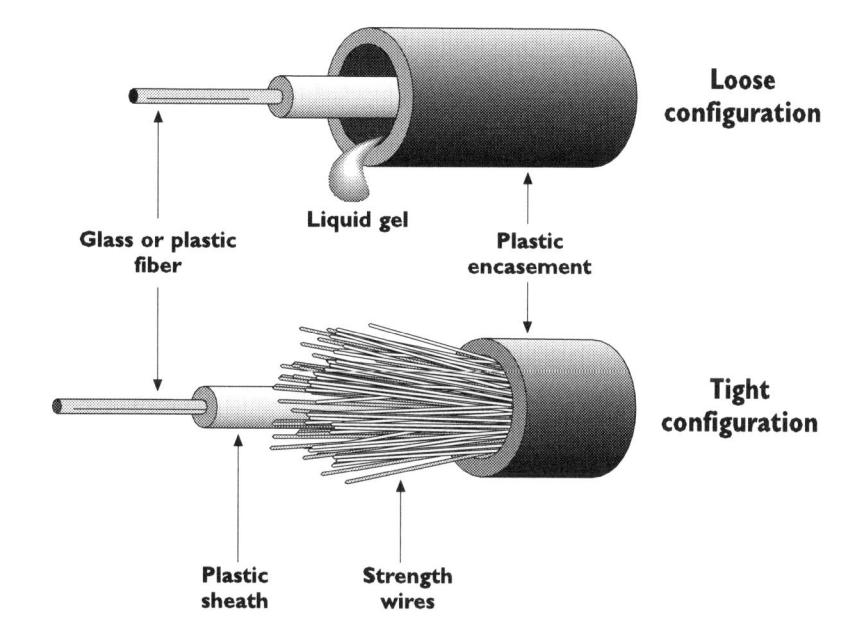

Twisted Pair

Twisted-pair cable consists of two insulated strands of copper wire twisted together to provide EMI shielding. *Unshielded twisted-pair cable* (known as UTP), which does not contain an outer shield, and *shielded twisted-pair cable* (STP) reside within the spectrum of twisted-pair cable.

STP STP cable is very resistant to EMI, because a layer of shielding has been added over the twisted cable, as shown in Figure 1.15. Like coax, STP is difficult to work with and fairly expensive. In a Token Ring environment, STP cables are connected with IBM data connectors from a workstation to a Multistation Access Unit (MAU).

UTP UTP cable is rated in categories. Categories 3 and 5 are data-grade cable. In most cases, Category 3 data cable has been replaced by Category 5 cable because of Category 3's inability to maintain a stable connection with any bandwidth greater than 10Mbps. Because Category 5 cable offers a data capacity of 100Mbps and is less expensive than either STP or coax, it is the preferred medium of many network administrators. UTP cable's big disadvantage is that it requires more network hardware, because it is used with

FIGURE 1.15

Shielded twisted-pair cable

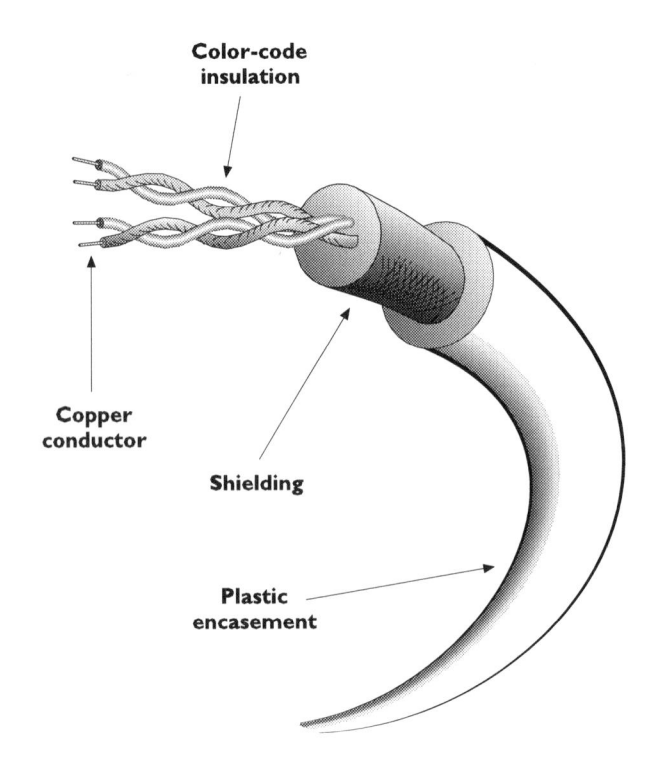

star and mesh topologies, which require a point of contact with the server. UTP cable uses the RJ-45 connector, which is discussed later in this unit. In most cases, each UTP cable has four pairs of copper. Figure 1.16 shows an example of a UTP cable.

Distance and Speed

Every type of networking medium has certain restrictions. The Network+ exam tests you primarily on the restrictions on Ethernet implementations. Table 1.3 shows some of the cable specifications, distance limitations, network speed, and other special notes about each Ethernet implementation.

Connector Types

Many types of connectors are used with computers today. In Ethernet networks, however, two types of connectors are most commonly used: RJ-45 and BNC.

FIGURE 1.16

Unshielded twisted-pair cable

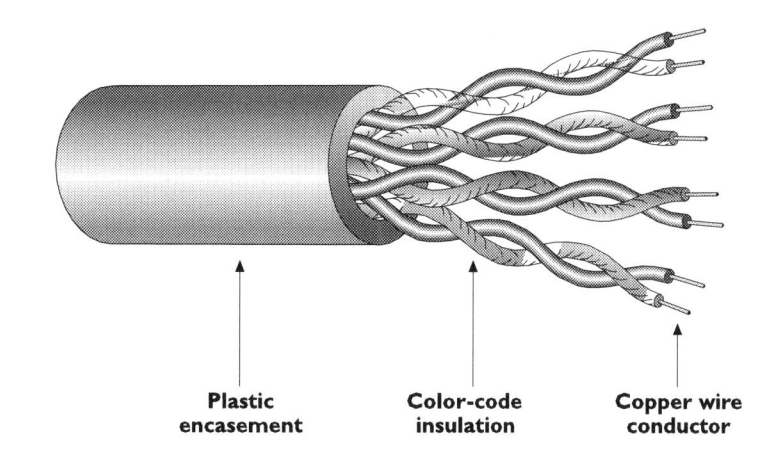

Plastic encasement | Color-code insulation | Copper wire conductor

TABLE 1.3: Cable specifications

Implementation	Maximum Segment Distance	Minimum Segment Distance	Speed	Description
10Base2	185 meters	0.5 meter	10Mbps	Coaxial cable, 925 meters total maximum, with 5 segments, 3 populated segments, 4 repeaters with 30 devices
10Base5	500 meters	2.5 meters	10Mbps	2.46 kilometers total maximum, with 500-meter segments, 100 nodes per segment
10BaseT	100 meters	0.6 meter	10Mbps	512 nodes per segment, 5 segments, 4 repeaters, 1,024 nodes
100BaseT4	100 meters	0.6 meter	100Mbps	512 nodes per segment, 5 segments, 4 repeaters, 1,024 nodes; four pair Cat 3, 4, or 5 wires

TABLE 1.3: Cable specifications *(continued)*

Implementation	Maximum Segment Distance	Minimum Segment Distance	Speed	Description
100BaseTX	100 meters	0.6 meter	100Mbps	Two pair Cat 5 wires or Type 1 STP
100BaseFX	2.5 kilometers	1 meter	100Mbps	Fiber-optic cable with a plastic or glass core
100BaseVG	100 meters	0.6 meter	100Mbps	Four pair Cat 3 UTP wires, but uses Demand priority instead of CSMA/CD for media access

To convert meters to feet, multiply by 3.28.

RJ-45

An RJ-45 connector is used in a UTP environment (such as 10BaseT or 100BaseT Ethernet). The connector looks like a telephone connector but is larger. A phone connector (RJ-11) may have up to six copper wires, whereas an RJ-45 connector has up to eight copper wires (see Figure 1.17).

FIGURE 1.17
RJ-45 connector

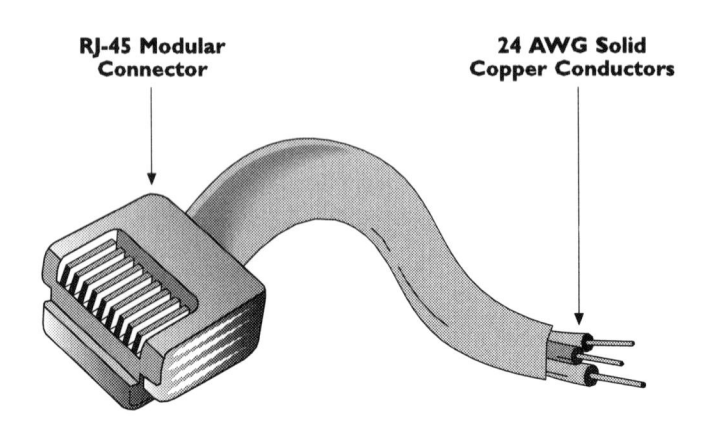

> The RJ in both RJ-11 and RJ-45 stands for Registered Jack.

BNC

A BNC connector (see Figure 1.18) is used in a coaxial network. The BNC connector has three parts: a cable connector, a T connector, and a terminator. The cable connectors attach to the opposing sides of the T connector, one cable coming in and one cable going out. The third side of the T connector is then attached to the network interface card (NIC). In a bus-topology network, the first and last devices in the chain have a terminator rather than a second cable connector.

FIGURE 1.18
BNC connector

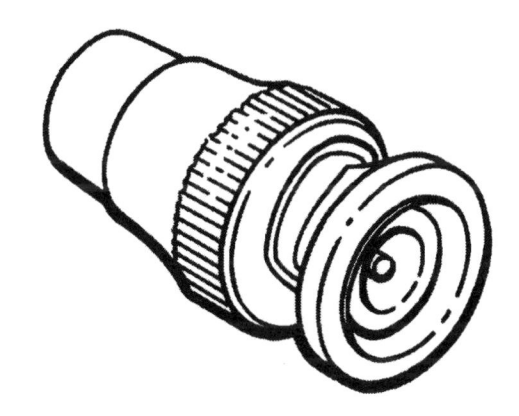

Networking Elements

Many elements create a networking environment, including both entities that you can touch and concepts that you must understand. All these items are collectively known as *network elements*. Components in this category range from large WAN router devices to the smaller, yet very important, baseband and broadband transmission signals.

Duplex Communications

Full and half duplexing are rules that govern network communication. *Half duplexing* occurs when two devices can send and receive across the network medium, but not at the same time. *Full duplexing* provides the capability to send and to receive simultaneously by using one portion of the medium to send data and another portion to receive data. An example of full duplex is a four-wire cable used with two wires dedicated for transmission and two wires dedicated for reception.

Network Categories

Networks are broken into many categories, defined by geographical boundaries and distances. LAN (local area network), MAN (metropolitan area network), and WAN (wide area network) are the main types of networks. The line that separates the different categories of networks is fading as technology advances.

LAN

A LAN exists in a limited area, such as within a building, spanning room to room or floor to floor. A LAN can be connected in many ways, a few of them which are described earlier in this unit. LAN is a general definition for a network that exists within a single building.

MAN

A MAN connects different buildings. A MAN is most commonly a network that has a 75-kilometer radius and that uses a high-speed telecommunications connection.

WAN

A WAN consists of multiple individual networks that are connected, as shown in Figure 1.19. A WAN also has a radius larger than an average state and requires the use of telecommunications connections.

Computer Roles on a Network

Networking is achieved when devices such as workstations, servers, and hosts are connected with the capability to communicate. Each device plays a different role in networking.

FIGURE 1.19
A sample WAN

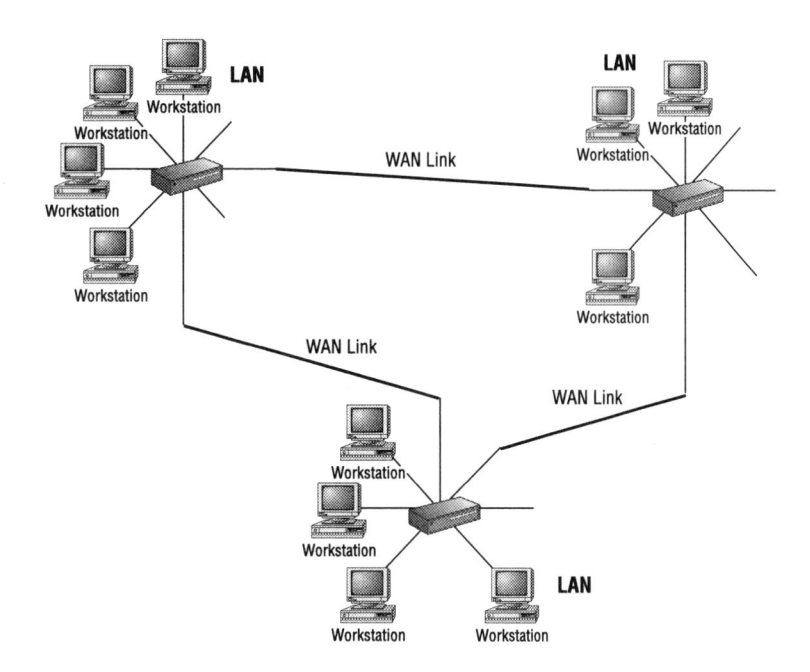

Workstation

A *workstation* (or *client*) connects to a server to access shared applications and data. The device does not have to be powerful, because a workstation generally does not need the amount of processing power that a server does. A workstation must have a network interface card and can house several devices (such as CD-ROM drives, printers, and tape drives) that can be shared across the network.

Server

A *server* is a large-capacity PC that houses shared data. In most cases, a server is loaded with specialized software, such as the network operating system. A network can be built with or without a server. When a server is used, the network is called a *client-server network*. When a server is not used, and the workstations communicate directly with one another, the network is called a *peer-to-peer network*.

Host

A *host* is a unit that provides processing for an attached device. A mainframe can be a host for terminals, or a workstation can be a host for a printer. *Host* is also a general term used to signify a computer.

Common Connection Devices

Three of the most common devices that make the connections on a network are the cable, NIC, and router. Other connection devices are used, but these components are used for the majority of the connections on a network.

Cable

A *cable* is a physical medium that carries data between devices on a network. Cable types are discussed in detail earlier in this unit.

Network Interface Card (NIC)

An NIC connects a device to the network medium and enables communication with other devices (along with the correct software). The type of NIC used on a network depends on the cable type and the network topology.

Router

A *router* is a device that reads network addresses and channels (*routes*) packets to the proper destination. A router uses artificial intelligence and route-discovery protocols to make intelligent decisions about which routes particular packets should take. Routers are used to connect similar or dissimilar networks and to translate between different network-layer protocols.

Bandwidth

Bandwidth—the amount of data that a cable can carry—typically is restricted by the medium that is being implemented. This section discusses two types of bandwidth: baseband and broadband.

Baseband

A *baseband* signal is a direct-current pulse along a single channel that uses a cable's full bandwidth capability and does not allow any other types of signals. When a multiplexor is used, multiple types of signals can be transmitted across a baseband connection. A digital signal is used in a baseband connection.

Broadband

A *broadband* signal sends data in a carrier wave along multiple channels, allowing other signals to travel along the same cable. Broadband carries more data than baseband but uses a much more complex pattern. An analog signal is used in broadband connections. An example of broadband is a television signal.

Gateway

A *gateway* translates or converts dissimilar protocols and data between different networking systems. Some types of gateways, for example, act as IP translators by converting IPX data and sending it to an outside IP source.

STUDY QUESTIONS

Basic Network Structure

1. In a ring topology, each device is connected to _____ other devices.

2. In a bus topology, the _____ and _____ device in the chain are terminated.

3. True or false: In a star topology, a break in the connection between the center device and one device affects all devices.

4. True or false: In a bus topology, no devices are affected by a break in the cable.

5. In a _____ topology, a central device is required to manage network signals.

6. A mesh topology exists when every device on the network connects with _____.

7. A network's _____ connects all servers and segments.

8. _____ is a general term for any short (cable) section of the network.

9. True or false: Workstations generally reside on a backbone.

10. True or false: Mesh topologies are commonly used for LANs today.

11. Physical star-topology networks use a central device called a _____.

STUDY QUESTIONS

12. A _____ indicates how a network is physically designed.

Major Network Operating Systems

13. NetWare, Unix, and NT are all _____ bit network operating systems.

14. NLMs are used in which network operating system? _____

15. NDS originated with what network operating system? _____

16. NTFS was created for which network operating system? _____

17. Which operating system has many flavors? _____

18. True or false: Unix is a 128-bit, single-threaded, multitasking NOS.

19. Solaris is an example of which type of NOS? _____

20. NDS is based on _____.

21. To implement file and folder security on Windows NT, you must have implemented _____ on the server.

22. To be able to administrate NDS from Windows 9x, you must use the _____ client.

STUDY QUESTIONS

Major Protocols

23. Of the IPX/SPX, TCP/IP, and NetBEUI protocols, which one cannot be routed? _____

24. Which protocol requires a unique 4-byte address consisting of four sets of decimal numbers, separated by periods? _____

25. Within the IPX/SPX protocol stack, which protocol is responsible for routing? _____

26. Which protocol confirms successful delivery within the IPX/SPX protocol stack? _____

27. Eight bits are an _____ in TCP/IP addresses.

28. Which protocol does Unix use by default? _____

29. Which protocol does NetWare 4 use by default? _____

30. True or false: TCP/IP addresses must be assigned dynamically by a server.

31. What does TCP/IP stand for? _____

32. Which protocol do Windows products use almost exclusively? _____

STUDY QUESTIONS

33. Which protocol was designed mainly for use with NetWare, but now is used by other NOSes, including Windows NT? _____

34. TCP/IP is primarily used on the _____.

Fault Tolerance and High Availability

35. What is fault tolerance?
_____
_____

36. Mirroring is also known as RAID level _____.

37. _____ creates an exact duplicate of all data on a physical drive on an identical physical drive.

38. Striping can be done in two ways: with and without _____.

39. Striping with parity (RAID 5) places the parity information on _____ drive.

40. Striping with parity (RAID 3) places the parity information on _____ drive.

41. Duplexing is different from mirroring, because in duplexing, each hard drive has its own _____.

STUDY QUESTIONS

42. Duplexing is taxing on a server, because the server has to process twice as many _____ requests.

43. Why should tape backups be tested on an ongoing basis?
_____

44. True or false: A volume cannot span multiple physical drives.

45. Striping with parity is RAID level _____.

46. Duplexing, in addition to two disks, requires two _____.

The OSI Model

47. The _____ helps hardware and software vendors work together.

48. The _____ layer is responsible for the physical aspects of the network, including the connections, the media, and the conversion of upper-layer data to electrical impulses.

49. The _____ layer is responsible for the creation, transmission, checking, and receipt of data packets.

50. The _____ layer is responsible for establishing and maintaining logical connections.

STUDY QUESTIONS

51. IPX exists primarily at which layer of the OSI model? _____

52. The _____ layer is responsible for reliable end-to-end communications.

53. The _____ layer ensures that the connection is maintained until the transmission is complete.

54. The _____ layer is responsible for the way that data is represented to the upper layers, including compression and encryption.

55. The _____ layer defines the various network services that are provided to network clients.

56. UDP operates primarily at the _____ layer of the OSI model.

57. The IP protocol (part of the TCP/IP protocol suite) operates at which layer of the OSI model? _____

58. A MAC address operates at which layer of the OSI model? _____

59. NCP operates primarily at the _____ layer of the OSI model.

60. ASCII is a function of the _____ layer of the OSI model.

61. What does OSI stand for? _____

STUDY QUESTIONS

62. The TCP protocol operates at the _____ layer of the OSI model.

63. A network interface card operates at the _____ layer of the OSI model.

64. SMB operates at the _____ layer of the OSI model.

65. FTP and HTTP operate primarily at the _____ layer of the OSI model.

Networking Media and Connectors

66. True or false: A local area network should be run over a television cable.

67. Cat 3 and Cat 5 are categories of what type of cable? _____

68. 100BaseT has a maximum distance of _____ meters.

69. 10BaseT has a maximum distance of _____ meters.

70. The minimum distance for 100BaseTX is _____ meter(s).

71. A _____ is a physical medium that transfers data between devices.

72. The maximum distance of a 10Base2 segment is _____ meters.

73. The most common connector used with 10BaseT and 100BaseT is _____.

STUDY QUESTIONS

74. _____ is the cable type that is immune to interference and eavesdropping.

75. 10Base2 typically uses a _____ connector.

76. What does the *RJ* in RJ-45 or RJ-11 stand for? _____

77. Which 100Mbps Ethernet standard(s) can run over Category 3 wire?

_____

78. Which 100Mbps Ethernet implementation uses fiber-optic cabling? _____

79. True or false: Fiber-optic cable is shielded.

80. True or false: Coaxial cable is shielded.

81. True or false: UTP cable is shielded.

Networking Elements

82. Half duplexing occurs when two devices can _____, but not at the same time.

83. What do the acronyms LAN, MAN, and WAN stand for?

_____

_____

_____

STUDY QUESTIONS

84. A peer-to-peer network exists when no _____ is used.

85. What do devices in a peer-to-peer network communicate with? _____

86. What does a network interface card do?
_____

87. What device channels data to a given location on a network? _____

88. What type of signal uses a direct-current pulse? _____

89. Dissimilar protocols are translated by a _____.

90. Which type of network signal separates network transmission paths into discrete frequency ranges (or bands)? _____

SAMPLE TEST

1-1 What OSI-model layer provides services for the Network layer and uses the Physical layer to transmit and receive data?

    A. The Data Link layer

    B. The Physical layer

    C. The Network layer

    D. The Application layer

1-2 A company is rebuilding its network infrastructure and is trying to find the topology that would best suit it. The most important item that the company is looking for is fault tolerance. Price and the future addition of workstations are not factors. What type of topology would you recommend?

    A. Star

    B. Ring

    C. Star and bus

    D. Mesh

1-3 What is a function of RAID 3?

    A. Striping without parity

    B. Mirroring

    C. Striping with parity on one drive

    D. Striping with parity on all drives

Unit 1 • Network Fundamentals

SAMPLE TEST

1-4 A company is rebuilding its network infrastructure and is trying to find the topology that would best suit it. The most important item that the company is looking for is easy expansion; ease of troubleshooting is a secondary factor. What type of topology would you recommend?

   A. Star

   B. Ring

   C. Star and bus

   D. Mesh

1-5 Microsoft Windows NT 3.*x* can be managed from which locations?

   A. The server console

   B. Any workstation (with appropriate tools and rights)

   C. Any remote location (with a modem)

   D. All of the above

   E. A, B

1-6 Which protocol can use static and dynamic assignments of workstation addresses?

   A. IPX/SPX

   B. TCP/IP

   C. NetBEUI

   D. HTTP

1-7 NetBEUI is based on what other protocol?

   A. NetPLUS

   B. NetBIOS

C. NetWORK

D. NetWARE

1-8 Mirroring is also known as what RAID level?

    A. 0

    B. 1

    C. 2

    D. 3

1-9 Why is duplexing taxing on a server?

    A. The server has more than one drive.

    B. The server has extra disk controller cards.

    C. The server has to process twice as many read/writes.

    D. It is not taxing on the server.

1-10 Pick the correct order for the OSI model.

    A. Network, Session, Presentation, Physical, Data Link

    B. Physical, Data Link, Network, Transport, Session, Presentation, Application

    C. Physical, Data Link, Network, Transport, Presentation, Session

    D. Data Link, Network, Transport, Presentation, Session, Physical, Application

1-11 Which type of cable is the most resistant to electromagnetic interference?

    A. Unshielded twisted-pair

    B. Shielded twisted-pair

SAMPLE TEST

   C. Coaxial

   D. Fiber-optic

1-12 Novell NetWare 4.*x* can be managed from which locations?

   A. The server console

   B. Any workstation (with Novell client software and appropriate rights)

   C. Any remote location (with a modem)

   D. B and C

1-13 Which type of cable commonly uses an IBM data connector?

   A. Unshielded twisted-pair

   B. Shielded twisted-pair

   C. Coaxial

   D. Fiber-optic

1-14 Which type of cable uses an RJ-45 connection?

   A. Unshielded twisted-pair

   B. Shielded twisted-pair

   C. Coaxial

   D. Fiber-optic

1-15 Select the correct statistics for 10Base2.

   A. 200 meters maximum, 0.5 meter minimum, 10Mbps speed

   B. 185 meters maximum, 0.5 meter minimum, 10Mbps speed

SAMPLE TEST

    C. 150 meters maximum, 0.6 meter minimum, 10Mbps speed

    D. 500 meters maximum, 0.6 meter minimum, 2Mbps speed

1-16 What OSI-model layer is at the bottom of the OSI model?

    A. The Data Link layer

    B. The Physical layer

    C. The Network layer

    D. The Application layer

1-17 What OSI-model layer is responsible for logical network addressing and routing?

    A. The Transport layer

    B. The Session layer

    C. The Network layer

    D. D. The Application layer

1-18 Select the correct statistics for 10Base5.

    A. 100 meters maximum, 0.6 meter minimum, 100Mbps speed

    B. 500 meters maximum, 2.5 meters minimum, 10Mbps speed

    C. 300 meters maximum, 1.5 meters minimum, 10Mbps speed

    D. 185 meters maximum, 0.6 meter minimum, 10Mbps speed

1-19 The Transport layer sits between what layers of the OSI model?

    A. Physical and Data Link

    B. Application and Interface

SAMPLE TEST

C. Sub and Lower

D. Network and Session

1-20 What is full duplexing?

A. Increasing the speed of the data that is transmitted

B. Installing a second network interface card and a second network cable

C. The capability to send and receive data simultaneously through the same connection

D. Making two copies of all data sent

1-21 Select the correct specification for 100BaseT.

A. 100 meters maximum, 0.6 meter minimum, 100Mbps speed

B. 330 meters maximum, 3 meters minimum, 100Mbps speed

C. 150 meters maximum, 0.6 meter minimum, 100Mbps speed

D. 500 meters maximum, 3 meters minimum, 100Mbps speed

1-22 If a network were to span London, England; Phoenix, Arizona; Sydney, Australia; and Moab, Utah, what would it be called?

A. A WAN

B. A LAN

C. A MAN

1-23 What does a network interface card do?

A. Allows a device to connect to the Internet

B. Connects a device to the network medium

SAMPLE TEST

    C. Stores user data

    D. Translates data between different protocols

1-24 What type of device translates dissimilar protocols between networks?

    A. Gateway

    B. Router

    C. Switch

    D. NIC

1-25 Why is striping with parity (RAID 5) the most fault-tolerant of all disk fault-tolerance methods?

    A. Data is stored offline.

    B. Data is striped across all the drives, along with its parity information.

    C. Data is copied in sections on each drive, and parity information is copied to a single drive.

    D. Data is stored on multiple drives using multiple disk controllers.

1-26 A baseband signal uses what amount of the bandwidth?

    A. All the bandwidth

    B. None of the bandwidth

    C. The majority of the bandwidth

    D. The minority of the bandwidth

UNIT 2

The Physical Layer

Test Objectives: The Physical Layer

- **Given an installation, configuration, or troubleshooting scenario, select an appropriate course of action if a client workstation does not connect to the network after you install or replace a network interface card. Explain why a given action is warranted. The following issues may be covered:**
  - Knowledge of how the network card is usually configured, including EEPROM, jumpers, and Plug-and-Play software
  - Use of network-card diagnostics, including the loopback test and vendor-supplied diagnostics
  - The ability to resolve hardware resource conflicts, including IRQ, DMA, and I/O base address

- **Identify the use of the following network components and the differences among them:**
  - Hubs
  - Switching hubs
  - MAUs
  - Repeaters
  - Transceivers

> **NOTE** Exam objectives are subject to change at any time without notice and at CompTIA's sole discretion. Please visit CompTIA's Web site (www.comptia.org) for the most current exam-objectives listing.

The Physical layer is the bottom layer of the OSI model. The physical layer defines all physical aspects of network protocols, including transforming packets and datagrams from higher-level protocols into the electrical signals that are placed on the wire. Network components such as NICs and cables are some of the items that the Physical layer helps define. The ability to troubleshoot devices and protocols at the Physical layer is an important skill for a network technician. The majority of network failures occur at the Physical layer.

Troubleshooting on the Physical Layer

Troubleshooting on the Physical layer refers to many topics, including troubleshooting the protocols and devices that operate at the physical layer. This section discusses troubleshooting NICs. Topics covered include configuration, diagnostics, and connection problems due to cabling or other errors on the LAN.

Network Interface Card Configuration

NICs are the cards that you install in the computer to connect your computer to the various physical network media. NICs can be configured in many ways, each dependent upon the given hardware and software. The use of Plug-and-Play software, EEPROM (Electronically Erasable Programmable Read-Only Memory) chips, and jumpers are three ways to configure the IRQ and I/O address on an NIC.

Plug and Play

Plug and Play (PnP) is the capability of a computer to automatically detect a new device and automatically configure it with the appropriate settings (I/O address, IRQ, memory address, and so on). The PnP option is integrated into many of the operating systems that are available today.

> **WARNING:** To take advantage of Plug and Play, a network interface card must be PnP-compliant.

The system should automatically configure an NIC by using the PnP options. Configuring an NIC with PnP normally requires the technician to do the following things:

- Power off the system
- Install the NIC
- Power on the system
- Allow the operating system to find the new NIC
- When prompted, install the correct driver
- Reboot and test the new NIC

The PnP software takes the responsibility of assigning the NIC an IRQ, I/O address, and any other necessary resources, such as a DMA (Direct Memory Access) channel. The software accomplishes these tasks by tracking all system devices, what resources they require, and what resources remain available for future assignment. For further details on PnP software on a specific system, refer to the operating system's documentation.

To install and configure older NICs or cards that are not PnP-compliant, use EEPROM or jumper configurations.

EEPROM and Jumpers

You can use two methods to configure non–PnP-compliant NICs: EEPROM configurations or jumpers.

EEPROM (Electronically Erasable Programmable Read-Only Memory) is a chip that resides on the NIC and that contains the unique settings for the IRQ and I/O address. The EEPROM can be configured by a special application, which is available from the NIC's manufacturer.

> **WARNING:** When you use EEPROM or jumpers to configure the NIC, ensure that the IRQ and I/O address are not in use by any other device on the system.

Jumpers are small plastic cubes with metal conductors inside that are used to physically set the IRQ and I/O address of an expansion card by shorting across two pins with the metal part of the jumper. To configure the jumpers for a particular setting, refer to the NIC's documentation.

Network Interface Card Settings

In addition to knowing how to configure NICs, you must know how to make a few of the default settings on the NICs you are installing, as well as the default settings of some of the hardware in a computer. Table 2.1 lists common IRQ and I/O addresses of hardware components. You must know this information when you install a networked computer, so that the new network card won't conflict with any hardware already installed in the computer. By default, most NICs are configured with an IRQ of 10 and an I/O address of 300h.

TABLE 2.1: Common IRQ and I/O addresses of hardware components

Device	IRQ	I/O Address
COM1\COM3	4	3F8h\3E8h
COM2\COM4	3	2F8h\2E8h
LPT1	7	378h
LPT2	5	278h
Network interface card	10	300h

When an NIC has been installed and configured correctly, but is receiving errors or is not communicating with the network, the next step is running NIC diagnostics.

Network Interface Card Diagnostics

When you are troubleshooting an NIC, using a manufacturer-supplied diagnostic test can help tremendously. Most diagnostic applications run the NIC through a series of internal tests and external loopback tests. The first step is running internal diagnostics, which test the components and functions of the card itself.

If the NIC has passed all internal diagnostics but is still receiving errors, the next step is to use a loopback plug and run external diagnostics. The external diagnostics use either a loopback plug or a second system elsewhere on the network running an echo program to return the diagnostic signals to the sending NIC. A *loopback plug* is a plug that fits into the port on an NIC and is wired in such a way as to connect the sending wires to the receiving wires, causing the network signal to loop back—hence, the name. An *echo program*, on the other hand, is a program designed to test network functionality through the use of *echoes* (packets that the receiving station sends back automatically). This type of program runs on a workstation on the same segment as the station being tested. The program's function is to respond automatically to the signals sent by the computer running the diagnostics.

The echo-system diagnostic program tests the NIC's capability to send and receive data across the network. When you use an echo system, you can cable it—with a crossover cable—directly to the workstation that you are testing.

When the NIC has passed all diagnostics, the next step in troubleshooting is checking the cabling.

> **NOTE** The infrastructure of a LAN can cause many connection problems. A standard unshielded twisted-pair network has four main points of failure: device to wall plate, wall plate to patch panel, patch panel to network component (hub, switch, or router), and network component to backbone (or main distribution point). The simple way to troubleshoot a LAN connection failure is to test it piece by piece. When the workstation hardware has been confirmed as working correctly, check to see whether other devices on the same network segment are working correctly. If they are, test the device when it is connected to a different port on the network device. Continue working through each port until the device connects correctly.

Understanding Networking Components

There are many types of networking components, each of which has advantages and disadvantages. A few of the most common components are hubs, switches, MAUs, repeaters, and transceivers.

Hubs

A *hub*, simply defined, is a network component that creates a central point to which devices physically attach. Hubs are mainly used with twisted-pair media, in a star or mesh topology (as shown in Figure 2.1). Hubs are broken into three primary categories: passive, active, and intelligent.

FIGURE 2.1
A hub used in a star topology

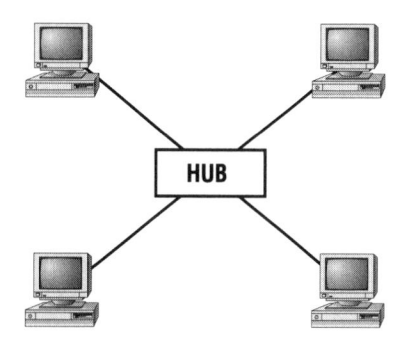

Passive Hubs

A *passive hub* is a network component that simply passes along any data that it receives; it does not amplify or regenerate the signal. ARCNet networks often use passive hubs.

> **NOTE** A passive hub can also be known as a dumb or workgroup hub.

Due to the fact that a passive hub does not have any type of processing capabilities, it passes along all signals received to all ports (connections). When you use a passive hub, remember that the maximum distance that media can be from the hub is 100 meters (10BaseT).

Active Hubs

An *active hub* is similar to a passive hub but has a few added features, including the capability to boost the signal and provide a small amount of management capability if it is Simple Network Management Protocol (SNMP)-compliant. As an active hub passes along a signal, it also boosts that signal, which can increase the maximum media cable length. The capability to boost the signal is similar to that of a repeater, as discussed in the "Repeaters" section later in this unit. The major drawback of these devices is the fact that they boost both the data portion of the signal and line noise. For that reason, repeaters and active hubs must follow the 5-4-3 rule. The *5-4-3 rule* states that for multiple network segments connected with repeaters, you can have a maximum of five segments and four repeaters, and up to three of the five segments can be populated with workstations. (The other two segments connect the populated segments.) An active hub requires electrical power to operate.

Intelligent Hubs

An *intelligent hub* acts more like a switch than either a passive or an active hub. Intelligent hubs can provide more management and a basic level of port switching called per-port switching. *Per-port switching* forwards packets based on the packet's address. This capability enables the component to send data intended for a specific device directly to that device and not broadcast the data to all its ports. An intelligent hub cannot be programmed on a per-port basis and does not provide any type of high-level fault tolerance.

Switching Hubs

A *switching hub*, or a *switch*, is a network component that can provide three services:

Per-port switching: Functions in the same manner as an intelligent hub, but a switch has the capability to learn the address of a device.

Per-port management: Allows the switch to be programmed with specific details on what type of device resides at each port. A switch can be programmed to know that a printer resides on port 1 and a workstation resides on port 2, for example. By knowing what type of device resides at each port, a switch can provide a better level of management.

High-level fault tolerance: Achieved in the switching environment because of a switch's capability to disable individual ports on command. If a specific segment on a network fails, a switch can disable all ports leading to that segment and allow the rest of the network to remain unaffected.

Multistation Access Units (MAUs)

Multistation access units, or MAUs (also called MSAUs), are the central devices that make the physical and logical connections in Token Ring networks. Although MAUs are similar in size and shape to hubs, they are very different; they connect all ports internally to provide the logical ring for a Token Ring network.

MAUs use IBM data connectors in ring topologies. MAUs also contain two specialized ports: a ring in and a ring out. These ports allow MAUs to be connected to other MAUs, ring in on the first to ring out on the second, and ring out on the first to ring in on the second.

Repeaters

A *repeater* is a network device that regenerates network signals. As a signal travels along a network media, it begins to lose its strength, thus allowing more data corruption to take place. When network media must be run beyond the recommended distance, you could add a repeater to regenerate the signal. When you use repeaters, remember that most types regenerate only the specific protocols for which they were designed and cannot perform any routing or segmenting.

> **Note:** Remember from the discussion of hubs earlier in this unit that repeaters must follow the 5-4-3 rule.

Transceivers

Transceivers are network components included on all NICs that convert a digital signal from the NIC to the appropriate analog signal for transmission on the network media, or vice versa. An NIC for a twisted-pair network, for example, contains a transceiver that converts the NIC's internal signal to a series of electrical pulses that can be transmitted out the RJ-45 connector. Transceivers can also be purchased as external adapters to convert between media types. If you have an NIC with a BNC adapter for coaxial media, but you have a twisted-pair network, you could use an external transceiver to convert the BNC connector to an RJ-45.

STUDY QUESTIONS

Troubleshooting on the Physical Layer

1. Plug and Play is integrated with what? _____

2. True or false: Any type of NIC works with Plug and Play.

3. On an NIC, Plug and Play automatically assigns the _____ and the I/O address.

4. EEPROM or _____ are used in non-Plug-and-Play NICs.

5. EEPROM is programmed by means of a specialized _____, which is provided by the card's manufacturer.

6. Jumpers are used to _____ set the IRQ and I/O address.

7. _____ and _____ tests are two of the types of diagnostics that an NIC can be run through.

8. _____ diagnostics test components located on the NIC.

9. External diagnostics use a _____ plug or an _____ program.

10. An external echo program diagnostic test helps test an NIC's capability to _____ and _____ data.

11. What is the default IRQ setting for an NIC? _____

STUDY QUESTIONS

12. What is the default I/O address for an NIC? _____

13. Name two points of failure on a LAN infrastructure.

_____

_____

Understanding Networking Components

14. Name three networking components discussed in this unit.

_____

15. Star and _____ are two types of topologies that use hubs.

16. The three types of hubs are: _____

17. A passive hub simply _____ any data that it receives.

18. True or false: Passive hubs have a large amount of processing capability.

19. The maximum recommended cable distance from a hub is _____ meters (10BaseT).

20. Name some of the differences between a passive hub and an active hub.

_____

21. One drawback of active hubs is that they boost _____ as well as data.

STUDY QUESTIONS

22. Per-port switching is available in _____ hubs.

23. True or false: An intelligent hub cannot be programmed on a per-port basis.

24. A switch is a network component that can provide per-port _____, per-port _____, and high-level fault tolerance.

25. A _____ has the capability to learn a device's address.

26. Per-port management allows a switch to be _____ with specific information about what type of device is located on each of its ports.

27. Fault tolerance is achieved in a switching environment because of a switch's capability to _____ a given port on command.

28. MAUs are used in a _____ environment.

29. True or false: MAUs are not powered and have no intelligence.

30. A _____ is used to boost a signal on a long cable run.

31. True or false: A repeater boosts any type of signal that it receives.

32. A transceiver is a network component that is built into all _____.

33. Transceivers can be purchased as external adapters to _____ between existing media.

SAMPLE TEST

2-1 You configure EEPROM by doing what?

    A. Using a special application

    B. Shorting pins, with a jumper

    C. Using a Plug-and-Play operating system

    D. None of the above

2-2 An NIC has been installed in a workstation. There are no hardware conflicts, and the cabling is known to be good, but the NIC still does not connect. What should you do next?

    A. Use the NIC's external diagnostics to test the NIC's components

    B. Use the NIC's internal diagnostics to test the NIC's components

    C. Replace the NIC

    D. None of the above

2-3 A new NIC has passed all internal diagnostics, and it has no hardware conflicts and good cabling, but it still does not connect. What tests could help diagnose this problem?

    A. The echo-server test

    B. A scandisk

    C. A self test

    D. A loopback test

2-4 To find the proper jumper settings for an NIC, you can do the following things:

    A. Look at the NIC's documentation

    B. Call the NIC manufacturer's technical-support line

    C. Go to the manufacturer's Web site

    D. All of the above

62 Unit 2 • The Physical Layer

SAMPLE TEST

2-5 What is the default IRQ and I/O address for most NICs?

    A. IRQ 10 & I/O address of 2FFh

    B. IRQ 12 & I/O address of 3FFh

    C. IRQ 15 & I/O address of 300h

    D. IRQ 10 & I/O address of 300h

2-6 You have just installed an NIC in a new Microsoft Windows 95 system, but the system could not find the card. The steps that you followed were turning off the power, installing the card, and powering on the system. What is the first thing that you should do now?

    A. Reboot

    B. Try a different NIC

    C. Confirm that the NIC is Plug-and-Play-compliant

    D. Try the NIC in a different computer

2-7 You have moved a good workstation to a newly cabled office. The NIC is known to have a good workstation-to-wall-plate patch cable at 100BaseT. The workstation does not connect. What is the first thing to check?

    A. The wall-plate-to-patch-panel cable

    B. The NIC

    C. The patch-panel-to-hub cable

    D. The workstation-to-wall-plate patch cable

2-8 What network component only passes along a signal (has no management capability)?

    A. Switch

    B. Passive hub

SAMPLE TEST

    C. Repeater

    D. Transceiver

2-9 What type of hub has the capability to boost a signal but cannot do any type of port switching?

    A. Active

    B. Passive

    C. Intelligent

    D. Routing

2-10 One drawback of an active hub is the fact that it:

    A. Boosts all incoming noise

    B. Cannot be programmed on a per-port basis

    C. Has no management capability

    D. Boosts only a specific type of signal

2-11 What network component has no power and no intelligence, and uses IBM data connectors?

    A. Passive hub

    B. MAU

    C. Transceiver

    D. Switch

2-12 Per-port switching, but not per-port programming, is available in what type of network component?

    A. Switch

    B. Router

SAMPLE TEST

   C. Intelligent hub

   D. Active hub

2-13 Per-port management is available in what network component?

   A. Switch

   B. Router

   C. Intelligent hub

   D. Active hub

2-14 A repeater increases a network signal's capability to:

   A. Travel over longer distances

   B. Resist magnetic interference

   C. Travel at faster speeds

   D. None of the above

2-15 A transceiver is a network component that resides on almost all network interface cards. What is its purpose?

   A. To convert between protocols

   B. To convert between media

   C. To convert between segments

   D. To convert between LAN speeds

SAMPLE TEST

2-16 A workstation with a 100Mbps card connects to the network only at 10Mbps. A known-good workstation was plugged into the same connection, using its NIC cable. The symptoms were the same. What do you check?

    A. The wall-plate-to-patch-panel cable

    B. The NIC

    C. The wall-plate-to-NIC cable

    D. The workstation-to-wall-plate cable

2-17 A switch achieves fault tolerance because of its capability to:

    A. Stop unauthorized users from logging in

    B. Disable a given port on command

    C. Connect to multiple workstations through a single NIC

    D. Track what Web sites are accessed

UNIT 3

The Data Link Layer

Test Objectives: The Data Link Layer Concepts

- **Describe the following Data Link layer concepts:**
  - Bridges (what they are and why they are used)
  - The 802 specs, including the topics covered in 802.2, 802.3, and 802.5
  - The function and characteristics of MAC addresses

Exam objectives are subject to change at any time without notice and at CompTIA's sole discretion. Please visit CompTIA's Web site (www.comptia.org) for the most current exam-objectives listing.

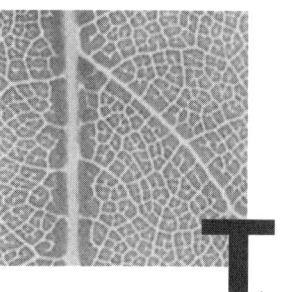

The Data Link layer is primarily responsible for the creation, transmission, and receipt of data packets. One feature of the Data Link layer is that it is divided into two sublayers: the *Logical Link Control* (LLC) and the *Media Access Control* (MAC). Bridges, the 802 standards, and MAC addressing are a few of the items that reside within the Data Link layer.

Bridges

A *bridge* is a network device that divides a single network into two distinct segments, isolating traffic on each side of the bridge but allowing certain packets to cross. A bridge allows packets from one network segment to pass to another network segment. If a packet reaches the bridge, and it is destined for a node on its own network, the bridge does not let the packet pass. This system is very useful in a network that contains one segment with heavy traffic and another segment with light traffic. Allowing the packets from a heavily used segment to pass into the light-traffic network would severely affect the performance of the light-traffic segment. Figure 3.1 shows the operation of a bridge.

FIGURE 3.1
Standard bridge operation

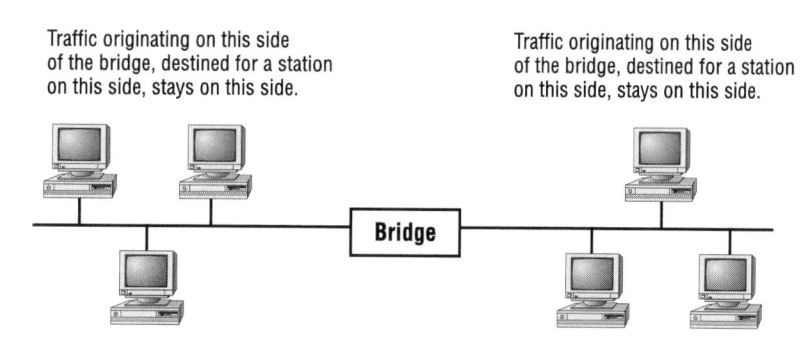

Traffic originating on this side of the bridge, destined for a station on this side, stays on this side.

Traffic originating on this side of the bridge, destined for a station on this side, stays on this side.

Traffic originating on one side of the bridge, destined for a station on the other side, is allowed to cross the bridge.

There are two types of bridges. The first type—an *MAC bridge*—operates at the MAC sublayer, whereas the second type—an *LLC bridge*—works at the LLC sublayer. A bridge that operates on the MAC sublayer can connect only networks that use the same architecture (Ethernet to Ethernet only, for example). A bridge that operates on the LLC sublayer can connect different architectures (Ethernet to Token Ring, for example).

The IEEE 802 Standards

The Institute for Electrical and Electronics Engineers (IEEE) developed the 802 standards to create a basis for the physical and electrical connection of networks. The 802 standards consist of many levels. The most important ones to know for the Network+ exam are the 802.2, 802.3, 802.4, and 802.5 standards.

802.2

The 802.2 standard defines the LLC layer for the other 802 standards. The LLC acts as an interface between the lower-layer protocols. In most cases, other 802 standards work in conjunction with the 802.2 standard.

802.3

The 802.3 standard was created from the original Digital Intel and Xerox (DIX) Ethernet, so networks based on 802.3 technologies are called *Ethernet*. The standard uses CSMA/CD (Carrier Sense Multiple Access with Collision Detection) as the media-access method. This media-access method listens for any other computer that is trying to transmit. If no other station is transmitting, it attempts its transmission. The sending station then listens to determine whether any other computer tried to transmit at the same time—a situation that is called a *collision*. If the sending station "hears" a collision, it backs off for a random amount of time and then retries the transmission. This standard also defines the 1Base5, 10Base2, 10Base5, 10BaseT, 10BaseF, and 10Broad36 physical topologies. Table 3.1 lists the specifications of these topologies.

TABLE 3.1: 802.3 physical topologies

Physical Topology	Maximum Distance Between Segments	Data Rate	Cable Type	Most Commonly Used Topology
1Base5	250 meters	1Mbps	UTP	Star
10Base2	185 meters	10Mbps	Thin coaxial	Bus
10Base5	500 meters	10Mbps	Thick coaxial	Bus
10BaseT	100 meters	10Mbps	Twisted-pair	Star
10BaseF	4 kilometers	10Mbps	Fiber-optic	Star
10Broad36	1,800 meters	10Mbps	75-ohm coaxial	Bus

802.4

The 802.4 standard was created for the Manufacturing Automation Protocol (MAP). The standard has a 10Mbps data rate and uses a bus topology. The 802.4 standard uses Token Passing technology as its media-access method. *Token Passing* is a media-access method that uses a special packet called a *token* to regulate access to the network medium. A station can transmit only when it has the token. To transmit, the token must not be in use by any other station. The station that has data to transmit takes the token, modifies the token to indicate that it is in use, and transmits both the data and token. When the data is received, the original sender modifies the token to indicate that the token is free, and the process begins again.

> **NOTE:** 802.4 is *not* ARCnet.

802.5

The 802.5 standard is derived from IBM's Token Ring networking technology. The standard uses a 4Mbps or 16Mbps data rate and is most commonly used in a logical ring with a physical star, using MAUs. The 802.5 standard also uses Token Passing technology as its media-access method.

MAC Addresses

MAC addresses reside within the MAC sublayer of the Data Link layer of the OSI model. A MAC address is a unique, factory-assigned number. The standard address layout for a MAC address is a set of six pairs of hexadecimal numbers separated by colons, in this format: xx:xx:xx:xx:xx:xx. An example of an MAC address is 45:a3:7h:33:2B:fc. The IEEE committee assigns a portion of this address to the manufacturer; the manufacturer assigns the rest of the address. An MAC address is also referred to as the *physical address*.

On very rare occasions, an MAC address has a duplicate on the same network. In such a case, an MAC-address conflict occurs, and you may receive errors on both stations. To solve this problem, you need to replace one of the devices. This action resolves the conflict, because the devices no longer have the same MAC address. If you don't resolve the conflict, neither device can receive packets because other network stations won't know which MAC address is the correct one.

> **NOTE** Not every network device has a hard-wired MAC address. Some NIC manufacturers provide the capability to change the MAC address with special software, to address the rare possibility of an MAC-address conflict.

STUDY QUESTIONS

The Data Link Layer Concepts

1. The Data Link layer is divided into two sublayers: the _____ and the _____.

Bridges

2. If a packet reaches a bridge, and it is destined for a device on the same network that it originated from, the bridge _____ the packet.

3. True or false: A bridge does not mediate the traffic between two networks.

4. True or false: A bridge can operate at either the MAC sublayer or the LLC sublayer of the Data Link layer.

The IEEE 802 Standards

5. 1Base5, 10Base2, and 10Base5 are part of the _____ standard.

6. The LLC is defined by the _____ standard.

7. _____ is defined by the 802.5 standard.

8. The MAP (Manufacturing Automation Protocol) was the basis for the _____ standard.

STUDY QUESTIONS

9. Which common network technology most closely resembles the IEEE 802.5 standard?

_____

10. What is the maximum segment length for a 10BaseT network segment?

_____

MAC Addresses

11. True or false: All MAC addresses can be assigned and changed by a network administrator.

12. True or false: F0.11.56.A1.99.A0 is an example of an MAC address.

13. True or false: MAC addresses are located at the Data Link layer of the OSI model.

SAMPLE TEST

3-1 You are the administrator of a network. The network has two segments and is plagued by large quantities of traffic that originate from one segment. Which network device could you place between the two segments to restrict the heavy traffic to only one of the segments?

   A. Hub

   B. Transceiver

   C. Bridge

   D. Modulator/demodulator

3-2 The 802.2 standard defines what layer or sublayer?

   A. MAC

   B. LLC

   C. Data Link

   D. JMS

3-3 A 4Mbps and 16Mbps data rate are used in what 802 standard?

   A. 802.10

   B. 802.5

   C. 802.3

   D. 802.4

3-4 If an MAC address is duplicated on the same network, how would you correct the problem?

   A. Move the MAC address to the LLC sublayer

   B. Reassign the MAC address

   C. Rebuild the network

   D. Replace the device

SAMPLE TEST

3-5 Which of the following specifications applies to 10BaseT?

    A. 185 meters maximum, 10Mbps, thin coaxial, bus topology

    B. 1 meter maximum, 10Mbps, fiber-optic, star topology

    C. 1,800 meters maximum, 10Mbps, 75-ohm coaxial, bus topology

    D. 100 meters maximum, 10Mbps, twisted-pair, star topology

3-6 Which of the following specifications applies to 10Broad36?

    A. 185 meters maximum, 10Mbps, thin coaxial, bus topology

    B. 1 meter maximum, 10Mbps, fiber-optic, star topology

    C. 1,800 meters maximum, 10Mbps, 75-ohm coaxial, bus topology

    D. 100 meters maximum, 10Mbps, twisted-pair, star topology

3-7 Which of the following specifications applies to 10Base2?

    A. 185 meters maximum, 10Mbps, thin coaxial, bus topology

    B. 1 meter maximum, 10Mbps, fiber-optic, star topology

    C. 1,800 meters maximum, 10Mbps, 75-ohm coaxial, bus topology

    D. 100 meters maximum, 10Mbps, twisted-pair, star topology

3-8 A bridge operates at which OSI-model layer?

    A. Physical

    B. Data Link

    C. Network

    D. Transport

SAMPLE TEST

3-9 Which networking component can you use to connect an Ethernet and a Token Ring network?

    A. Repeater

    B. Bridge

    C. Transceiver

    D. MUX

3-10 The factory presets what address on an NIC?

    A. DNS address

    B. TCP address

    C. MAC address

    D. OSI address

3-11 Which of the following is *not* an 802 specification?

    A. 802.5

    B. 802.2

    C. 802.3

    D. 802.15

3-12 What 802 specification describes an architecture that is similar to Ethernet?

    A. 802.1

    B. 802.2

    C. 802.3

    D. 802.4

UNIT 4

The Network Layer

Test Objectives: The Network Layer

- **Explain the following routing and Network layer concepts, including:**
  - The fact that routing occurs at the Network layer
  - The difference between a router and a brouter
  - The difference between routable and nonroutable protocols
  - The concept of default gateways and subnetworks
  - The reason for employing unique network IDs
  - The difference between static and dynamic routing

NOTE: Exam objectives are subject to change at any time without notice and at CompTIA's sole discretion. Please visit CompTIA's Web site (www.comptia.org) for the most current exam-objectives listing.

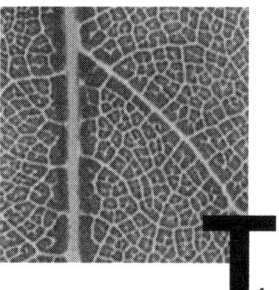

The Network layer's main responsibility is moving data to its specified destination between independent networks, or *internetworks*. Routing and gateways are two of the methods that the Network layer uses to accomplish this task.

Routing

Routing—the most important function of the Network layer—is the process by which packets are sent over various paths on their way to a destination. Routing provides a path for a node on one network to send packets to a node on another network. The functions of routing include route selection and route discovery.

Routers

Routers are the network devices that perform routing. Routers operate at the Network layer and are very complex devices. These devices use artificial intelligence and route-discovery protocols to select the individual route that a packet takes on its way to its destination. The router gets its information from a table, called the *routing table*, that it stores internally. This table is built either manually, by the administrator, or dynamically, through the use of route-discovery protocols (discussed later in this unit). Routers connect multiple networks into an internetwork. Each network connects to a port on the router. Figure 4.1 shows several routers and their routing tables.

Brouters

A *brouter*, or a *bridging router*, is a combination of a bridge and a router. A brouter works on both the Network and Data Link layers. A brouter attempts to deliver a packet to its destination by using the Network-layer information (routing the packet, for example). If the delivery attempt fails,

FIGURE 4.1

Routers and their terminology

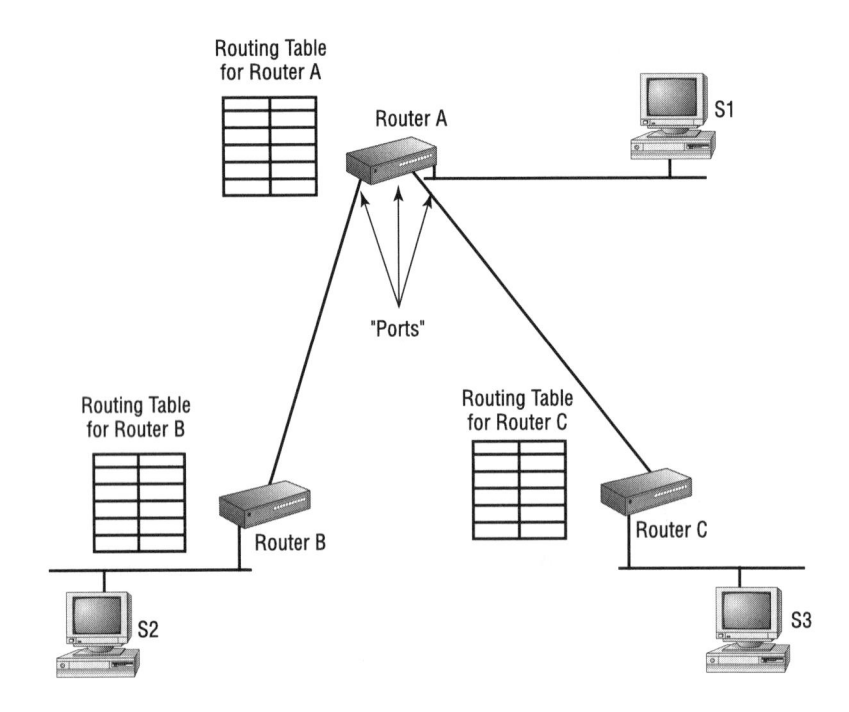

a router would discard the packet, but a brouter attempts to deliver that packet by using either Data Link layer information or the MAC address (bridging the packet, for example).

Routable Protocols

A *protocol* is the set of rules that govern network communications. A *routable protocol* is any protocol that contains Network-layer address information and that can be routed. Not all protocols are routable. Remember that within the same protocol stack, one protocol may be routable, but another may not be. Within the IPX/SPX protocol stack, for example, the IPX protocol is routable, but the SPX protocol is not. The main examples of routable protocols are:

- TCP/IP via IP
- IPX/SPX via IPX

Following are dynamic protocols that are used in routers:

- BGP (Border Gateway Protocol)
- EGP (Exterior Gateway Protocol)
- Integrated IS-IS (Integrated Intermediate System to Intermediate System)
- OSPF (Open Shortest Path First)
- RIP (Routing Information Protocol)
- RTMP (Routing Table Maintenance)
- SPF (Shortest Path First)

Route Selection

The optimum path for packets can be selected and a routing table can be built through dynamic or static route selection. Both dynamic and static route selection use a table of networks to route protocols.

Dynamic Route Selection

Dynamic route selection uses route-determination protocols such as RIP and OSPF to determine what routes exist and how to get there. This information is then placed in the routing table. Dynamic routing is used when routers are required to constantly adjust to network changes. The router reads the routing table and determine the path with the lowest cost.

> **Note:** Cost is a function of estimating both time and distance. The more time transmission takes or the farther data has to travel, the more expensive the path is.

Dynamic routing is the most efficient routing method. When a change occurs within the network, the router can reroute automatically to accommodate the change.

Static Route Selection

Static route selection occurs when an administrator modifies the routing table manually. An administrator or a specialized computer creates the table. The router cannot deviate from the path listed in the table. The static routing method forces the packets to travel along the prescribed path. This method creates a large amount of management overhead, because the network administrator must update the routing table manually any time the network changes.

Static routers minimize network traffic because they do not broadcast their routes. Routers that use the RIP protocol broadcast their entire routing table every 30 seconds. Following is an example of a static (generic) `route add` command:

`route add` *`network ID`* *`subnetmask`* *`default gateway`*

`route add` is the command.
`network ID` is the destination network number, such as 131.107.1.0.
`subnet mask` is the subnet mask for the entire network, such as 255.255.0.0.
`default gateway` is the IP of the router port that connects to your network.

Default Gateways

A *gateway* is a networking device that translates between different types of network protocols at any layer of the OSI model. A gateway can consist of hardware, software, or a combination. On TCP/IP networks, routers are often referred to as *gateways* when they connect one TCP/IP network to another TCP/IP network. When you configure TCP/IP on any host that connects to a router, you must specify a default gateway. The default gateway is the router connection to which all TCP/IP packets are sent on their way to a destination network (packets bound for a destination outside the local network).

Subnetworks

A *subnetwork* is a network that is part of a larger network. Individual devices within a subnetwork can use one type of protocol and can connect to the larger network with a single routing-protocol connection.

STUDY QUESTIONS

Routing

1. _____ and gateways are two of the tools that the Network layer uses.

2. Routing provides a _____ for a node on one network to send packets to a node on another network.

3. A brouter works on what two layers of the OSI model? _____ and _____

4. True or false: All protocols are routable.

5. _____ routing occurs when a router constantly adjusts to network changes.

6. _____ routing occurs when a prewritten routing table is used.

7. The static routing method forces packets to travel along a prescribed _____.

8. The _____ routing method involves a great deal of management overhead, because the administrator must update the routing table manually whenever the network changes.

Default Gateways

9. A _____ is a network device that connects to and translates between different types of networks.

10. A _____ is a network that resides within a larger network.

11. True or false: Nodes in a subnetwork must use multiple protocols to connect to a larger network.

SAMPLE TEST

4-1 If a brouter fails to deliver a packet by using Network-layer information, what does it do next?

   A. Tries using the Transport layer

   B. Drops the packet

   C. Tries using the Data Link layer

   D. Sends the packet to all devices on the network

4-2 A network administrator asks you what device you would use to connect a Token Ring network to an Ethernet network. What device would you suggest?

   A. Hub

   B. Filter

   C. Media converter

   D. Gateway

4-3 Which of the following protocols is routable?

   A. TCP/IP

   B. IPX/SPX

   C. NetBEUI

   D. RIP

4-4 Static routing occurs when a router does which of the following things?

   A. Uses a prewritten routing table for the paths

   B. Divides the packets and sends them to a different server

   C. Updates and changes paths by itself

   D. Routes any protocol

SAMPLE TEST

4-5 Which of the following statements are false?

    A. A gateway is a networking device that connects and translates between different types of networks.

    B. A gateway consists of hardware and/or software.

    C. A gateway is a networking device that allows only a backup connection between different types of networks.

    D. A gateway consists of software only.

4-6 Which type of routing requires the most management: static or dynamic?

    A. Static

    B. Dynamic

    C. Both require the same amount

    D. Neither requires any management

4-7 Which of the following is *not* a routable protocol?

    A. BGP

    B. RIP

    C. OSPF

    D. NETROUTE

4-8 A satellite office is connected to a larger company's network. What would you call the satellite office's network?

    A. Subnetwork

    B. Internetwork

SAMPLE TEST

C. Compact network

D. Reduced network

4-9 Which type of route discovery adds traffic to a network?

A. Static

B. Dynamic

C. Fault-tolerant

D. Subnet

4-10 A user complains to you that although she can communicate with anyone in her office, she cannot communicate with anyone outside her office. Which entry in her workstation's TCP/IP configuration would you inspect?

A. IP address

B. Subnetmask

C. WINS server

D. Default gateway

4-11 All workstations in an office can communicate with one another except for one workstation. The network uses the TCP/IP protocol. What do you suspect is the problem?

A. IP address

B. Default gateway

C. Subnet mask

D. Brouter

UNIT 5

The Transport Layer

Test Objectives: The Transport Layer

- **Explain the following Transport layer concepts:**
  - The distinction between connectionless and connection-oriented transport
  - The purpose of name resolution, either to an IP/IPX address or a network protocol

Exam objectives are subject to change at any time without notice and at CompTIA's sole discretion. Please visit CompTIA's Web site (www.comptia.org) for the most current exam-objectives listing.

The Transport layer is the fourth layer from the bottom in the OSI model, above the Physical, Data Link, and Network layers. and immediately below the Session layer. The lower layers together are responsible for the movement of packets from their source to their destination. The Transport layer is primarily responsible for transferring data at specified speeds and error rates, end-to-end data transportation, and flow control; it also establishes a logical connection between the sending host and the receiving host. This layer resides in the middle of the OSI model, separating the upper from the lower layers. The Transport layer is responsible for name resolution and network transport protocols.

Transport Options

Generally speaking, the Transport layer is responsible for reliable, end-to-end data transmission. To accomplish this task, the layer uses one of two transport methods: connection-oriented or connectionless.

Connection-Oriented Transmissions

Connection-oriented transmissions use acknowledgments for each packet sent, to establish a virtual connection between sender and receiver. It is important to remember that the receiver sends an acknowledgment for each packet (flow control), indicating that it received the packet correctly. If a packet is received in error, the sender is informed, either by a negative acknowledge or by a timeout; then the packet is retransmitted. Transmission Control Protocol (TCP) is connection-oriented. Connection-oriented transmissions have the following characteristics:

- The packets follow a single route.
- They are very reliable.

- They are slower and less efficient than other methods due to packet acknowledgments.

Connectionless Transmissions

Connectionless transmissions are transmissions that occur without a virtual connection between sender and receiver. When a connectionless transmission is used, the packets are sent to their destinations via any available path. The packets must be numbered, due to the fact that they are sent in random order through random connections and may become lost or duplicated. The sender merely sends the packets to the intended receiver. The receiver does not send an acknowledgment for each packet that arrives, so packets can be lost. If a packet is lost, the receiver knows, because one of the packets in the sequence is missing. The receiver then sends a packet to the original sender, saying, in effect, "I missed packet # x." The original sender returns packet # x as a reply. The TCP/IP User Datagram Protocol (UDP) and the IPX protocol (part of the IPX/SPX protocol stack) are examples of connectionless transport protocols.

Connectionless transmissions have the following characteristics:

- They are faster and more efficient than connection-oriented transmissions.

- They are less reliable due to lack of acknowledgments.

Name Resolution

Name resolution is the process of mapping an alphanumeric name to the numeric address of a network device (usually, a computer). Name resolution occurs on both IPX/SPX- and TCP/IP-based networks. A workstation could be referred to as ROOM102 instead of its TCP/IP address of 198.152.11.3, for example. Name resolution is initiated by either of two entities: the service requester or the service provider.

Service-Requester-Initiated

Service-requester-initiated name resolution occurs when the requester asks for a numeric address, using the alphanumeric name. The requester accomplishes this task by broadcasting a special packet, asking for the network address of a device. If a device wants to communicate with ROOM102, it sends out a broadcast, asking, in effect, "Will ROOM102 give me its address?" DNS (TCP/IP), Windows Internet Name Service (WINS/Microsoft), and NDS (NetWare 4.*x*'s global naming service) are service-requester-initiated name-resolution protocols.

Service-Provider-Initiated

Service-provider-initiated name resolution occurs when a network device broadcasts a special packet that contains the device's name and network address. This information is stored on other network devices for future use. A network device might broadcast a message that says, in effect, "Hi, my name is ROOM102, and my address is 198.152.11.3." Network devices consistently cache and maintain a local list of all the network entities, their names, and their network addresses. Service Advertisement Protocol (SAP/NetWare) uses a service-provider-initiated name-resolution method. NetWare 3.*x* servers periodically use the IPX SAP protocol to broadcast their names and addresses.

STUDY QUESTIONS

The Transport Layer

1. The Transport layer resides where in the OSI model ? _____

Transport Options

2. The Transport layer of the OSI model resides between the _____ and _____ layers.

3. A transmission within the subnet layer may be _____ or connectionless.

4. True or false: In a connection-oriented transmission, packets are numbered.

5. Which connection type confirms a connection before transmitting packets?

6. True or false: A connectionless transmission sends packets by using any available path.

7. In a connectionless transmission, packets are numbered because they are sent in _____ order.

8. TCP is an example of which connection type? _____

9. UDP is an example of which connection type ? _____

STUDY QUESTIONS

Name Resolution

10. Name resolution is the process of mapping _____ to a network device's numeric address.

11. _____ and _____ are methods of name resolution.

12. Service-requester-initiated name resolution occurs when the requester asks for a _____ address by using the alphanumeric name.

13. In _____, a server contains all network names and addresses, and performs the resolution between the two at the request of a workstation.

14. Service-provider-initiated name resolution occurs when a special packet is broadcast, containing the name and the _____.

15. What device broadcasts an address during service-provider-initiated name resolution? _____

SAMPLE TEST

5-1 The Transport layer is responsible for providing the transfer of data at which of the following?

   A. Cable types and distances

   B. Distances and speeds

   C. Speeds and error rates

   D. Error rates and cable types

5-2 Which name-resolution service asks for a device's address?

   A. Service-provider-initiated

   B. Service-requester-initiated

   C. Service-device-initiated

   D. Service-preceding-initiated

5-3 How does a connection-oriented transmission work?

   A. The sender sends numbered packets over any possible path.

   B. The sender and the receiver connect, the receiver broadcasts a packet saying that it is ready to accept packets, the packets are sent from last to first, and the connection is broken.

   C. The sender broadcasts numbered packets to all devices on the network until the intended receiver broadcasts back that it has received all packets.

   D. The sender and the receiver connect and confirm the connection; the sender sends the packets (unnumbered and along the same path) and breaks the connection.

5-4 What is the name of the process of mapping an alphanumeric name to a network device's network address?

   A. Number mapping

   B. Name resolution

SAMPLE TEST

    C. Alpha devices

    D. Name assigning

5-5 Which name-resolution service broadcasts its name and address?

    A. Service-provider-initiated

    B. Service-requester-initiated

    C. Service-device-initiated

    D. Service-preceding-initiated

5-6 How does a connectionless transmission work?

    A. The sender sends numbered packets over any possible path.

    B. The sender and the receiver connect, the receiver broadcasts a packet saying that it is ready to accept packets, the packets are sent from last to first, and the connection is broken.

    C. The sender broadcasts numbered packets to all devices on the network until the intended receiver broadcasts back that it has received all packets.

    D. The sender and the receiver connect, and confirm the connection; the sender sends the packets (unnumbered and along the same path) and then they both break the connection.

5-7 The Transport layer resides above which three layers of the OSI model?

    A. Physical, Network, Application

    B. Physical, Data Link, Network

    C. Physical, Data Link, Session

    D. Network, Session, Application

SAMPLE TEST

5-8 Which connection type is considered to be the most reliable for network communications?

   A. Connection-oriented

   B. Connectionless

   C. Connectionfull

   D. Connection-free

5-9 Which connection type is the most efficient?

   A. Connection-oriented

   B. Connectionless

   C. Connectionfull

   D. Connection-free

5-10 Which name-resolution protocol uses service-provider-initiated name resolution?

   A. NDS

   B. DNS

   C. RIP

   D. SAP

5-11 The names of network hosts are translated into network addresses by what OSI-model Transport-layer technology?

   A. Service lookup

   B. Name resolution

   C. System identification

   D. Network management

SAMPLE TEST

5-12 What is the name of the global naming service in Novell NetWare 4.*x*?

   A. WINS

   B. FBLA

   C. NDS

   D. Bindery

5-13 What is the name of the Windows and NetBIOS name-resolution service?

   A. WINS

   B. FBLA

   C. NDS

   D. Bindery

UNIT 6

TCP/IP Fundamentals

Test Objectives: TCP/IP Fundamentals

- **Demonstrate knowledge of the following TCP/IP fundamentals:**
  - The concept of IP default gateways
  - The purpose and use of DHCP, DNS, WINS, and host files
  - The identity of the main protocols that make up the TCP/IP suite, including TCP, UDP, POP3, SMTP, SNMP, FTP, HTTP, and IP
  - The idea that TCP/IP is supported by every operating system and millions of hosts worldwide
  - The purpose and function of Internet domain name server hierarchies (how e-mail arrives in another country)

- **Demonstrate knowledge of the fundamental concepts of TCP/IP addressing, including:**
  - A, B, and C classes of IP addresses and their default subnet mask numbers
  - The use of port number (HTTP, FTP, SMTP) and port numbers commonly assigned to a given service

- **Demonstrate knowledge of TCP/IP configuration concepts, including:**
  - The definition of *IP proxy* and why it is used
  - The identity of the normal configuration parameters for a workstation, including IP address, DNS, default gateway, IP proxy configuration, WINS, DHCP, host name, and Internet domain name

---

NOTE Exam objectives are subject to change at any time without notice and at CompTIA's sole discretion. Please visit CompTIA's Web site (www.comptia.org) for the most current exam-objectives listing.

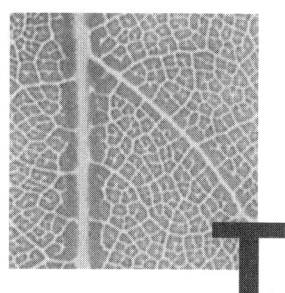

The *Transmission Control Protocol/Internet Protocol* (TCP/IP) stack of protocols has become very popular in the world of networking. TCP/IP was designed specifically for use on the Internet, and with the explosion of Internet use worldwide, more companies are connecting to the Internet. To make their networks easier to manage, companies choose to standardize on TCP/IP, because they can use it on both their networks and the Internet. All network operating systems now support TCP/IP utilities and protocols. Companies all over the world are now standardizing on TCP/IP protocols (including SMTP, FTP, and HTTP) so that they have only one suite of protocols to manage.

The TCP/IP suite is compatible with all common desktop operating systems, including the following:

- Microsoft Windows 95/98
- Microsoft Windows NT
- IBM OS/2
- Apple Macintosh
- Unix (including Linux, SCO, and UnixWare)

TCP/IP Fundamentals

As stated earlier in this unit, TCP/IP is a suite of protocols, which means that many individual protocols work together to facilitate network communication. You must understand a few fundamental components before using TCP/IP in a workstation environment. Each of these components affects the compatibility and manageability of the TCP/IP stack. These fundamental components are:

- Default gateways
- Windows TCP/IP concepts

- Individual TCP/IP protocols
- Domain server hierarchies

IP Default Gateways

Whenever you set up a network with TCP/IP and multiple routers, you need to specify a default gateway at the workstation. The IP *default gateway* is a parameter that tells the TCP/IP stack where it should send all traffic that is not local (that has a different network address from the network on which the workstation resides). You should fill in this parameter with the TCP/IP address of the primary router for that network segment.

Windows TCP/IP Concepts

Before configuring the TCP/IP stack on a Windows 9*x* or NT workstation, you must understand four concepts:

- Dynamic Host Configuration Protocol (DHCP)
- Domain Name System (DNS)
- Windows Internet Naming Service (WINS)
- Host files

Dynamic Host Configuration Protocol (DHCP)

In large TCP/IP networks (more than 100 users), configuring all TCP/IP parameters on every workstation can be a time-consuming task. For this reason, a protocol was developed to allow automatic assignment of TCP/IP configuration information at system startup. This protocol—DHCP—is used in TCP/IP networks to automatically assign to a host a TCP/IP address, subnet mask, and default gateway. When you use DHCP, you can assign TCP/IP information in either of two ways:

- Static assignment
- Dynamic assignment

Static Assignment When you use the static method to assign TCP/IP addressing information, you must preassign an address to a device. To do so, you add the device, referenced by its Media Access Control (MAC) address, computer name, and a TCP/IP address to a table in the DHCP server configuration program. When a DHCP server receives a request from a station for an IP address, it looks up the station's MAC address in the table and responds with the TCP/IP information assigned to that station's MAC address in the table. In the static addressing method, DHCP's only function is to pass to the workstation the TCP/IP configuration information that the DHCP server looks up in the DHCP table. This process is called *client reservation*.

Dynamic Assignment   Dynamic assignment occurs when a TCP/IP address is temporarily leased to a device by a DHCP server. To use the dynamic method of assigning TCP/IP addresses, you must specify a range of addresses (called a *pool* of addresses) that are available to be temporarily assigned, or leased, to a device. The TCP/IP address lease expires when the device is disconnected from the network. That TCP/IP address then becomes available to be assigned to the next device that requests an address. This arrangement prevents users from hogging a TCP/IP address.

DHCP servers can operate in what is often called automatic mode, in which they assign addresses to hosts automatically upon powerup. The address is leased to the client computer for a specified period (such as three days). This is a function of dynamic addressing, but it is often referred to as automatic mode or semipermanent mode.

Domain Name System (DNS)

DNS works on the Transport layer and provides Internet-domain-name-to-TCP/IP-address mapping for clients. This process is also known as *name resolution*. DNS is a hierarchical system of unique names (called *domain names*) used on the Internet to resolve the hierarchical name structures for various domains. When DNS performs name resolution, it first looks up the source address and then the destination address. In a browser request for www.hotmail.com, for example, DNS resolves this name to IP address 207.82.252.251.

Windows Internet Naming Service (WINS)

WINS is Microsoft's proprietary name-resolution service tool. This service is similar to DNS, but WINS uses a database to hold NetBIOS computer names and their TCP/IP addresses (instead of DNS host names and TCP/IP addresses). NetBIOS computer names are limited to 15 characters. WINS is used in place of an lmhosts file because the lmhosts file requires the manual entry of all computer-name to IP-address mappings, whereas WINS entries are automatic and change dynamically. WINS is used in place of an `lmhost` file to allow NetBIOS to be used to access servers across a router.

Host Files

DNS and WINS are examples of server-based name-resolution systems. If your network is simple enough that it doesn't need a DNS server, you can use host files. *Host file* is a general term that describes any text file that is used to associate host names with an IP address. A Unix computer uses a host name; a Microsoft computer uses a NetBIOS computer name. The two most common host files are `hosts` and `lmhosts`.

hosts File The `hosts` file (which actually is a file named `hosts` or `hosts.txt`) is the workstation equivalent of DNS. It is a list of DNS host names and their associated TCP/IP addresses. A TCP/IP stack can look in this file to find the address of a station, rather than use DNS requests to a DNS server.

lmhosts File The `lmhosts` file, which is the static equivalent of WINS, is a list of NetBIOS computer names and their associated TCP/IP addresses. Entries in this file allow computer NetBIOS names to be accessed over a TCP/IP network.

Individual TCP/IP Protocols

The TCP/IP protocol stack is constructed of many individual protocols. Only when these protocols are used together can they provide the desired stability for a network connection. The following sections describe a few of the protocols in the TCP/IP stack.

TCP

Transmission Control Protocol (TCP) is a connection-oriented and stream-oriented Transport-layer protocol. TCP uses IP to deliver packets. The stream portion of this protocol is similar to Novell's SPX.

UDP

User Datagram Protocol (UDP) is a connectionless protocol that works at the Transport layer. UDP uses IP at the Network layer. UDP can be used in place of TCP, but it is known as a thin protocol, because it cannot accomplish all the things that TCP can.

POP3

Post Office Protocol 3 (POP3) is an Application-layer protocol. It is used to access and transfer e-mail from mail post offices that use POP3 to a client computer running a POP3 e-mail client.

SMTP

Simple Mail Transfer Protocol (SMTP) is an Application-layer protocol used to provide simple e-mail services. SMTP uses TCP to send and receive. SMTP itself resides on the Application layer. The Unix network operating system uses SMTP to transfer e-mail between servers.

SNMP

Simple Network Management Protocol (SNMP) is used to provide network management. SNMP works at the Application layer to provide for the collection and manipulation of communication statistics by a manager computer.

FTP

File Transfer Protocol (FTP) resides on the Application layer and uses TCP to move packets at the Transport layer. The main use for FTP is to move or copy files and navigate directories between hosts.

HTTP

Hypertext Transfer Protocol (HTTP) is the primary protocol used on the World Wide Web (WWW). HTTP allows Web clients to interact and to transfer packets between Web servers and Web browsers. HTTP performs this process by using *Hypertext Markup Language* (HTML). A workstation's Web browser contains the configuration for HTML. HTTP operates primarily at the Application layer.

IP

Internet Protocol (IP) is the protocol in TCP/IP that is responsible for network addressing and internetwork routing. This protocol works on the Network layer and uses the Data Link layer to transmit packets. IP is responsible for giving a local address to a host. IP also uses packet switching to help ensure the delivery of its packets.

Domain Server Hierarchies

Internet domains can be assigned on a geographical or an organizational basis. An organizational domain contains domains that are arranged by a similar group or activity. At the time that this book was published, there were seven top-level organizational domains, which are listed in Table 6.1.

TABLE 6.1 Organizational Internet domains

Domain Name	Interpretation
com	Commercial organization
edu	Educational institution
gov	Government organization
int	International organization
mil	U.S. military
net	Networking organization
org	Not-for-profit organization

At the time that this book was published, there were 59 top-level geographical domains. A geographical domain most commonly represents a country. Table 6.2 lists the geographical domains.

TABLE 6.2: Geographical Internet domains

Domain Name	Interpretation	Domain Name	Interpretation	Domain Name	Interpretation
aq	Antarctica	fr	France	nl	Netherlands
ar	Argentina	gb	Great Britain	no	Norway
at	Austria	gr	Greece	nz	New Zealand
au	Australia	hk	Hong Kong	pl	Poland
be	Belgium	hr	Croatia	pr	Puerto Rico
bg	Bulgaria	hu	Hungary	pt	Portugal
br	Brazil	ie	Ireland		
ca	Canada	il	Israel	se	Sweden
ch	Switzerland	in	India	sg	Singapore
cl	Chile	is	Iceland	si	Slovenia
cn	China	it	Italy	su	Soviet Union
cr	Costa Rica	jp	Japan	th	Thailand
cs	Czech and Slovak Republics	kr	South Korea	tn	Tunisia
de	Germany	kw	Kuwait	tw	Taiwan
dk	Denmark	li	Liechtenstein	uk	United Kingdom
ec	Ecuador	lt	Lithuania	us	United States
ee	Estonia	lu	Luxembourg	ve	Venezuela
eg	Egypt	lv	Latvia	yu	Yugoslavia
es	Spain	mx	Mexico	za	South Africa
fi	Finland	my	Malaysia		

TCP/IP Addressing

A *TCP/IP address* (or *IP address* for short) is a unique, dotted-decimal numeric address that uniquely identifies a host on a TCP/IP network. The address consists of 4 bytes or 4 octets (an *octet* is a collection of 8 binary digits) separated by a period, as in the following example:

199.58.210.34

Each number in an IP address can range from 0 to 255, although the numbers 0 and 255 have special uses (0 refers to the network itself, and 255 is used to refer to all hosts on the network), so only 1 to 254 are actually available.

> **Note:** Remember that 1 byte is equal to 8 bits.

Addresses are broken into two parts: the network and the node. The *network* portion indicates the portion of the IP address that refers to the network. The *node* portion indicates the identity of the station on that particular network. The *class* of an address determines which part of the address is the network and which part is the node. Some utilities add a third portion, called the *port address* (although the actual numbered address is not visible as part of a TCP/IP address), that its services use to communicate with one another.

Network Address Classes

The network portion of an address is divided into three main classes:

- Class A
- Class B
- Class C

The class determines which portion of the TCP/IP address is the network and which is the node. The decimal number in the first octet of the address indicates the class of an address. If the first number is between 0 and 127 (as in 45.102.19.2), the address is a Class A address. The first octet refers to the network, and the last three octets refer to the individual nodes on that network. You can indicate this address scheme by using a subnet mask. A *subnet mask* is a set of numbers that illustrates the class of an address, using the number 255 for the network portion of the address and zeroes for the node portion in standard address classes. The subnet mask for a Class A address is 255.0.0.0, indicating that the first octet is the network portion (notice the 255); the last three octets are zeroes, indicating that you can use those numbers to identify hosts on that network.

You can have up to 127 Class A networks (numbered 0 through 127), and each Class A network can have up to 16,777,216 hosts. Classes B and C are similar, except that they have more networks and fewer hosts per network. Table 6.3 describes the three classes of TCP/IP addresses.

TABLE 6.3: TCP/IP classes

TCP/IP Class	Class A	Class B	Class C
Format	net.node.node.node	net.net.node.node	net.net.net.node
Default Subnet	255.0.0.0	255.255.0.0	255.255.255.0
Range for First Octet	1 – 127	128 – 191	192 – 223
Sample Address	125.162.102.134.	158.192.102.123	204.124.142.126
Total Node Addresses per Network	$(2^{24})-2$: 16,777,214	$(2^{16})-2$: 65,534	$(2^{8})-2$: 254
Total Network Addresses	$2^{(8-1)}$: 127	$2^{(16-2)}$: 16,384	$2^{(24-3)}$: 2,097,152

Port Numbering

At any time, any number of TCP/IP services (such as FTP and HTTP) can be running on a TCP/IP host. A port number allows TCP/IP transport protocols (TCP and UDP) to differentiate the upper-layer TCP/IP protocol or service (such as FTP, HTTP, or DNS) on a host to which it should deliver a packet. The port numbers are assigned by the Internet Engineering Task Force (the standards body that works on developing Internet standards, including TCP/IP) when the new protocols are introduced.

Use of Port Numbers

Each service on a TCP/IP host—SNMP, ICMP, FTP, and so on—is assigned a unique port. A client application formats the request for the service that it wants by addressing the packet to the host's IP address and the service's specific port number. When the host that is hosting the service receives the TCP/IP packet, it knows the service for which the packet is destined because of the port number.

Commonly Assigned Port Numbers

Table 6.4 lists some individual protocols/services in the TCP/IP protocol stack and their associated port numbers.

TABLE 6.4 Default ports

Protocol	Default Port
FTP	21
Telnet	23
SMTP	25
HTTP	80
POP3	110
NTTP	119

TCP/IP Configuration Concepts

To have use of the TCP/IP stack for an Internet connection, a workstation must have the TCP/IP protocol and the correct network adapter driver installed. After these items are installed, they must be configured. You must understand two major concepts to configure TCP/IP correctly:

- IP proxy
- Workstation configuration parameters

IP Proxy

A TCP/IP proxy, or *IP proxy*, is a network service that makes Internet requests on behalf of a workstation on your network. This technology is also known as *network address translation*. IP proxies act as translators between a LAN and the Internet, intercepting all requests going out to the Internet and replacing the sender's IP address with that of the IP proxy. When the response comes from the Internet, the response is addressed to the IP proxy instead of to a particular workstation. The proxy replaces its own address in the response with the address of the station for which the response is destined and then sends the packet on the internal network. This technology is useful when you want to use a single TCP/IP address over the Internet (or have only one TCP/IP address available), regardless of what workstation is sending it. An IP proxy also allows an administrator to manage Web connections on a port-per-port basis.

Workstation TCP/IP Configuration Parameters

Generally speaking, TCP/IP is fairly simple to configure for most computers; you have to configure only a few parameters. Quite a few optional parameters add extra TCP/IP functionality to a workstation when they are implemented. The available configuration parameters include the following:

- Host IP address and subnet mask
- DNS information
- Default gateway
- IP proxy configuration (optional)
- WINS (optional)
- DHCP (optional)
- Host name
- Internet domain name

IP Address and Subnet Mask

When you are configuring a workstation for TCP/IP, you must configure an IP address and a subnet mask on the TCP/IP stack of the workstation. The workstation cannot communicate on a TCP/IP network unless you configure at least those two parameters. The IP address must be unique on that network to uniquely identify that station on the network. The subnet mask indicates what kind of IP address is being used on that workstation. If your network is connected to the Internet, your Internet Service Provider assigns a block of TCP/IP addresses (usually, a range of dotted-decimal numbers) and a subnet mask for you to use. If you aren't connected to the Internet (or aren't going to be connected in the future), you can pick any IP addressing scheme that you want to use, as long as the class of address and subnet mask match.

You must input the IP address and the subnet mask in the TCP/IP protocol configuration for your particular operating system. The location where you enter this information varies between operating systems. In Windows $9x$, you open the Network Control Panel (choose Start ➤ Settings ➤ Control Panel) and double-click Network); click the TCP/IP protocol; and click Properties. You can then enter the TCP/IP address and subnet mask in the dialog box, in the fields designated for them. Reboot your system, and the system will have basic TCP/IP communications capabilities.

DNS

When you configure a workstation to use DNS, you must set three parameters: the DNS server's IP address, the local host name, and the Internet domain name of the host that you are configuring. Where you configure these parameters depends on the operating system. In Windows $9x$, you add this information to the DNS tab of the TCP/IP Protocol Properties dialog box, which you access from the Network Control Panel as described in the preceding section.

Default Gateway

The *default gateway* is a parameter that indicates to the TCP/IP stack where this workstation should send all packets that are destined for other networks. You must specify the default gateway on the workstation if you want this workstation to be able to send packets to hosts on other networks. The address that you type for this parameter is the IP address of the router interface (connection) that connects your workstation's network segment to the Internet. By default, this parameter is blank; you must fill it in to be able to send IP packets to other networks.

As is true of the other parameters, where you configure this parameter depends on the OS. To configure the default gateway in Windows 9*x*, you still use the properties of the TCP/IP protocol, but you enter the information in the Gateway tab of the TCP/IP Properties dialog box.

IP Proxy Configuration

Many IP proxy servers are available, including Microsoft's and Novell's, and each IP proxy has a different method of configuration. Most IP proxies, however, don't require any workstation configuration. The server is configured with two IP addresses: one on the NIC that connects to the Internet, and the other on the NIC that connects to the internal network. All IP addresses on the internal network (LAN and proxy server) can use any IP addressing scheme, as long as it fits within a certain class. The IP proxy is configured to translate a browser request between these two addresses. Access to the proxy server is configured through the browser. In Windows 95, on the Desktop, right-click the browser's icon and choose Properties; then choose the Connection folder. The second radio button allows you to choose a proxy server. Choose a radio button and then enter either the proxy server's name or its IP address.

> **NOTE** This parameter is optional; it is required only if your network uses an IP proxy to access the Internet.

WINS

You must configure the WINS parameter on TCP/IP workstations that run any version of Microsoft Windows (including 9*x* and NT). This parameter indicates to the Windows machine what method it should use to resolve NetBIOS computer names over TCP/IP. To configure WINS on a workstation, you must enable WINS and specify a primary WINS server. To configure WINS on a Microsoft Windows 95/98 workstation, for example, choose Start ➤ Settings ➤ Control Panel ➤ Network ➤ TCP/IP ➤ Properties ➤ WINS Configuration.

DHCP

No specific parameter tells a workstation which DHCP server to use (unlike the other TCP/IP parameters). To use DHCP to assign a TCP/IP address, you must direct a workstation to use the DHCP server. This setting is usually the default in most Windows TCP/IP stacks. The setting usually is a check box that asks a variant of "Obtain an IP address automatically?" If you change this setting, you must configure the workstation with a static IP address and subnet mask. If you accept the default setting, the DHCP server automatically assigns an IP address and a subnet mask, as well as any other parameters configured on the DHCP server, such as the default gateway.

Host Name

The *host name* is the DNS name of a particular workstation. You must configure the host name so other workstations on the network can identify this workstation by DNS name, rather than just by IP address. You can assign host names in many ways, depending on the OS that you are using. On Windows 9x workstations, you use the DNS tab of the TCP/IP Properties dialog box to configure the host name of that workstation. By default, this parameter is blank. This parameter tells the workstation what host name to use in all TCP/IP communications.

Internet Domain Name

The final parameter that you should configure on a workstation is the Internet Domain Name of the network on which this workstation resides. You obtain this information from the Internet Service Provider to which you are connecting, if you do not have your own domain name. This parameter is optional. If you fill in this parameter, this workstation knows what Internet domain it is part of and can use that information in future TCP/IP communications. You configure this parameter in different places in different operating systems, but in Windows 9x, you use the DNS tab of the TCP/IP Properties dialog box.

STUDY QUESTIONS

TCP/IP Fundamentals

1. Name three operating systems that are compatible with a TCP/IP stack.
_____

2. What TCP/IP component do you use to statically, dynamically, or automatically assign a TCP/IP address? _____

3. Which DCHP assignment method uses a manually assigned (dedicated) TCP/IP address?
_____

4. Which DHCP assignment method uses a leased address for a pool of available TCP/IP addresses? _____

5. Which DHCP assignment method is a combination of the other two assignment methods?
_____

6. What TCP/IP component is Microsoft's proprietary NetBIOS name-resolution tool?
_____

7. WINS is similar to what other TCP/IP protocol? _____

8. Internet domains can be assigned on a geographical or an _____ basis.

9. Name four of the seven current top-level organizational Internet domains.
_____

STUDY QUESTIONS

10. aq is what type of Internet domain? _____

11. True or false: ne is the geographical Internet domain for the Netherlands.

12. What is the geographical Internet domain for the United States of America? _____

13. True or false: The TCP protocol, within the TCP/IP stack, is a connectionless protocol.

14. Name the protocol in the TCP/IP stack that routes packets. _____

15. On a Microsoft Windows 95/98 workstation using the TCP/IP stack, DNS mappings are stored in which local file? _____

16. On a Microsoft Windows 95/98 workstation using TCP/IP, NetBIOS computer-name mappings are stored in which local file? _____

17. Which protocol in the TCP/IP stack can you use in place of the TCP protocol? _____

18. Which protocol in the TCP/IP stack is used for network management? _____

19. SMTP resides on which layer of the OSI model? _____

STUDY QUESTIONS

20. Which protocol in the TCP/IP stack is mainly used to copy files and navigate directories? _____

21. Which protocol in the TCP/IP stack allows transfers between Web browsers and Web servers? _____

TCP/IP Addressing

22. What TCP/IP component allows an operating system to differentiate the service to which it should forward a packet? _____

23. What is the default port for Telnet? _____

24. What is the default port for POP3? _____

25. What is the default port for NTTP? _____

26. What is the default port for HTTP? _____

27. What is the default port for SMTP? _____

28. What is the default subnet mask for the address 204.153.163.38? _____

29. What is the default subnet mask for the address 17.30.108.44? _____

STUDY QUESTIONS

30. What is the default subnet mask for the address 150.200.14.33? _____

31. How many nodes can you have per network using a Class A TCP/IP address?
_____

32. How many bits are in 1 byte (in standard IP configurations)? _____

33. What is the default subnet mask for a Class A TCP/IP address? _____

34. What is the range of network addresses for the first byte in a Class A TCP/IP address?
_____

35. What is the default subnet mask for a Class B TCP/IP address? _____

36. What is the range of network addresses for the first byte in a Class B TCP/IP address?
_____

37. What is the default subnet mask for a Class C TCP/IP address? _____

38. What is the range of network addresses for the first byte in a Class C TCP/IP address?
_____

39. How many network addresses are available in a Class B TCP/IP addressing scheme?
_____

40. How many node addresses per network are available in a Class B TCP/IP addressing scheme? _____

STUDY QUESTIONS

41. The TCP/IP address 207.34.102.2 is an example of a Class _____ address.

TCP/IP Configuration Concepts

42. For a workstation to connect to the Internet, it must have what protocol stack loaded, along with the correct network adapter driver? _____

43. Name the five items listed in this unit that you should configure when you install the TCP/IP stack.

_____, _____, _____,
_____, _____

44. To have all workstations on a network broadcast a single TCP/IP address, what parameter should you use? _____

45. To set DNS on a workstation, what three DNS parameters do you need to configure?

_____, _____, _____

46. When a TCP/IP address is assigned with a static connection, you need to set the default gateway and what other component? _____

47. On a Microsoft Windows 95/98 workstation, how do you configure WINS?

_____

48. If your workstation resides on a network that is connected to the Internet, what parameter (in addition to an IP address and subnet mask) must you configure for packets to be sent to the Internet properly? _____

STUDY QUESTIONS

49. What IP address gets sent to a Web server when you are browsing the Web, using an IP proxy? _____

50. Which Windows 9x TCP/IP parameters are optional when you are configuring a workstation for browsing the Internet and Web sites?
_____

SAMPLE TEST

6-1 What is the default TCP/IP port for FTP?

   A. 25

   B. 21

   C. 80

   D. 119

6-2 A Microsoft Windows 95/98 workstation on a network that is connected to the Internet has been configured with a static TCP/IP address. What other parameters must you set on the workstation?

   A. Subnet mask

   B. Default gateway

   C. DHCP address

   D. Primary WINS server

6-3 What service would you use to assign an IP address, a subnet mask, and a default gateway automatically?

   A. WINS

   B. DHCP

   C. DNS

   D. lmhosts

6-4 You want to broadcast a single IP address across the Internet, regardless of which PC is used. What TCP/IP component do you use to accomplish this task?

   A. Cache

   B. Host

SAMPLE TEST

    C. Proxy

    D. Bridge

6-5 What parameters do you specify to configure a DNS lookup?

    A. Server IP address

    B. Host name

    C. Internet domain name

    D. Windows NT domain name

6-6 What local file can you alter on a Windows 95/98/NT machine to resolve www.sybex.com to its network address?

    A. hosts

    B. lmhosts

    C. iphosts

    D. nthosts

6-7 Which TCP/IP parameters can you configure on a workstation?

    A. IP address

    B. DHCP server address

    C. DNS server

    D. WINS server

6-8 What protocol performs name resolution on a non-NetBIOS network?

    A. WINS

    B. DNS

SAMPLE TEST

C. DHCP

D. lmhosts

6-9 What local file can you alter on a Windows 95/98/NT machine to resolve the NetBIOS name \\ntfsone to its TCP/IP network address?

A. hosts

B. lmhosts

C. iphosts

D. nthosts

6-10 What is the default TCP/IP port for SMTP?

A. 25

B. 21

C. 80

D. 119

6-11 Which TCP/IP protocol is primarily used for network management?

A. HTTP

B. SMTP

C. SNMP

D. FTP

6-12 What TCP/IP protocol does your client use to download e-mail from a server?

A. SMTP

B. POP3

SAMPLE TEST

C. SNMP

D. FTP

6-13 What is the default TCP/IP port for HTTP?

A. 21

B. 25

C. 80

D. 119

6-14 What TCP/IP protocol is used to transfer files between two hosts?

A. FTP

B. SNMP

C. TCP

D. UDP

6-15 What TCP/IP protocol is used to assign a logical address to a host?

A. TCP

B. UDP

C. IP

D. SMTP

6-16 If you have been assigned an IP address of 223.123.75.142, what is the default subnet mask?

A. 255.255.255.220

B. 255.255.255.255

C. 228.123.75.142

D. 255.255.255.0

SAMPLE TEST

6-17 What TCP/IP protocol is used to transfer files from a Web server to a Web browser?

   A. SMTP

   B. HTTP

   C. ICMP

   D. OSPF

6-18 What is the default subnet mask for a Class C TCP/IP address?

   A. 255.255.255.0

   B. 255.255.0.0

   C. 255.255.255.255

   D. 255.0.0.0

6-19 Which of the following are valid Internet domains?

   A. com

   B. edu

   C. fre

   D. fr

6-20 Which of the following is a valid Class B TCP/IP address?

   A. 126.34.98.0

   B. 225.34.11.3

   C. 199.165.213.3

   D. 191.67.23.1

SAMPLE TEST

6-21 What is the default subnet mask for a Class A TCP/IP address?

    A. 255.255.255.0

    B. 255.255.0.0

    C. 255.255.255.255

    D. 255.0.0.0

6-22 In which TCP/IP class does the address 171.32.123.10 belong?

    A. Class A

    B. Class B

    C. Class C

    D. Class D

6-23 What is the default TCP/IP port for NTTP?

    A. 80

    B. 110

    C. 117

    D. 119

6-24 What are the minimum network software components required to connect a Microsoft Windows 95/98 machine to the Internet?

    A. TCP/IP protocol

    B. Client for NetWare Networks

    C. Network adapter driver

    D. NetBEUI protocol

SAMPLE TEST

6-25 What are the minimum steps required to configure WINS on a Microsoft Windows 95/98 workstation?

    A. Enable WINS resolution

    B. Disable WINS resolution

    C. Enter primary WINS server

    D. Enter secondary WINS server

6-26 Which of the following TCP/IP addresses is a valid Class C address?

    A. 199.334.4.44

    B. 10.2.233.0

    C. 191.67.23.1

    D. 199.165.213.3

    E. 225.34.11.3

6-27 Which of the following are valid TCP/IP protocols?

    A. DHCP

    B. TCP

    C. RIP

    D. OSPF

UNIT 7

TCP/IP Suite: Utilities

Test Objectives: TCP/IP Suite: Utilities

- **Explain how and when to use the following TCP/IP utilities to test, validate, and troubleshoot IP connectivity:**
  - ARP
  - NBTSTAT
  - NETSTAT
  - FTP
  - Ping
  - ipconfig
  - winipcfg
  - tracert
  - Telnet

Exam objectives are subject to change at any time without notice and at CompTIA's sole discretion. Please visit CompTIA's Web site (www.comptia.org) for the most current exam-objectives listing.

The TCP/IP stack includes utilities that can be very useful for troubleshooting and configuring TCP/IP connections. ARP, NBTSTAT, NETSTAT, FTP, Ping, ipconfig/winipcfg, tracert, and Telnet are a few of the most commonly used utilities.

ARP

ARP (Address Resolution Protocol) resides on the Network layer of the OSI model. The TCP/IP ARP utility is used to display the *ARP table*, which is the file that contains TCP/IP name-resolution information. Figure 7.1 shows an example of the output of the ARP command used with the -a switch.

FIGURE 7.1
ARP-output display

```
Interface: 204.153.163.3 on Interface 2
   Internet Address      Physical Address    Type
   204.153.163.2         00-a0-c9-d4-bc-dc   dynamic
   204.153.163.4         00-a0-c0-aa-b1-45   dynamic
```

ARP maps TCP/IP addresses to MAC addresses. The Data Link layer, which includes the MAC layer, manages a table of TCP/IP-to-physical-address mappings. If a TCP/IP address is requested and is not in the table, ARP sends out a discovery packet. The ARP utility is a useful troubleshooting tool because of its capability to display and modify the TCP/IP-to-physical-address table. The ARP utility, like other command-line utilities, has switches that are used with it to change the way that the utility works. Figure 7.2 shows the different switches that are integrated with the ARP command.

FIGURE 7.2

ARP command switches

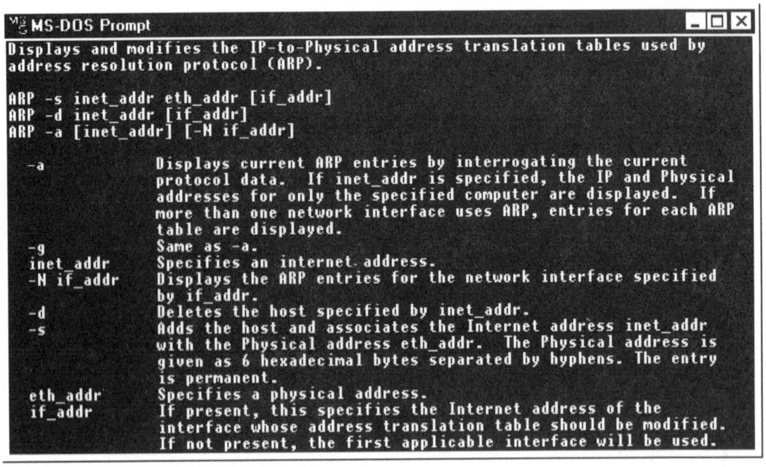

```
Displays and modifies the IP-to-Physical address translation tables used by
address resolution protocol (ARP).

ARP -s inet_addr eth_addr [if_addr]
ARP -d inet_addr [if_addr]
ARP -a [inet_addr] [-N if_addr]

   -a          Displays current ARP entries by interrogating the current
               protocol data. If inet_addr is specified, the IP and Physical
               addresses for only the specified computer are displayed. If
               more than one network interface uses ARP, entries for each ARP
               table are displayed.
   -g          Same as -a.
   inet_addr   Specifies an internet address.
   -N if_addr  Displays the ARP entries for the network interface specified
               by if_addr.
   -d          Deletes the host specified by inet_addr.
   -s          Adds the host and associates the Internet address inet_addr
               with the Physical address eth_addr. The Physical address is
               given as 6 hexadecimal bytes separated by hyphens. The entry
               is permanent.
   eth_addr    Specifies a physical address.
   if_addr     If present, this specifies the Internet address of the
               interface whose address translation table should be modified.
               If not present, the first applicable interface will be used.
```

NBTSTAT

The *NBTSTAT* (NetBIOS-TCP/IP Statistics) utility allows an administrator to view a device's current NetBIOS (computer name) information that uses TCP/IP connections (also called NetBIOS over TCP/IP or NBT). This utility can be useful for troubleshooting a WINS name-resolution error. Figure 7.3 shows the features and commands that are built into the NBTSTAT utility.

FIGURE 7.3

NBTSTAT command switches

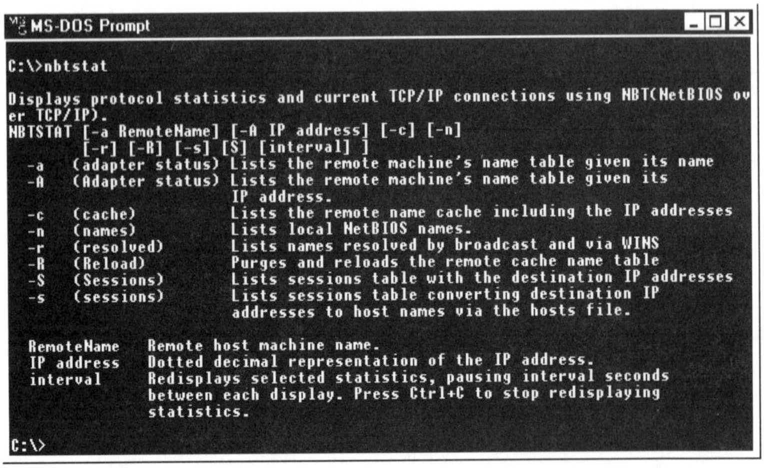

```
C:\>nbtstat

Displays protocol statistics and current TCP/IP connections using NBT(NetBIOS ov
er TCP/IP).

NBTSTAT [-a RemoteName] [-A IP address] [-c] [-n]
        [-r] [-R] [-s] [S] [interval] ]

   -a   (adapter status) Lists the remote machine's name table given its name
   -A   (Adapter status) Lists the remote machine's name table given its
                         IP address.
   -c   (cache)          Lists the remote name cache including the IP addresses
   -n   (names)          Lists local NetBIOS names.
   -r   (resolved)       Lists names resolved by broadcast and via WINS
   -R   (Reload)         Purges and reloads the remote cache name table
   -S   (Sessions)       Lists sessions table with the destination IP addresses
   -s   (sessions)       Lists sessions table converting destination IP
                         addresses to host names via the hosts file.

   RemoteName   Remote host machine name.
   IP address   Dotted decimal representation of the IP address.
   interval     Redisplays selected statistics, pausing interval seconds
                between each display. Press Ctrl+C to stop redisplaying
                statistics.

C:\>
```

NETSTAT

The *NETSTAT* utility displays all the current connections that a workstation is holding. The utility also can display the ports and statistics of current connections. Command switches allow the NETSTAT utility to display the router table. All the switches built into this utility make it very useful for diagnosing what protocols are running and where they are going at any time. Figure 7.4 shows the NETSTAT utility's help file, which displays all the command switches.

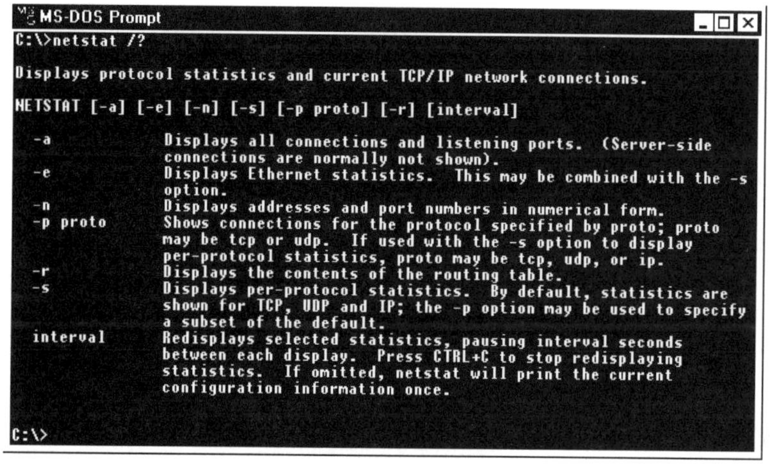

FIGURE 7.4
NETSTAT command switches

```
C:\>netstat /?
Displays protocol statistics and current TCP/IP network connections.

NETSTAT [-a] [-e] [-n] [-s] [-p proto] [-r] [interval]

  -a          Displays all connections and listening ports. (Server-side
              connections are normally not shown).
  -e          Displays Ethernet statistics. This may be combined with the -s
              option.
  -n          Displays addresses and port numbers in numerical form.
  -p proto    Shows connections for the protocol specified by proto; proto
              may be tcp or udp. If used with the -s option to display
              per-protocol statistics, proto may be tcp, udp, or ip.
  -r          Displays the contents of the routing table.
  -s          Displays per-protocol statistics. By default, statistics are
              shown for TCP, UDP and IP; the -p option may be used to specify
              a subset of the default.
  interval    Redisplays selected statistics, pausing interval seconds
              between each display. Press CTRL+C to stop redisplaying
              statistics. If omitted, netstat will print the current
              configuration information once.

C:\>
```

FTP

FTP (File Transfer Protocol) uses the TCP transport protocol to move or copy files. The FTP protocol is mainly used in a TCP/IP environment to transfer files to a workstation. This protocol works at the three top layers of the OSI model: Session, Presentation, and Application. At each layer, the FTP utility and protocol have a different function:

- At the Session layer of the OSI model, the FTP protocol supports connection creation, release, and file transfer.

- At the Presentation layer of the OSI model, the FTP protocol manages translation, which gives this protocol the capability to transfer files between hosts.
- At the Application layer of the OSI model, the FTP protocol provides network services in the form of file and collaborative services.

Ping

Ping (Packet Internet Groper) is an application that determines whether a TCP/IP host can be reached and is responding. This application sends an echo packet, using the Internet Control Message Protocol (ICMP), and if the echo packet reaches its destination, the receiver sends an echo-reply packet back to the original sender. Figure 7.5 shows an example of a Ping response. Ping can test whether TCP/IP is loaded and working properly on the local machine by pinging address 127.0.0.1 or executing a `ping localhost` command.

FIGURE 7.5

Ping Sample output

```
ping 204.153.163.2

Pinging 204.153.163.2 with 32 bytes of data:

Reply from 204.153.163.2: bytes=32 time<10ms TTL=128
Reply from 204.153.163.2: bytes=32 time=1ms TTL=128
Reply from 204.153.163.2: bytes=32 time<10ms TTL=128
Reply from 204.153.163.2: bytes=32 time<10ms TTL=128
```

Ping can also deliver the time that it took the echo packet to travel to its destination and back. Figure 7.6 shows the command switches that are integrated with the `ping` command.

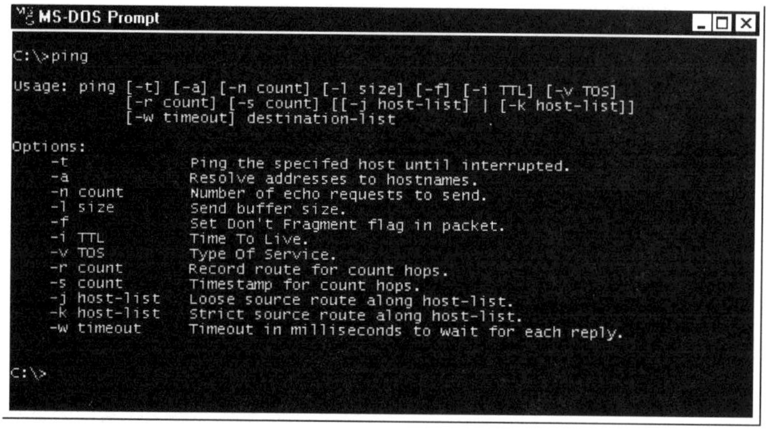

FIGURE 7.6

Ping command switches

```
C:\>ping
Usage: ping [-t] [-a] [-n count] [-l size] [-f] [-i TTL] [-v TOS]
            [-r count] [-s count] [[-j host-list] | [-k host-list]]
            [-w timeout] destination-list

Options:
    -t              Ping the specifed host until interrupted.
    -a              Resolve addresses to hostnames.
    -n count        Number of echo requests to send.
    -l size         Send buffer size.
    -f              Set Don't Fragment flag in packet.
    -i TTL          Time To Live.
    -v TOS          Type Of Service.
    -r count        Record route for count hops.
    -s count        Timestamp for count hops.
    -j host-list    Loose source route along host-list.
    -k host-list    Strict source route along host-list.
    -w timeout      Timeout in milliseconds to wait for each reply.

C:\>
```

ipconfig/winipcfg

The functions of the ipconfig and winipcfg utilities are very similar. Both utilities allow an administrator to retrieve TCP/IP statistics for review and to release or renew current TCP/IP connections. The main difference is that the ipconfig utility (see Figure 7.7) is used primarily by Microsoft Windows NT, whereas the winipcfg utility (see Figure 7.8) is used by Microsoft Windows 95 and 98.

FIGURE 7.7

Microsoft Windows NT's ipconfig

```
C:\>ipconfig

Windows NT IP Configuration

Ethernet adapter E100B1:

        IP Address. . . . . . . . . . : 204.153.163.2
        Subnet Mask . . . . . . . . . : 255.255.255.0
        Default Gateway . . . . . . . :
```

FIGURE 7.8

Microsoft Windows 95/98's winipcfg

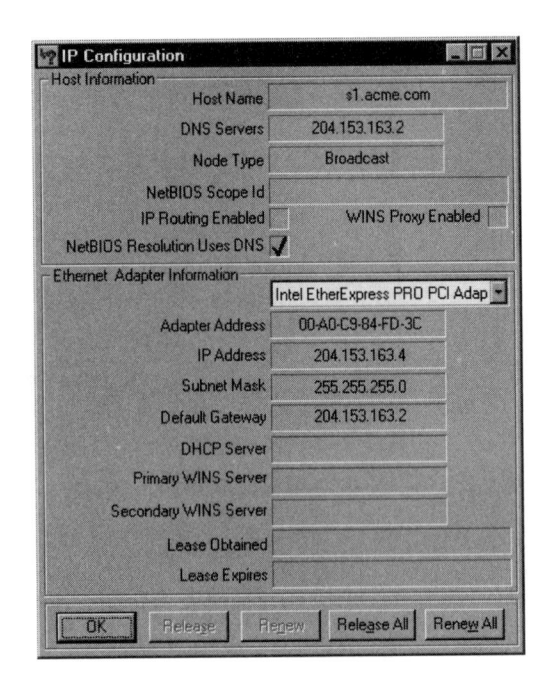

tracert

The *tracert* (trace route) utility traces the routes that a packet takes while traveling to its destination. Figure 7.9 shows an example of tracert's display.

FIGURE 7.9

Sample tracert output

```
C:\>tracert www.yahoo.com
Tracing route to www10.yahoo.com [204.71.200.75]
over a maximum of 30 hops:

  1   110 ms    96 ms   107 ms  fgo1.corpcomm.net [209.74.93.10]
  2    96 ms   126 ms    95 ms  someone.corpcomm.net [209.74.93.1]
  3   113 ms   119 ms   112 ms  Serial5-1-1.GW2.MSP1.alter.net [157.130.100.185]
  4   133 ms   123 ms   126 ms  152.ATM3-0.XR2.CHI6.ALTER.NET [146.188.209.126]
  5   176 ms   133 ms   129 ms  290.ATM2-0.TR2.CHI4.ALTER.NET [146.188.209.10]
  6   196 ms   184 ms   218 ms  106.ATM7-0.TR2.SCL1.ALTER.NET [146.188.136.162]
  7   182 ms   187 ms   187 ms  298.ATM7-0.XR2.SJC1.ALTER.NET [146.188.146.61]
  8   204 ms   176 ms   186 ms  192.ATM3-0-0.SAN-JOSE9-GW.ALTER.NET [146.188.144.133]
  9   202 ms   198 ms   212 ms  atm3-0-622M.cr1.sjc.globalcenter.net [206.57.16.17]
 10   209 ms   202 ms   195 ms  pos3-1-155M.br4.SJC.globalcenter.net [206.132.150.98]
 11   190 ms     *      191 ms  pos0-0-0-155M.hr3.SNV.globalcenter.net [206.251.5.93]
 12   195 ms   188 ms   188 ms  pos4-1-0-155M.hr2.SNV.globalcenter.net [206.132.150.206]
 13   198 ms   202 ms   197 ms  www10.yahoo.com [204.71.200.75]

Trace complete.
```

When used in conjunction with other programs, tracert is a useful utility for diagnosing slow or incorrectly routed protocols. Figure 7.10 shows the utility's command switches.

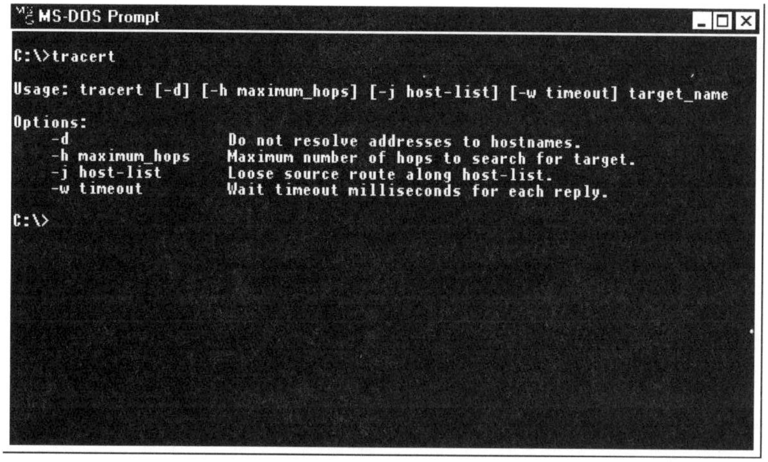

FIGURE 7.10

tracert command switches

```
C:\>tracert

Usage: tracert [-d] [-h maximum_hops] [-j host-list] [-w timeout] target_name

Options:
    -d                  Do not resolve addresses to hostnames.
    -h maximum_hops     Maximum number of hops to search for target.
    -j host-list        Loose source route along host-list.
    -w timeout          Wait timeout milliseconds for each reply.

C:\>
```

Telnet

The Telnet utility can access remote applications by using terminal emulation. Telnet can also diagnose specific ports by connecting to them. Like the FTP protocol, the Telnet protocol works at the three top layers of the OSI model: Session, Presentation, and Application. At each layer, the Telnet protocol and application perform different functions, including the following:

- Telnet works at the Session layer of the OSI model to provide dialogue control, connection creation, release, and file transfer.

- At the Presentation layer of the OSI model, Telnet manages translation by using the byte order and character codes.

- At the Application layer of the OSI model, Telnet provides the functions used for remote operations.

STUDY QUESTIONS

ARP

1. At which layer of the OSI model does ARP operate? _____

2. Which TCP/IP utility maps addresses to the Data Link layer and manages a table of logical-to-physical-address mappings? _____

3. The ARP command switch -g is the same as what other ARP command switch?
_____

4. What does the ARP command switch -d do?
_____

NBTSTAT

5. Which TCP/IP utility displays NetBIOS information over a TCP/IP connection?
_____

6. What does the NBTSTAT command switch -R do?
_____

7. To list the session table with the destination TCP/IP address, which command switch should be added to NBTSTAT? _____

8. Which TCP/IP utility displays all current connections that a workstation has?
_____

STUDY QUESTIONS

9. To display all connections and listening ports, what command switch should you add to the NETSTAT utility? _____

10. What does the NETSTAT command switch -r do?
_____

FTP

11. Which TCP/IP utility transfers files and operates at the top three layers of the OSI model?
_____

12. FTP uses which TCP/IP transport protocol? _____

13. Which TCP/IP utility can you use to transfer files between hosts with different operating systems? _____

Ping

14. Which TCP/IP utility determines whether a host can be reached and is responding?
_____

15. What does the Ping utility do if the command switch -a is added?
_____

16. To run a `ping` command until interrupted, what command switch do you use?
_____

ipconfig/winipcfg

17. What TCP/IP utility does Microsoft Windows NT use to display TCP/IP statistics? _____

18. What TCP/IP utility does the Microsoft Windows 95/98 operating system use to display TCP/IP statistics? _____

tracert

19. What TCP/IP utility tracks and displays the route that a packet takes from its source to its destination? _____

20. What does the tracert utility do if the command switch -d is added?
_____

Telnet

21. What TCP/IP utility accesses remote applications by using terminal emulation? _____

22. At which three layers of the OSI model does Telnet reside?
_____

SAMPLE TEST

7-1 Which TCP/IP utility can you use to determine whether an IP host can be contacted and is responding?

    A. FTP

    B. HTTP

    C. ARP

    D. Ping

7-2 Which TCP/IP utility should you use to test whether a Web server is responding on TCP/IP port 80?

    A. Ping

    B. Telnet

    C. tracert

    D. NETSTAT

7-3 Which utility displays this output?

```
Reply from 192.123.223.212: bytes=32 time=230ms TTL=244
Reply from 192.123.223.212: bytes=32 time=271ms TTL=244
Reply from 192.123.223.212: bytes=32 time=214ms TTL=244
Reply from 192.123.223.212: bytes=32 time=234ms TTL=244
```

    A. FTP

    B. Ping

    C. ARP

    D. HTTP

7-4 Which Ping switches verify that a local TCP/IP interface is working properly?

    A. `Ping host`

    B. `Ping localhost`

SAMPLE TEST

    C. `Ping 127.0.0.1`

    D. `Ping address-server`

7-5 Which TCP/IP utility displays the following?

```
Interface: 10.132.123.12
  Internet Address     Physical Address      Type
  10.132.123.12        00-e0-b0-5b-0e-ac     dynamic
```

    A. tracert

    B. NBTSTAT

    C. ARP

    D. NETSTAT

7-6 Which TCP/IP utility displays the number of routers through which an IP packet passes from its source to its destination?

    A. Ping

    B. Telnet

    C. tracert

    D. FTP

7-7 Which protocol can map TCP/IP addresses to Data Link layer addresses?

    A. AFP

    B. MAP

    C. ARP

    D. NBT

SAMPLE TEST

7-8 Which ARP command switch displays the currently cached ARP entries?

    A. ARP

    B. ARP -a

    C. ARP /a

    D. ARP -c

7-9 Which Microsoft Windows TCP/IP utility allows an administrator to view statistics of NetBIOS running over TCP/IP?

    A. NETSTAT

    B. NetBIOS

    C. NBTSTAT

    D. Ping

7-10 Which NBTSTAT command switch lists all NetBIOS names that a computer has resolved and their associated IP addresses?

    A. /r

    B. /R

    C. -r

    D. -R

7-11 Which NBTSTAT command switch purges and reloads a NetBIOS name cache?

    A. /r

    B. /R

    C. -r

    D. -R

SAMPLE TEST

7-12 Which TCP/IP utility displays all the current connections for a workstation?

    A. NETSTAT

    B. NetBIOS

    C. NBTSTAT

    D. Ping

7-13 Which NETSTAT command switch shows all connections and their associated ports?

    A. -a

    B. -n

    C. -r

    D. -s

7-14 Which transport protocol does the TCP/IP protocol FTP use?

    A. UDP

    B. TCP

    C. IP

    D. ICMP

7-15 Which TCP/IP utility displays the current TCP/IP configuration for a Windows NT workstation?

    A. NETSTAT

    B. ipconfig

    C. winipcfg

    D. tracert

SAMPLE TEST

7-16 Which TCP/IP utility displays the current TCP/IP configuration for a Windows 95 workstation?

    A. NETSTAT

    B. ipconfig

    C. winipcfg

    D. D.tracert

7-17 Which ipconfig command switch can display detailed information about the current TCP/IP configuration?

    A. /ALL

    B. /RELEASE

    C. /RENEW

    D. /VERBOSE

7-18 Which TCP/IP protocol allows a user to access host applications by using terminal emulation?

    A. FTP

    B. tracert

    C. Telnet

    D. TCP

7-19 Which TCP/IP utility can you use to test whether TCP/IP port 25 is operational?

    A. Ping

    B. Telnet

    C. tracert

    D. NETSTAT

UNIT 8

Remote Connectivity

Test Objectives: Remote Connectivity

- **Explain the following remote-connectivity concepts:**
  - The distinction between PPP and SLIP
  - The purpose and function of PPTP and the conditions under which it is useful
  - The attributes, advantages, and disadvantages of ISDN and PSTN (POTS)

- **Specify the following elements of dial-up networking:**
  - The modem-configuration parameters that must be set, including serial port IRQ, I/O address, and maximum port speed
  - The requirements for a remote connection

NOTE: Exam objectives are subject to change at any time without notice and at CompTIA's sole discretion. Please visit CompTIA's Web site (www.comptia.org) for the most current exam-objectives listing.

Remote connectivity allows a user to dial in, connect to a network, run applications, and transfer files. The Network+ exam tests your knowledge of remote-connectivity concepts, such as protocols and services, and dial-up networking configuration and practices. This unit discusses these remote-connectivity concepts.

Remote-Connectivity Concepts

The most important remote-connectivity concepts to understand are protocols and types of connection services. PPP, SLIP, PPTP, ISDN, and PSTN are a few of the concepts that are involved with remote connectivity. The first three protocols—PPP, SLIP, and PPTP—provide for connection and data transfer over remote connections. ISDN and PSTN are services that connect devices for dial-in and remote connections.

Point to Point Protocol (PPP)

Point to Point Protocol (PPP) is the protocol used to provide TCP/IP services over point-to-point links (such as serial and parallel connections). PPP supports asynchronous, dial-up, or synchronous ISDN media. PPP works across a single layer of the OSI model: the Data Link layer. A Link Control Protocol (LCP) included in PPP creates, maintains, and terminates a Data Link connection. PPP supports PAP (Password Authentication Protocol), CHAP (Challenge-Handshake Authentication Protocol) for username and password authentication of connections, and the compression of data. These features were not available in PPP's precursor, Serial Line Internet Protocol.

Serial Line Internet Protocol (SLIP)

Serial Line Internet Protocol (SLIP) is a protocol that encapsulates and frames packets for use over a serial line. SLIP is an industry standard developed in 1984 to support TCP/IP over low-speed serial lines. SLIP resides on two layers of the OSI model: the Physical and Data Link layers. The protocol does not do any type of error checking or packet addressing.

SLIP is widely being replaced by PPP. PPP builds on the SLIP specification, adding login, password, and error correction. The main difference between PPP and SLIP is that PPP uses only the Data Link layer of the OSI model, whereas SLIP has both a Data Link and a Physical layer component. As a result, PPP can be used over many types of physical media, whereas SLIP is limited to use over serial links.

Figure 8.1 shows the relationships of the PPP and SLIP protocols to the OSI model.

FIGURE 8.1

PPP and SLIP relationships to the OSI model

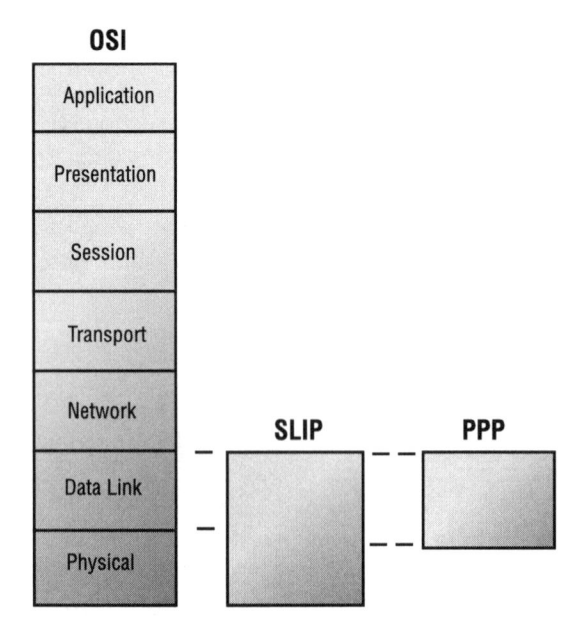

Point to Point Tunneling Protocol (PPTP)

Point to Point Tunneling Protocol (PPTP) transfers Internetwork Packet Exchange (IPX) and NetBEUI packets across a TCP/IP WAN (such as the Internet) inside TCP/IP packets. The IPX and NetBEUI packets are wrapped in a TCP/IP packet and sent across the TCP/IP WAN, where they are unwrapped and sent on their way. PPTP uses the TCP/IP suite to transfer these packets across a dial-up or dedicated TCP/IP connection.

PPTP resides higher in the OSI model than PPP and SLIP do (the Network layer and up), and it can't be used without another transport protocol (specifically, TCP/IP). PPTP has the capability to encapsulate most protocols, and it can create a very secure connection to the Internet or between two networks across the Internet. The latter of these two options is the most useful implementation of PPTP.

Figures 8.2 and 8.3 show examples of how PPTP is used to deliver IPX packets between two networks and between a remotely connected workstation and a host network, respectively. PPTP maintains a secure connection by creating a situation in which the TCP/IP suite does not need to be used on the host workstation.

FIGURE 8.2
Using PPTP to encapsulate LAN TCP/IP over the Internet between two networks

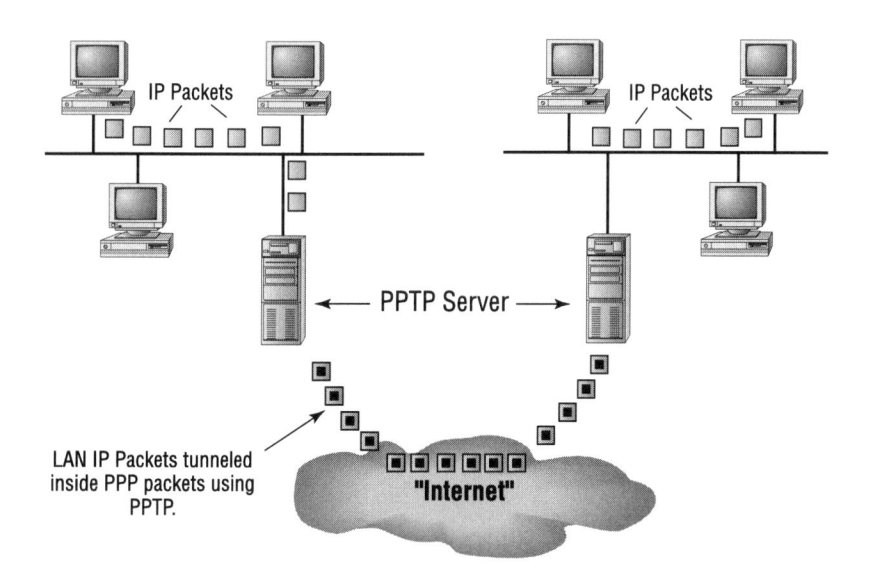

FIGURE 8.3
Using PPTP to encapsulate TCP/IP over the Internet between a remote workstation and a host network

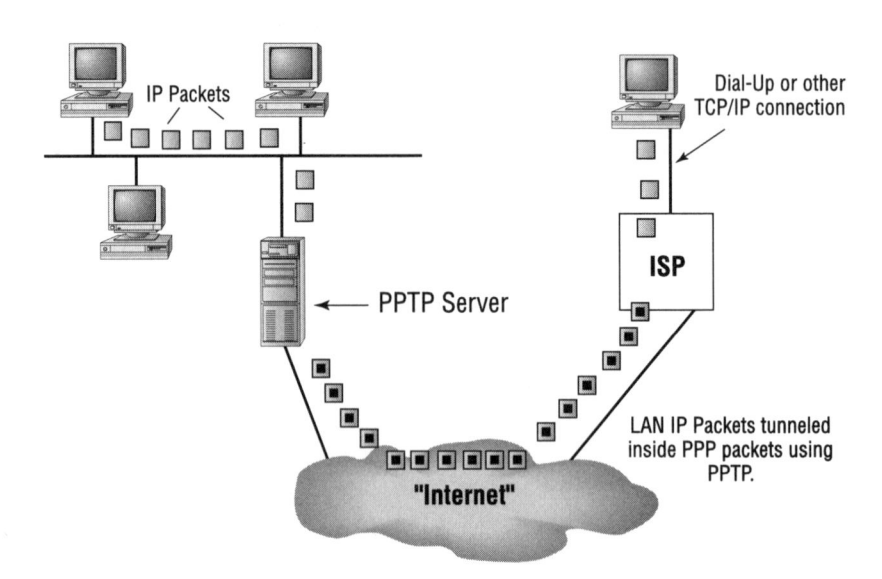

Integrated Services Digital Network (ISDN)

Integrated Services Digital Network (ISDN) is an all-digital, wide area network connection type that uses the standard copper phone wires that come in to most homes. ISDN can communicate with a true digital signal from the sender to the receiver, using circuit- or packet-switched connections. ISDN has become popular for point-to-point WAN links and home-office Internet connections. A single ISDN line can carry video, voice, and data. Bit pipes are used with ISDN lines to transfer data across different channels.

A typical ISDN line—called a *Basic Rate Interface* (BRI)—contains two *Bearer* (B) channels and a *Data* (D) channel. The B channels are 64Kbps each and can be connected for a combined data rate of 128Kbps. The D channel is 16Kbps in a BRI, is used for connection management, and does not carry data. A *Primary Rate Interface* (PRI), by comparison, has 23 B channels and one 64Kbps D channel, for a combined data rate of 1.536Mbps.

Table 8.1 shows the channels that are available, along with their data rates.

ISDN has become very popular in the past two years because of its advantages:

TABLE 8.1	ISDN Channel	Data Rate
ISDN channels and their data rates	A	4KHz analog
	B	64Kbps digital
	C	8Kbps or 16Kbps digital
	D	16Kbps or 64Kbps digital
	E	64Kbps digital
	H	384Kbps, 1,536Kbps, or 1,920Kbps digital

Speed: Data-transmission speeds of up to 1.536Mbps are possible by combining multiple B channels.

Relatively low cost: ISDN is relatively inexpensive compared with many other digital communications technologies for short transmission distances (within the same city, for example).

Flexibility: ISDN can carry both voice and data over the same communications link.

Like any other technology that has advantages, ISDN also has its share of disadvantages. These disadvantages include:

Complexity: ISDN is not a networking technology that an average user can set up. ISDN requires many components, including an ISDN modem (called a *terminal adapter*, or TA) and possibly a router and NIC.

Distance-related pricing: The farther your ISDN link has to go to connect to a site, the more the link costs. Although ISDN is cheaper than most other digital point-to-point connections, it can be more expensive if the link is between sites in different states.

Limited availability: ISDN is not available in all markets. The number of areas in the United States and abroad that have ISDN support is growing annually, but the medium is still not universal. ISDN is fairly common in Europe, however.

Public Switched Telephone Network (PSTN)

The *Public Switched Telephone Network* (PSTN) is the nationwide network of telephone circuits that provides switched-circuit communications from end to end. Standard analog telephones use this network when people make telephone calls. As technology advances, more and more people are connecting to the Internet and working from home. Because almost every home in the United States has telephone access, PSTN is the most popular method of making a remote connection to a corporate network.

PSTN uses a single pair of copper wires to carry data from the transmission source to the destination. This network is an analog network, and you must use a modem to transmit data over PSTN.

PSTN is the most common remote-access network technology in use today, mainly because it has several advantages and few disadvantages. Following are some of the advantages:

Wide availability: PSTN is available in almost every home in the United States (and in most homes abroad).

Ease of use: Setting up a connection over PSTN is simple—so simple, in fact, that almost every computer sold today comes with a modem, allowing the buyer to connect to the Internet over PSTN.

Low cost: If you have a telephone and a computer in your house, you already have the means to make a remote-access connection. All you need is a modem for the computer and a remote-access account on the system that you need to access.

Long-distance connections: PSTN connections can go for miles because they use analog transmissions, which don't suffer from distance limitations, as digital transmissions do.

PSTN has two main disadvantages:

Speed: Currently, the Federal Communications Commission (FCC) limits PSTN connection speeds to 53Kbps. The FCC is currently discussing lifting this restriction, however.

Analog connections: Although analog connections permit transmission over great distances, they cannot provide the speed or complexity required by many high-speed network-communications methods.

Dial-Up Networking

Dial-up networking (also called *remote-access networking*) allows users to connect to a corporate network by using some kind of remote-access method. The Network+ exam tests your knowledge of dial-up networking concepts—specifically, modem configuration. This section examines the requirements for a remote-access connection and explains how to configure a modem for use with a remote workstation.

Remote-Connection Requirements

Connecting a remote workstation to a network involves a few requirements. The remote workstation must have the following:

- The correct telephone equipment, including telephone lines and service
- A modem, installed and configured with the proper communications software
- The correct protocols installed
- A good connection to the host computer

The host device (the host can be a server, such as RAS Server) must have the following:

- An account created for the remote user, with the proper dial-in privileges
- The capability to accept incoming connections
- The permissions to allow an incoming connection to browse the network or access specific applications

Modem-Configuration Parameters

A *modem* (modulator/demodulator) converts a digital signal to an analog signal that can be transmitted via telephone lines, and vice versa. This process is illustrated in Figure 8.4.

A modem is needed for a remote asynchronous connection. This device can be installed in the computer as an expansion card or connected to it via a serial cable as an external device. When you install a modem in a computer

FIGURE 8.4
Modem transmission

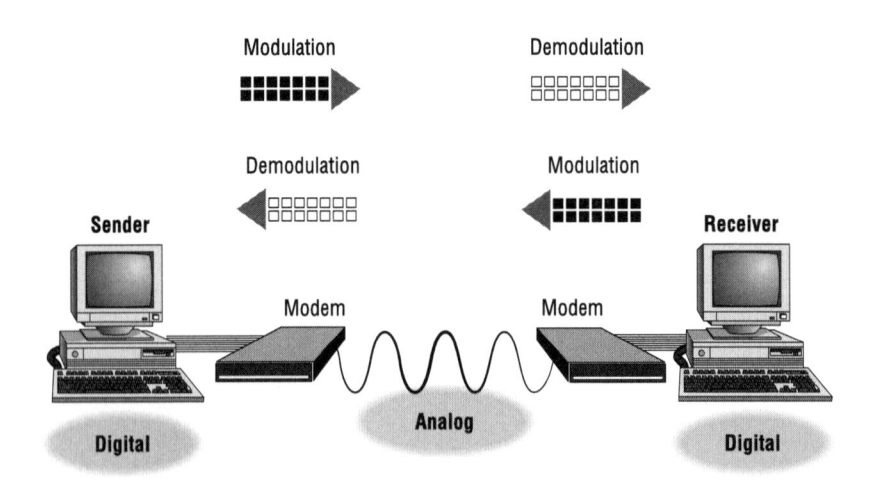

as an expansion card (the most popular option), you must configure the COM port, IRQ, and I/O address. When you use a PnP operating system and a PnP-compatible modem, the workstation can perform the configuration process automatically. In conjunction with PnP, you can use the Windows 9x Device Manager to check or modify the modem's hardware-configuration settings.

If the computer is not PnP-aware, you can configure the modem by using jumpers or dip switches to set the parameters. *Jumpers* are small plastic blocks with metal clips inside that fit over a set of pins on the modem, thus shorting across the pins and making an electrical connection. Which pins are shorted depends on which setting you want to make. The modem's documentation indicates which pins correspond to which settings.

DIP switches are blocks of small sliding or toggle switches that are set in patterns. The pattern indicates the particular setting. The modem's documentation indicates which patterns correspond to which hardware settings, where appropriate.

When you install a modem on your computer for dial-up networking, you need to consider the following:

- Maximum port speed
- Modem hardware settings

Maximum Port Speed

Maximum port transmission speed is the highest speed at which a serial port can transmit and receive data. Serial-port transmissions are controlled by special chips called *UART* (Universal Asynchronous Receiver/Transmitter) chips. UART chips are a key component of proper modem operation; these devices manage the serial input and output for a device. Because they can perform a finite number of serial operations per second, the chips are the limiting factor in maximum port speed—and in maximum modem transmission speed as well.

UART chips can be installed on an internal modem and are installed in a workstation system board. Following are some of the functions that UART chips perform:

- Add required stop, start, and parity bits
- Control the timing of a transmission
- Monitor the status of the serial port
- Strip framing bits from a transmitted character

The type of UART chip determines the maximum transmission speed at which the modem can communicate. Most internal modems have the appropriate UART chips built in, so having the appropriate UART chips isn't a real issue. External modems rely on the UART chips on the computer's system board to manage the functions mentioned in the preceding list. If you connect a newer, faster modem to the serial port on a computer that has an older set of UART chips, you may be limiting the maximum speed at which the external modem can connect. For an external modem to connect at speeds of up to 115,200bps, for example, the workstation must have a 165*xx* UART chip installed.

Modem Hardware Settings

You must also configure the modem to respond to a particular COM port. The *COM port* is a port-address name that the operating system can call when it has serial data to send. COM ports are assigned to all serial devices in a computer, including external serial ports.

COM Settings for External Modems If you are using an external modem, you simply hook the modem to an available serial port and then configure the dial-up software to look for the modem on the serial port's corresponding COM port address.

COM Settings for Internal Modems For the operating system to use an internal modem correctly, the modem must be set to a COM port that doesn't conflict with another serial device in the computer. Additionally, each COM port has default IRQ and I/O addresses, which you can change, if necessary. Be aware, however, that of the four COM port addresses available, only two IRQ addresses are used.

Table 8.2 lists the four COM ports, their default IRQs, and their default I/O addresses. Most Intel-based PCs can use the COM ports' associated default IRQ and I/O addresses.

> **NOTE** On some older modems, you set the COM port on the modem by setting the IRQ and I/O address to correspond to the COM port's default address.

TABLE 8.2 PC COM ports and their default IRQ and I/O addresses

COM Port	Default IRQ	Default I/O
COM1	4	3F8
COM2	3	2F8
COM3	4	3E8
COM4	3	2E8

STUDY QUESTIONS

Remote Connectivity

1. A _____ connection allows a user to dial in, connect to a network, run applications, and transfer files.

Remote-Connectivity Concepts

2. Name the three protocols described in this unit that are used for the connection and data transfer in remote connections. _____ , _____ , and _____ .

3. _____ and _____ are services described in this unit that connect devices for dial-in and remote connections.

4. What remote-access protocol described in this unit has only a Data Link-layer implementation? _____

5. The SLIP protocol resides across what layer(s) of the OSI model? _____

6. PPTP uses what protocol suite to transfer tunneled (or encapsulated) IPX and NetBEUI packets across a dial-up or dedicated Internet connection? _____

7. Of the PPP, SLIP, and PPTP protocols, which one can create the most secure connection? _____

8. True or false: An ISDN line communicates with a fully analog signal.

STUDY QUESTIONS

9. Video, voice, and _____ can be transferred across an ISDN line.

10. Which is easier to configure, ISDN or PSTN? _____

11. True or false: The Federal Communications Commission restricts maximum transmission speed over PSTN.

Dial-Up Networking

12. A modem converts _____ signals from a phone line to _____ signals that a computer can use.

13. A modem can transfer a signal along what public network? _____

14. When you install and configure a new modem, you must configure the _____, so that the operating system knows which serial device to send the data to.

15. The _____ can help you configure a modem in Windows 9x.

16. What UART chip do you need to use an external modem with speeds up to 115,200bps? _____

17. List the three items that a host device must have to accept remote connections.

_____
_____
_____

STUDY QUESTIONS

18. What device discussed in this unit is needed for an asynchronous PSTN connection?
_____

19. What is the default I/O address for COM1? _____

20. 20. What is the default I/O address for COM2? _____

SAMPLE TEST

8-1 A Web browser, an FTP client, and dial-up components have been installed and configured on a workstation. Which protocol could you use to browse the Internet and to access FTP files?

    A. PPP

    B. IPX/SPX

    C. NetBIOS

    D. PSTN

8-2 What TCP/IP protocol resides at the Physical layer and the Data Link layer of the OSI model?

    A. PPP

    B. SLIP

    C. PPTP

    D. PSTN

8-3 You need to create a secure virtual network connection from a remote location to a central office by using the Internet. How do you achieve this connection?

    A. Use FTP and a direct connection from the remote location to the central office

    B. Use PPTP and a dial-up connection from the remote location to the local ISP

    C. Use SLIP and a dial-up connection from the remote location to the local ISP

    D. Use HTTP and a direct connection from the remote location to the central office

8-4 PPTP uses which transport protocol?

    A. IPX/SPX

    B. TCP/IP

SAMPLE TEST

   C. AppleTalk

   D. SNA

8-5 Which of the following phrases best describes ISDN?

   A. Readily available

   B. 64Kbps data rates or higher

   C. Easy to configure

   D. Least expensive implementation

8-6 Digital signaling from sender to receiver is used in which WAN technology?

   A. ISDN

   B. POTS

   C. X2

   D. Kflex

8-7 Which of the following hardware components are needed to create a remote, asynchronous connection?

   A. Keyboard

   B. Mouse

   C. Modem

   D. Monitor

8-8 Which protocol is used to encapsulate and frame packets for use over a serial connection?

   A. POP4

   B. ISDN

SAMPLE TEST

    C. PPP

    D. SLIP

8-9 Which of the following components are required for connecting to a central office from a remote location?

    A. The correct telephone equipment, including telephone lines and service

    B. The correct protocols installed and a good connection to the host computer

    C. The capability to accept incoming connections

    D. The capability to allow incoming connections to browse the network or access specific applications

    E. A modem, installed and configured with the proper communications software

    F. An account created for the remote user, with the proper dial-in privileges

8-10 When you install a modem in a Plug-and-Play operating system, how is the modem configured?

    A. By a special utility provided by the manufacturer

    B. By the user

    C. By the operating system

    D. By the factory before shipment

8-11 Which of the following parameters do you need to configure to use an internal modem?

    A. COM port

    B. IRQ

    C. DMA channel

    D. I/O address

SAMPLE TEST

8-12 PPP is mainly used to transmit what type of packets over the telephone system?

    A. IPX/SPX

    B. TCP/IP

    C. NetBIOS

    D. EtherTALK

8-13 What must you do to ensure that the following modems work simultaneously when they are installed in a single server? Both modems are known to be good. The first modem is set to COM3, IRQ 4, I/O 2F8h. The second modem is set to COM4, IRQ 3, I/O 2F8h.

    A. Change the IRQ of modem 1

    B. Change the I/O address of modem 1

    C. Change the IRQ of modem 2

    D. Change the COM port of modem 2

8-14 An ISDN connection can transfer what type of packets?

    A. Video

    B. Data

    C. Voice

    D. A and B only

8-15 What is PSTN?

    A. The Public Switched Telephone Network

    B. The Public Shared Transportation Network

    C. The Packet Sharing Transport Network

    D. The Private Sector Training Network

UNIT 9

Security

Test Objectives: Security

- **Identify good practices to ensure network security, including:**
    - Selection of a security model (user- and share-level)
    - Standard password practices and procedures
    - The need to employ data encryption to protect network data
    - The use of a firewall

Exam objectives are subject to change at any time without notice and at CompTIA's sole discretion. Please visit CompTIA's Web site (www.comptia.org) for the most current exam-objectives listing.

Network security means the restrictions placed on the individual users of a network to prevent unauthorized use of network resources. Many restrictions are placed on users, including when and where they access the network, what kinds of information they can access, and how they can access it.

Network security is a complex topic that encompasses every aspect of the network. Theoretically, an unauthorized user can access any part of a network that an authorized user can. The Network+ exam tests you on a few aspects of network security, including:

- Security models
- Standard password practices and procedures
- Data encryption
- Firewall use

Although the preceding items are the most popular aspects of network security, this list is by no means comprehensive. As a general rule, you should take whatever steps are necessary to prevent unauthorized access to your network.

Network Security Models

Network security models are the concepts that dictate how you approach network security. You can secure files that are shared over the network in two ways:

- At the share level
- At the user level

Although user-level security provides more control of files and is the preferred model, implementing share-level security is easier for the network administrator.

User-Level Security

User-level security is the security model that tracks user security from a central location. All requests to access shared resources pass through a security provider, which has the capability to grant or deny those requests. This type of security is most commonly used in a client-server network. User-level security is used in networks based on either Microsoft Windows NT or Novell NetWare operating systems.

Share-Level Security

Share-level security is the security model in which each user, or the administrator, sets a password on each resource that is shared across the network. These resources can include drives, directories, files, and printers. Share-level security is most commonly used in a peer-to-peer network (such as networks running Windows 9x or NT). This security model minimizes the time required to administer security on simpler networks, because the primary user of the machine hosting the resource has the capability to change other users' rights to the resources. This type of security is harder to manage in more complex networks, which may have hundreds of resources and thousands of users.

Passwords

Passwords are combinations of alphanumeric text strings that allow users to prove their identities. Users gain access to a network by entering the usernames that they have been assigned and the passwords that they have chosen. A password should be unique and known only by the user. If someone else knows a person's username and password, an unauthorized person could access the network and perform operations as that user. Possible implications are data loss and system instability (if the violated user happens to be one who has administrative rights). Entire drive contents can be deleted.

To keep a network as secure as possible, you must implement a strong password policy. A *password policy* is the set of rules that dictate what kinds of passwords can be used and how they are used. To create a strong password policy, keep the following key components in mind:

- The most secure passwords are those that expire on a regular basis. Users should be forced to change their passwords on a regular basis.

- A password should not be based on any word that appears in a dictionary.

- A password should never be based on a proper name.

- Users must not share their passwords with other users, within or outside the network. The most common breach of network security occurs when users reveal their passwords to other people.

- Passwords should contain a combination of letters, numbers, and symbols, because these combinations do not appear in a dictionary. Colt!45, for example, would be a fairly secure password, because it is a combination of letters and numbers separated by a symbol.

Encryption

Encryption is the process used to encode and decode data for transmission over a public network. Generally speaking, encryption works by running the data (represented as numbers) through a special encryption formula called a *key*. Both the sender and receiver know the key, which encrypts and decrypts the data.

Encryption is used in internal communication, external communication, and storage to keep the data from being viewed by people who aren't authorized to view it. Password files and data on servers contain important information that must be safeguarded; therefore, that data is often encrypted. Most NOSes automatically encrypt the username and password database so that the information can't be viewed by anyone who does not have proper access. Additionally, most NOSes encrypt the password during transmission from the workstation to the server. This practice ensures that the password stays secure during transmission and that no one could use network hacking tools to grab the password from the wire and use it to log into the network.

Many encryption techniques are available, and each uses a different method. Following are some examples of encryption methods:

- Data Encryption Standard (DES)
- SkipJack
- Rivest, Shamir, and Adleman (RSA)
- Pretty Good Privacy (PGP)

Firewalls

A *firewall* is a device that prevents unauthorized users from accessing sensitive data on a network. Firewalls usually are installed between an entire local area network and public networks (such as the Internet). Firewalls can also be installed between a network that contains private information and one that contains public information. All packets that go to and from the private network must pass through the firewall.

Firewalls usually are a combination of hardware and software. The hardware usually is a computer or dedicated piece of hardware (often called a *black box*) that contains two NICs: one that connects to the public side of the firewall (the NIC connected to the public network), and one that connects to the private side (the NIC that connects to the local network you are protecting). The software controls the way that the firewall operates and protects the network. The software examines all incoming and outgoing packets and rejects any suspicious packets.

Firewalls can protect protocols at any layer of the OSI model and are divided into categories based on their function. The three main firewall categories are:

Packet filtering: The firewall examines each packet as it passes through the firewall and then passes or rejects packets based on the information in the firewall's security configuration, which is called its Access Control List (ACL). A firewall of this type can filter packets by network address or by port address.

Application filtering: The firewall examines each packet as it passes through the firewall and then passes or rejects packets based on the information in its ACL, specifying which packets from network applications or services are allowed to pass.

Circuit filtering: The firewall examines the source and destination address and then views the path that each packet has taken. If the packet has taken a route other than the routes specified in the firewall's ACL, the packet is rejected.

> **NOTE** The combination of a firewall and a strong password policy is a good way to help minimize the risk of unauthorized access to sensitive data.

STUDY QUESTIONS

Network Security Models

1. This unit describes how network security can be assigned at the user level or the _____ level.

2. To keep data files on a server from being examined by unauthorized users, you should _____ the files.

3. Encrypting data before a transmission is a good way to _____ data.

4. Multiple accounts and privileges can be centrally managed with _____ security.

5. User-level security is most commonly used on a _____ network.

6. What type of security is being used when each user, or the administrator, sets a password on resources that are shared across the network? _____

7. What type of security is most commonly used in a peer-to-peer network? _____

Passwords

8. True or false: The most secure passwords are those that expire on a regular basis.

9. A strong password is made up of a combination of _____, _____, and _____.

STUDY QUESTIONS

10. Users should not share their network _____ with other users.

Encryption

11. What is encryption ?
_____
_____

12. A _____ generates the encryption formula used to encrypt the data.

13. RSA is an acronym for _____, _____, and _____.

Firewalls

14. A firewall is a device that prevents _____ from accessing data on a network.

15. True or false: A firewall can be installed only between a network and the outside world.

16. What are the three main firewall categories?
_____, _____, and _____.

18. How does a packet-filtering firewall work?
_____
_____
_____

STUDY QUESTIONS

19. How does a circuit-filtering firewall work?

SAMPLE TEST

9-1 Which type of security policy can minimize the time required to administrate security on a network?

    A. User-level

    B. Share-level

    C. Encryption-level

    D. Firewall-level

9-2 What security functions can a firewall perform?

    A. Authenticate all remote-access users

    B. Ensure that file and print resources are used by WAN but not LAN users

    C. Prevent local network users from creating unauthorized user accounts

    D. Prevent unauthorized network users from accessing sensitive data

9-3 How does user-level security differ from share-level security?

    A. Multiple accounts and privileges are centrally administered

    B. Privileges cannot be changed on a case-by-case basis

    C. One password is used for everyone to connect

    D. Fewer privileges are available to be set on resources

9-4 Which of the following statements describes a secure password policy?

    A. Passwords are random lengths.

    B. Passwords for all administrator accounts are identical.

    C. All network users change their passwords on a regular basis.

    D. Network users never change their passwords.

SAMPLE TEST

9-5 What can you do to ensure that sensitive data remains secure during transmission?

    A. Reformat the data to include unnecessary information that will confuse unauthorized users

    B. Use removable media to transfer data

    C. Set share-level security on the data before transmission

    D. Encrypt the data before transmission

9-6 What technology can you use to ensure that data files stored on a server are protected from unauthorized use by internal users?

    A. Firewall

    B. Network operating system

    C. Share-level security

    D. Encryption

9-7 Which of the following techniques could you use to help prevent network attacks by unauthorized users?

    A. Encrypt all passwords

    B. Set up a firewall to restrict access

    C. Set up additional user-level security

    D. D. Implement additional share-level security

9-8 What is the most secure type of password?

    A. A password that never expires

    B. A password that is based on a user's phone number

    C. A password on a shared resource

    D. A password that expires on a regular basis

SAMPLE TEST

9-9 Which of the following security options could you use to prevent unauthorized users from gaining access to your network?

    A. Establish a secure password policy

    B. Set high access privileges for a remote administrator account

    C. Encrypt share-level passwords

    D. Implement a firewall

9-10 Which of the following security measures protects data during transmission from the sender to the receiver so that it can't be viewed if it is captured?

    A. Firewall

    B. Encryption

    C. Security model

    D. Physical security

UNIT 10

Implementing a Network Installation

Test Objectives: Implementing the Installation of the Network

- **Demonstrate awareness that administrative and test accounts, passwords, IP addresses, IP configurations, relevant SOPs, and so on must be obtained before network implementation.**

- **Explain the impact of environmental factors on computer networks. Given a network-installation scenario, identify unexpected or atypical conditions that could either cause problems for the network or signify that a problem condition already exists, including:**
  - Room conditions (e.g., humidity, heat)
  - The placement of building contents and personal effects (e.g., space heaters, TVs, radios)
  - Computer equipment
  - Error messages

- **Recognize visually, or by description, common peripheral ports, external SCSI (especially DB-25 connectors), and common network components, including:**
  - Print servers
  - Peripherals
  - Hubs
  - Routers
  - Brouters

- **Given an installation scenario, demonstrate awareness of the following compatibility and cabling issues:**
  - The consequences of trying to install an analog modem in a digital jack
  - That the uses of RJ-45 connectors may differ greatly, depending on the cabling
  - That patch cables contribute to the overall length of the cabling segment

Exam objectives are subject to change at any time without notice and at CompTIA's sole discretion. Please visit CompTIA's Web site (www.comptia.org) for the most current exam-objectives listing.

You need to keep in mind many considerations when you perform a network implementation, including preinstallation items, environmental factors, and the physical aspects of a network. When you do not discuss or prepare for these details, you may run into serious obstacles, such as completion delays, down time, or an increase in the cost of an implementation.

Network Preinstallation

When you perform a preinstallation check, you must gather specific information that describes the network to the person who does the installation. This information includes administrative accounts, test accounts, and their passwords; individual TCP/IP addresses and configuration; the network's standard operating procedures (SOPs); protocol schemes; and a device-location map.

Accounts

All users require network accounts to gain access to the network. Every user should have his or her own user account. When you install new network hardware or software, you must have access to two types of accounts: administrative and test. You use each type of account for a different purpose during an installation.

Administrative Accounts

Administrative accounts, also called *maintenance accounts*, are the user accounts that have sufficient rights to perform network administration (add and delete users, install servers, and so on). You must know the administrative account name and password before installation, because you may need to be logged in as one of the administrative accounts to install any network hardware or software. The names of the administrative accounts differ, based on the type and version of NOS used on the network. All NOSes have a default administrative account that is used to administrate or manage the network. In most cases, the administrative account can be named something other than the default name. Table 10.1 lists the NOSes, versions, and associated default administrative accounts.

TABLE 10.1 Default administrative accounts for major NOSes

NOS	Version	Administrative Account
NetWare	3.x and earlier	supervisor
NetWare	4.x and later	admin (can be renamed)
Windows NT	4.x and earlier	administrator (can be renamed)
Unix	Various	root

Test Accounts

Test accounts are user accounts with security and environment settings similar to those of actual user accounts. You use these accounts to test network functionality after an installation or upgrade. You should obtain the names and passwords of test accounts before an installation or upgrade, so that you can test the network functionality before and after an installation. To differentiate them from normal user accounts, test accounts usually have names such as the following:

- test
- testuser
- user01

Passwords

If the new network is replacing an existing one, discovering the current administrative passwords is critical. To migrate data and users, most NOSes require you to have administrative access to all volumes on the server(s). If the new network is not replacing an existing network, you can use or modify the existing administrative accounts.

IP Addresses

When you install any network hardware device on a network that is running the TCP/IP protocol, you must obtain a valid IP address for the new device. If you are the network administrator for your company, you may already have a block of available TCP/IP addresses and can use one of them for the new device. If you are an outside network engineer who is coming in to install a new piece of hardware, you may need to ask the IS staff for a valid IP address for the new device.

You may not have to assign an IP address to the device manually if your network and the device are configured to use DHCP for IP address assignment. In such a case, the IP address for the device is assigned automatically when the device is brought online.

> TCP/IP addressing and DHCP are covered in detail in Unit 6.

IP Configuration

In addition to a valid IP address, you must have the network's TCP/IP configuration information at hand, so that you can enter the appropriate parameters for a new device. IP configuration information includes items such as the default gateway for the segment in which you are installing the device, and the subnet mask for that segment.

Relevant Standard Operating Procedures (SOPs)

Standard operating procedures (SOPs) are the company documents that indicate how things are done within the company. SOPs cover many items and often include network and technology-installation procedures and protocols: conventions for naming new devices, people who are in charge of installing new devices, conventions for documenting new devices, and so on. You must obtain and read the appropriate sections of the SOPs so that you understand the way that new devices should be installed according to the company's SOPs.

Protocols

Knowing what protocols are going to be used on a network is another important aspect of implementing a network. When you use some protocol stacks, you must know in advance what range of addresses to use. Following are some of the things that you must know when you use the TCP/IP stack:

- What class address(es) to use
- What subnet(s) to use
- How to assign TCP/IP addresses
- What range of addresses are blocked for static addressing
- What range of addresses are blocked for dynamic addressing

Environmental Factors Affecting Computer Networks

Electronic devices are fairly delicate, requiring a physical environment that is designed for electronic devices so that they can function properly. The Network+ exam tests you on the placement of a network device. The environmental factors listed in the Network+ exam include the following:

- Room conditions
- Device location
- Computer equipment
- Error messages

Room Conditions

One of the most important factors that contribute to device failure is improper environmental conditions in the room in which the network device is operating. Improper room conditions can shorten the life of the device or cause it to behave erratically. Room conditions include the following:

- Humidity

- Heat
- Air quality

Humidity

Humidity is the measure of the amount of saturation of water in the air. A humidity level of 0 percent indicates that there is no water in the air. A humidity level of 100 percent means that the air contains as much water as it can hold. The ideal humidity level for an environment that contains electronic devices is around 40 percent. If the humidity gets too high, moisture can begin to condense on equipment, possibly shorting out components. If the humidity gets too low, the result may be electrostatic discharge (ESD), a condition that causes static electrical charges to jump between two charged entities. ESD can damage electrical components.

Excessive Heat

All electronic components are sensitive to heat. If possible, all electronic devices would love to operate at 0°F, but this temperature level usually is not practical. For that reason, most network devices that contain any significant amount of electronics (including routers, computers, and servers) usually have built-in fans that draw in fresh air to cool the components. The devices are designed to operate most effectively at around 70°F.

A fan can't do its job, however, if it can't freely draw air into the device. For that reason, you should make sure to provide enough room in front of a device's fan for the fan to work properly. If airflow is restricted, the fan may not be able to cool the internal components properly, and device failure can result.

Air Quality

Air quality for computers is not something that many people think about. But just like human beings, network devices with fans need fresh, clean air to function properly for a long time. If a device (such as a computer or server) operates in a dusty, dirty environment, the device's fan will draw that dirty air into the device, where it will coat all the electronic components. This coating has the effect of insulating these components, causing them to run hotter. Additionally, the dirt or dust might get into the fan-motor bearings, plugging them and stopping the fan's operation. The fan will be unable to cool the components properly, and device failure will result.

Device Location

Determining the location for a new network device is a necessity when you install a new network device. You must determine the best location for the device, taking into account function, ease of access, physical security, and environmental factors. The new device should be placed in a location where the device can perform its function and is easily accessible for maintenance, but is protected from unauthorized physical access.

Network devices should be installed in locations away from sources of electromagnetic interference (EMI) and radio-frequency interference (RFI). EMI is electrical interference produced by any source of power (typically, high-current or high-voltage sources, such as compressor motors). If you run a network cable parallel to a power cable, the EMI produced by the power cable can introduce spurious signals into the network cable, causing network communication problems. RFI, on the other hand, is electrical interference produced by sources of radio waves, such as TV and radio transmitters. Sources of RFI can negatively affect the quality, speed, and reliability of network communications.

> **WARNING** Don't run network cables near fluorescent light fixtures in the ceiling, which are powerful sources of EMI.

Computer Equipment

Computer equipment (including workstations and servers) is slightly different from other network devices in terms of responding to environmental factors, because computers contain more electronics and moving parts. When a computer operates in a dusty or dirty environment, dirt and dust particles can enter the computer through the floppy-disk drive, causing it to malfunction. Other network devices, such as routers, don't have that problem, because they don't use floppy-disk drives.

In general, you should be extremely cautious about where you place computers, because they are highly susceptible to environmental problems. Hubs, for example, can often be placed where computers can't, because hubs don't contain sensitive electronics.

Error Messages

Error messages can be the result of environmental problems but typically are generated by device or program failure. An *error message* is a message displayed on either a workstation or server console, indicating that a problem exists somewhere in the system. Error messages can be generated by an application program (inability to access a subroutine or program-instruction execution failure), a backup or restore failure (improper termination or a verify failure), or in a server by the failure of a service to start or a hardware error. The nature of an error message often indicates whether the problem is related to environmental conditions. If an error message appears only sporadically, the problem can be an intermittent hardware failure or may be related to some environmental condition that is causing a network device to malfunction.

Network Elements

Network elements are a general category of the devices and connectors on a network. The Network+ exam tests you on your ability to recognize, visually or by description (mostly by description), the various network elements involved in implementing a network. These network elements include:

- Peripheral ports
- External SCSI connectors
- Network components

Peripheral Ports

Peripheral ports are the expansion ports on a computer used to connect peripherals (discussed later in this unit). Many port types exist, but the most common are the DB-*xx* series. DB-*xx* series ports are shaped like trapezoids and are categorized by the number of pins or sockets that they contain. A DB-9 female port, for example, contains nine sockets. The most common DB ports are DB-9 male (serial) and DB-25 female (parallel).

External SCSI Connectors

External SCSI connectors are the ports used to connect Small Computer Systems Interface (SCSI) devices to a computer or host device. The three types of connectors are DB-25, Centronics 50, and high-density 68-pin. The DB-25 connector (see Figure 10.1) is used mainly to connect external SCSI devices to Macintosh computers. The Centronics-50 connector (see Figure 10.2) is used most often to connect external SCSI disks. The high-density 68-pin connector, shown in Figure 10.3, is used in most SCSI implementations later than SCSI-2.

FIGURE 10.1
A DB-25 external SCSI connector

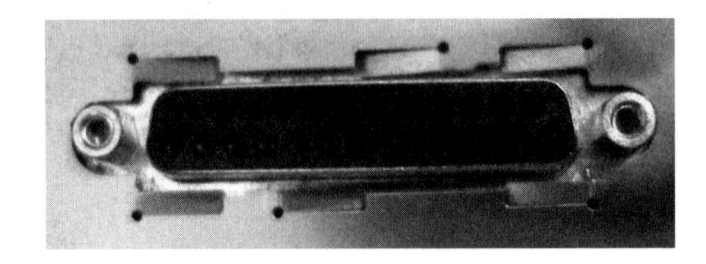

FIGURE 10.2
A Centronics-50 external SCSI connector

FIGURE 10.3
A high-density 68-pin external SCSI connector

Network Components

Network components are the components that make up a network. When you implement a new network or upgrade an older network, knowing what network components look like and what they do is very helpful.

Print Servers

A *print server* is a software device, hardware device, or a combination of the two that runs programs needed to create and operate print queues or spoolers. (*Queues* and *spoolers* are areas of the disk drive that contain the print jobs.) A print server manages and redirects print jobs to multiple printers, which typically are attached to the server. Print jobs can be prioritized and scheduled to print at a time when the printers are less busy. Some NOSes allow a print server to reside on a workstation connected to a printer, but others require the print server to reside on a file or application server. Novell NetWare 2.x and 3.x, for example, allowed a print server to reside on a dedicated workstation, but a print server for Novell NetWare 4.x must run on a file or application server.

Peripherals

Peripherals are hardware devices that may not be directly connected to the network, but are connected to a device that is directly connected. Most PC monitors, for example, are considered to be peripherals. Monitors usually are not directly connected to the network, but they are connected to a device (the user's workstation) that is. Following are some other examples of peripherals:

- Speakers
- Modems
- Printers
- Mice
- Keyboards

UPSes

An *Uninterruptible Power Supply* (UPS) is a device that provides continuous power to a computer or other network device. Most UPSes work by running the equipment off a battery inside the UPS and continuously charging that battery by using standard AC power. If the AC power goes out, the computer or electronic equipment continues to function until the battery runs out of power.

UPSes come in many shapes and sizes. The key to recognizing a UPS is recognizing that almost all of them have multiple power outlets and are very heavy, due to the batteries.

Patch Panels

A *patch panel* is a centralized location where all network cable runs interconnect. The patch panel has a group of modular connectors that are connected to the cable run on one side. On the other side, the connectors can be connected to any other location by a short network cable called a *patch cord*.

NICs

NICs probably are the most important components of any network. NICs are expansion cards that connect the electronics of a computer to the network medium. Every device connected to the network medium has an NIC.

> **NOTE:** NICs are discussed in more detail in Units 1 and 2.

Media Filters

A *media filter* is a passive device that can eliminate undesirable high-frequency line noise. A media filter can also convert the output from a Token Ring NIC to a signal that can be transmitted over other types of media—specifically, shielded twisted-pair cable.

Hubs and Switches

Hubs and switches are very similar in appearance, the major difference being their internal components. Hubs pass all packets, whereas a switch intelligently passes specific packets to particular ports. In most cases, the device is rectangular, as shown in Figure 10.4, and has multiple connection points for the network media.

FIGURE 10.4
A switch

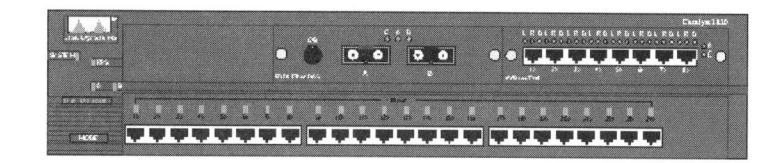

Some higher-end switches have the capability to accept different types of modules to expand the device's capabilities. These modules can include 100TX, 100FX, gigabit, and management modules.

> **NOTE** Hubs and switches are explained in greater detail in Unit 2.

Routers

A *router* is an intelligent network device that connects multiple network devices into an internetwork. Although a router is a complex device, you can't tell from its appearance. A router typically has a smooth face, with only logos and LEDs on the front, as shown in Figure 10.5. Some routers also have configuration ports on the front.

FIGURE 10.5
A front view of a router

The back of a router (see Figure 10.6) has ports for WAN links and for configuration, if they are not on the front. Empty slots are built into some models of routers; they allow the device to have many options installed. These options can include ISDN ports, fiber-optic connections, Ethernet ports, and Digital Subscriber Link (DSL) ports.

FIGURE 10.6
A back view of a router

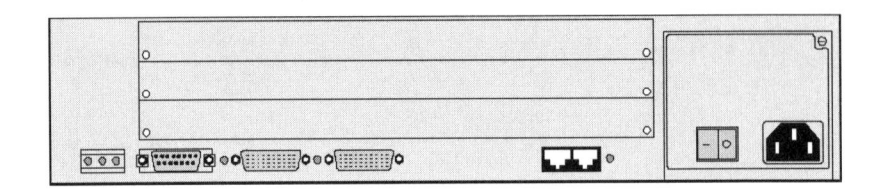

> Routers are discussed in greater detail in Unit 4.

Brouters

A *brouter* (bridging router) is a hybrid of a bridge and a router. A brouter responds to both a physical address (MAC) and a logical address (such as an IP address). A brouter looks very similar to a router. In fact, telling the difference between a router and a brouter based on looks alone is almost impossible. All differences are on a software level and reside within the devices themselves.

> Brouters are discussed in greater detail in Unit 4.

UTP Cable Installation Issues

Networks based on unshielded twisted-pair (UTP) cabling (the most common type of network cable) have certain installation issues that can cause problems with the operation of the network. The Network+ exam recognizes this fact and tests you on the main issues that cause problems in a UTP installation. Three of the most common issues are:

- Analog/digital signaling type
- RJ-45 connector use
- Patch cables and cable length

> Cabling technologies are discussed in greater detail in Unit 1.

Analog/Digital Signaling

UTP is used for two types of electrical signals: digital and analog. An *analog* electrical signal changes voltage over time and at any given instant is in transition between two voltages. A *digital* electrical signal, on the other hand, consists of voltages in an on/off pattern. The voltage rises to its set value in an instant, stays at that voltage for a period, and then is turned off in an instant. Figure 10.7 shows a comparison of analog and digital electrical signals.

FIGURE 10.7 Analog and digital electrical signals

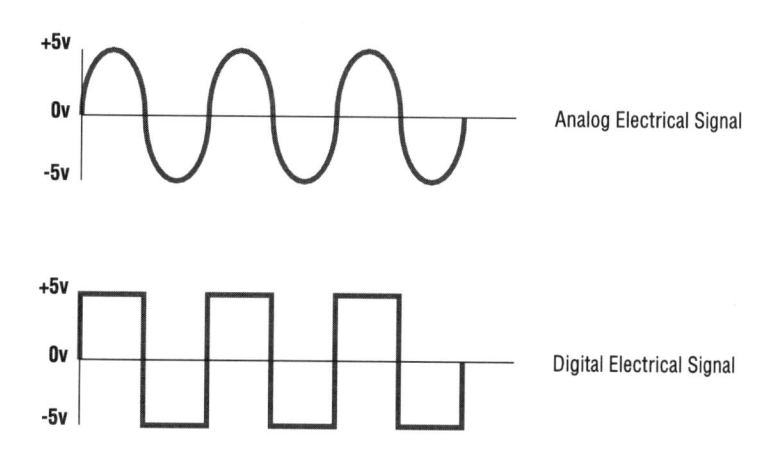

The analog-versus-digital concept becomes important during the installation of modems. To install a modem without problems, you must know what kind of telephone system you have. The telephone lines (and telephones) in most homes use analog signals. Most offices, on the other hand, use digital telephone systems. Modems are designed to send and receive analog electrical signals. If you install a modem in a computer and hook it to a digital telephone line, at the very least, the modem won't be able to dial. In a worst-case scenario, both the modem and the computer could be damaged.

RJ-45 Connectors

Another important consideration in installing a network based on UTP is making the proper connection of RJ-45 connectors to UTP cables. Standard Category 5 UTP cables have four pairs of wires twisted around one another. Each pair is color-coded, to identify it. The colors for each pair are orange, green, blue, and brown. One of the wires in each pair is solid-color; the other has a white stripe. The way that these wires are connected to individual pins in an RJ-45 connector is important, because 10BaseT Ethernet requires these connections to be made the same way on both ends of a cable. Two standards exist for wiring RJ-45 connectors. Both standards are agreed upon by the Electronic Industries Association and Telecommunications Industries Association, so they are called *EIA/TIA standards*. The cabling standards are EIA/TIA 568-A and EIA/TIA 568-B; Table 10.2 shows their colored-wire-to-pin connections.

TABLE 10.2 UTP colored-wire-to-pin connections

RJ-45 Pin	EIA/TIA 568-A	EIA/TIA 568-B
1	Green/white	Orange/white
2	Green	Orange
3	Orange/white	Green/white
4	Blue	Blue
5	Blue/white	Blue/white
6	Orange	Green
7	Brown/white	Brown/white
8	Brown	Brown

Patch Cables and Cable Length

When you plan UTP cable runs, remember that the maximum distance between the workstation and hub is 100 meters. Also remember that this 100-meter distance includes all sections of cable between the workstation and hub, including patch cables (both from the workstation to the wall plate and from the patch panel to the hub). If you have a 5-meter patch-cable run from the workstation to the wall plate, a 100-meter UTP-cable run from the wall plate to the patch panel, and a 3-meter patch-cable run from the patch panel to the hub, you have a total cable run of 108 meters. Even though the main cable run from the wall plate to the patch panel is 100 meters, the entire length of the cabling from the workstation to the hub (108 meters) is more than the allowed maximum for UTP (100 meters). Although in practice, this connection may actually work, according to the UTP distance specifications, it is too long. When cable runs are too long, workstations may have difficulty communicating. The symptoms can be corrupted data or no connection at all. Runs that are too long may not only affect a single workstation, but also slow the entire network.

> **NOTE** Fiber-optic cable is often used for cable installations longer than 700 meters, to circumvent many of the distance limitations of copper cables.

STUDY QUESTIONS

Network Preinstallation

1. The items that you should gather before performing a network implementation include the administrative passwords, current documentation, _____, and a device-location map.

2. What types of passwords do you need to gather for a network implementation? _____

3. When you use the TCP/IP stack, what information should you know in advance?
   _____
   _____
   _____

4. _____ is the default administrative account for Novell NetWare 4.x.

5. _____ is the default administrative account for Microsoft Windows NT 3.x.

6. Before you use some protocol stacks, you must know what range of _____ to use.

7. When you use the TCP/IP stack, you must know what _____ of addresses are blocked for dynamic addressing.

8. Knowing the _____ of all network devices is a necessity for implementing a new network.

9. True or false: The location of a server can be affected by many factors, including the environment.

STUDY QUESTIONS

Environmental Factors on Computer Networks

10. True or false: A server should be installed in a warm, damp room.

11. Copper-cored cable should not be placed under _____ lighting.

12. True or false: Under the counter of the break-room floor is a good location for a server.

13. True or false: The floor of the supply room is a good location for a server.

14. True or false: A shelf in a ventilated, secured supply room is a good location for a server.

15. True or false: The temperature in the server room does not matter.

16. True or false: Moisture is not a factor in selecting the placement of a server.

17. A server should be kept away from _____ and _____.

18. True or false: A copper-cored cable cannot be run in the same conduit as a high-voltage power line.

Network Elements

19. A print server consists of either _____ or hardware or both.

20. A _____ provides power protection for a network device.

STUDY QUESTIONS

21. UPSes contain a _____ to provide power to connected devices.

22. True or false: A patch panel needs power to operate.

23. A media filter is used on what type of network? _____

24. A media filter can convert from unshielded twisted-pair to _____ twisted-pair.

25. SCSI connectors use a _____ pin, _____ pin, or a _____ pin connector.

26. When you use an analog modem, what type of telephone line should you use? _____

27. True or false: The distance of a cable run is not a factor in installing a network.

28. The print-server software for Novell NetWare 4.*x* must execute on a _____; it cannot be executed on a workstation.

29. A UPS has multiple _____ and is very heavy due to the batteries.

30. A media filter is a passive device that can _____ undesirable high-frequency line noise.

STUDY QUESTIONS

UTP Cable Installation Issues

31. True or false: The length of a cable is relevant in an Ethernet network.

32. What type of cable is normally used for runs longer than 700 meters? _____

33. True or false: A modem uses a standard RJ-45 data cable.

34. Modems typically use an _____ connector.

35. A standard older modem communicates over what type of signal? _____

36. True or false: In an extreme case, a cable-TV cable can be used in place of a coaxial data cable.

SAMPLE TEST

10-1 What types of information would you need before starting a network upgrade?

   A. CEO's password

   B. Administrative password

   C. Network documentation

   D. IP-addressing scheme

10-2 Which of the following devices does a hub resemble?

   A. Switch

   B. SCSI connector

   C. UPS

   D. SPS

10-3 What is the default administrative account for NetWare 4.11?

   A. master

   B. administrator

   C. admin

   D. supervisor

10-4 Why should you know the administrative accounts before migrating a network?

   A. To have access to all volumes

   B. To have access to all servers

   C. All of the above

   D. None of the above

SAMPLE TEST

10-5 What is the default administrative account for Windows NT 4.x?

    A. master

    B. administrator

    C. admin

    D. supervisor

10-6 Which of the following can reside at a centralized location for all devices to interconnect?

    A. Media filter

    B. UPS

    C. Power outlet

    D. Patch panel

10-7 What network components can provide access to network print services?

    A. Print server

    B. Print administrator

    C. PCONSOLE.EXE

    D. Print manager

10-8 What information do you need when you use the TCP/IP protocol stack?

    A. What class address(es) to use

    B. What subnet masks to use

    C. What type of addressing to use

    D. None of the above

SAMPLE TEST

10-9 Which of the following would be a bad locations for a network server?

    A. Under the receptionist's desk

    B. A ventilated wiring closet

    C. A factory production floor

    D. A conference room

10-10 Which of the following statements about cables is true?

    A. No speed limit exists for copper-cored cable.

    B. No distance limit exists for fiber-optic cable.

    C. Both statements are true.

    D. Both statements are false.

10-11 Which of the following systems provides a continuous supply of power to the server?

    A. UPS

    B. SPS

    C. Surge protector/power strip

    D. Hub

10-12 What information should you know before beginning a network installation?

    A. Where the systems will be placed

    B. Where the cafeteria is

    C. How many users the network will have

    D. What departments the users are in

SAMPLE TEST

10-13 Which of the following network components has no electronic components?

  A. Brouter

  B. Patch panel

  C. Router

  D. Switch

10-14 Which of the following environmental factors should you consider for a network installation?

  A. Ventilation

  B. Temperature

  C. Security

  D. All of the above

10-15 An external SCSI interface can use which types of connectors?

  A. DB-25 female

  B. High-density 68-pin

  C. Centronics-36

  D. Centronics-50

10-16 Which of the following network devices can connect dissimilar cable types and perform frequency adjustments on a Token Ring network?

  A. Switch

  B. Media filter

  C. MAU

  D. Brouter

SAMPLE TEST

10-17 Which of the following locations would be bad for a copper-cored cable?

    A. Anywhere in the ceiling

    B. In shielded conduit

    C. Along a dedicated data cable path

    D. Cabled along with the power lines

10-18 What would be an ideal temperature range for a room that contains network servers?

    A. 110°F to 120°F

    B. 60°F to 70°F

    C. 90°F to 100°F

    D. 120°F to 130°F

10-19 A wall plate has three jacks: an RJ-45, marked Network; an RJ-11, marked Phone; and an RJ-11, marked Data. Which port should you use for a modem?

    A. Phone

    B. Network

    C. Data

    D. None of the above

10-20 Which of the following provides power to devices when a power failure occurs?

    A. ISA

    B. CPA

    C. SPS

    D. UPS

UNIT 11

The Change-Control System

Test Objectives: Administering the Change-Control System

- Demonstrate awareness of the need to document the current status and configuration of the workstation (i.e., providing a baseline) prior to making any changes.

- Given a configuration scenario, select a course of action that would allow the return of a system to its original state.

- Given a scenario involving workstation backups, select the appropriate backup technique from among the following:
  - Tape backup
  - Folder replication to a network drive
  - Removable media
  - Multigeneration

- Demonstrate awareness of the need to remove outdated or unused drivers, properties, etc., when an upgrade is successfully completed.

- Identify the possible adverse effects on the network caused by local changes (e.g., version conflicts, overwritten DLLs, etc.).

- Explain the purpose of drive mapping, and, given a scenario, identify the mapping that will produce the desired results, using Universal Naming Convention (UNC) or an equivalent feature. Explain the purpose of printer port capturing, and identify properly formed capture commands, given a scenario.

- Given a scenario where equipment is being moved or changed, decide when and how to verify the functionality of the network and critical applications.

- Given a scenario where equipment is being moved or changed, decide when and how to verify the functionality of that equipment.

- Demonstrate awareness of the need to obtain relevant permissions before adding, deleting, or modifying users.

- **Identify the purpose and function of the following networking elements:**
  - Profiles
  - Rights
  - Procedures/policies
  - Administrative utilities
  - Login accounts, groups, and passwords

Note: Exam objectives are subject to change at any time without notice and at CompTIA's sole discretion. Please visit CompTIA's Web site (www.comptia.org) for the most current exam-objectives listing.

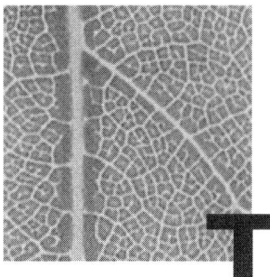

The *change-control system* is the main system that a network administrator uses to administrate the network. The change-control system manages all changes that occur, from performing installations and upgrades to adding users to the existing network. The Network+ exam includes only a few questions on the change-control system, including questions on the following topics:

- Documenting a workstation baseline
- Returning a system to its original state
- Performing workstation backups
- Removing unnecessary software components
- Understanding local changes that cause adverse network effects
- Performing drive mapping
- Verifying network and critical-application functionality
- Verifying equipment functionality
- Using permissions for administration
- Understanding network-administration concepts

All these topics are part of managing the moves, additions, and changes that occur daily on an average network.

> **NOTE** Although the unit covers many objectives, these objectives make up a small percentage of the actual questions on the exam (about 4 percent). Bear that fact in mind when you study this unit.

Documenting a Workstation Baseline

A *baseline* is a document that contains all the settings and information about how a workstation should operate. The baseline provides a starting point for making changes in a network, particularly in a server or workstation. If something goes wrong (during an upgrade, for example), you can use the baseline to try to return the workstation to its previous state.

When a workstation is first built, it is a good idea to document all the settings and statistics on it before installing any new hardware or software. This documentation can give you vital information for troubleshooting workstation and network errors. The documentation can include the following:

- Hardware specifications and settings
    - IRQ, I/O address, and DMA settings (in use and available)
    - Processor type
    - Memory (type, amount installed, available space)
    - Hard drive (type, size)
    - Monitor (type, size, settings)
    - Optional components (sound card, modem)
- Installed applications (versions, patches)
- Network (settings, addresses, protocols)
    - Client (version, type)
- Statistics (network, local)
    - Average transfer rates
    - Average request rates
    - Average boot time

You should update documentation after making any updates on a workstation or network level. This updated documentation can expedite the process of troubleshooting bugs in new upgrades, patches, or application conflicts. If a user complains that his workstation's sound card is not working, for example, you can check the baseline documentation to see whether that workstation ever had a sound card.

Returning a System to Its Original State

Not every upgrade or new software installation goes as smoothly as planned. Being able to restore a workstation to its original state when problems occur can greatly reduce administration time and effort. You can accomplish this task by creating an image of a workstation after its initial successful installation.

An *image* of a workstation is a single file (an exact copy of the hard drive) that contains the boot sector, the operating system, all programs, all files, and all the workstation-configuration information in compressed form. You use a workstation-imaging program to create images. An image file typically includes items such as the following:

- Disk configuration
- Operating system
- Operating-system configuration
- All application and data files

You can use an image file to return a system to its original state after an unsuccessful upgrade. The workstation is erased; then the image is applied to the workstation. This process is known as *dumping* an image to a workstation. Ghost (from Symantec) is one example of a disk-imaging and dumping program.

> **NOTE** An image file is only current as the date when the image was made. If data files or settings have changed since the image was made, the workstation after the image dump is current only to the date when the original image was made.

The first step in preparing an image is loading the workstation with the appropriate operating system (Microsoft Windows 95/98, Windows NT, OS/2, or Linux, for example), with all the appropriate drivers in place. The next step is installing any applications that are required on that workstation, such as an office-productivity suite (such as Microsoft Office or Corel Office) and Internet software. Then you can customize the user interface to your liking by adding wallpaper, screen savers, desktop shortcuts, and so on.

Finally, you can run the imaging software to create the image. The image should be stored on a storage medium large enough to store the single file. A single image file often is several hundred megabytes or larger (depending on the amount of information on the machine when it was imaged). When a workstation needs to be rebuilt, any additional files or applications loaded after the last image are lost. For this reason, you need to perform a backup for critical files that are stored on the workstation.

> **TIP** People often store workstation images on servers, because servers have enough capacity to store multiple images. In addition, servers typically are backed up every day.

Performing Workstation Backups

Workstations are the computers on the network where data is created and manipulated, as well as the interaction points with the users. The users often store the data that they create on their workstation. For this reason, the data on workstations often needs to be backed up.

> **TIP** Workstation backups are not recommended for any network, because they are complex and time-consuming. A better approach is to show users how to save data to the server. Tell users that their data will be safe on the server (because you will back it up) and that their workstations will not be backed up.

You can use many backup strategies for workstations. Some backup methods are similar to those that are used on servers (removable media, for example). Other methods, such as replication, take advantage of the workstation's capability and the network layout.

Workstation backup strategies can be divided into three major categories:

- Tape backup
- Other removable backup media
- Folder replication

The following sections briefly explain how to use these backup strategies to back up workstation data.

> **NOTE:** Backup types are covered in more detail in Unit 12.

Tape Backup

Tape backup is a backup method that uses a magnetic tape and tape drive installed on every workstation. Special software installed on the workstations automatically (at scheduled intervals) copies preselected directories (including their data) to the tape for archival purposes.

Using tape backups for workstations has the following advantages:

Simplicity: Tape backups are the simplest method of backing up a workstation. The tape-drive-and-software combination copies all files or selected workstation directories and files to the tape drive in the workstation automatically.

Large data capacity: Tape drives and media are available that can back up an entire workstation hard disk to a single tape.

Tape backups also have the following disadvantages:

High cost: Because every workstation must have a tape backup unit, and because tape backup units can cost anywhere from $100 on up apiece, this method can become very expensive very quickly.

Tape rotation: Even though the backups occur automatically, someone must change the tapes every day before a new backup is performed. If you are responsible for this task, you must visit every workstation every day, and this procedure can take a great deal of time if you have to visit 20 or more workstations. If users are asked to do their own tape rotation, however, they may not do it or may not do it properly; therefore, their data might be lost.

Other Removable Backup Media

Magnetic tape is not the only removable backup medium. Removable media include, but are not limited to, the following:

- Magnetic disks
- Optical discs and CD-ROMs
- Removable hard drives
- Multigeneration tape rotations

The following sections examine several types of removable media.

Magnetic Disks

Magnetic disks store data as magnetic flux patterns on a spinning disk. Jaz drives, Zip drives, LS-120 drives, and standard floppy disks are examples of removable magnetic disk media. Zip (100MB) and Jaz (1GB common) drives can store anywhere from 100MB to 2GB on a removable, portable disk. LS-120 disks look similar to standard 1.44MB or 720KB floppy disks, but a special drive is required to read and write to them. An LS-120 disk can store approximately 120MB of data.

> **NOTE:** An LS-120 drive can also read 1.44MB and 720KB disks.

Optical Discs and CD-ROMs

Optical discs and *CD-ROMs* (compact disc read-only memory) use a laser to read and write data from the disc. CD-ROM writers and rewriters are fast becoming commonplace as their prices drop. These devices can be used to back up large amounts of data (approximately 650MB) and can be read, but not written to, by most CD-ROM readers. With CD-ROM readers being standard on most workstations today, you can add a CD-ROM writer/rewriter without installing additional hardware.

Removable Hard Drives

A *removable hard drive* is a hard drive that has been installed in a special chassis for easy removal. Some removable hard drives are *hot-pluggable*, which means that they can be removed while power is still applied to the system. Hot-pluggable drives are most commonly used in RAID disk systems.

> **WARNING** Many removable hard drives are *not* hot-pluggable. Removing a non-hot-pluggable disk while power is applied can permanently damage it. Refer to the manufacturer's documentation to verify that a disk is hot-pluggable before you remove it with the power applied.

A removable hard drive can operate as the primary drive, with the operating system and applications stored on it, or it can operate as a second drive used only for file storage. Removable hard drives are an excellent choice for security and data transportation.

Folder Replication

Folder replication is a backup method in which local data is automatically copied to a server, where it is centrally backed up. The main reason for using this technology is because the fact that it is transparent to users. Users save their files to their local folders, as though the computer weren't connected to the network. The data in the folder is automatically copied to a central server by means of special replication software or services. Then the data on the central server is archived on tape or some other storage medium.

> **NOTE** Folder replication is a technology mainly used by Windows NT Server. Windows NT supports replication only for one specific folder and only for internal replication. Most other operating systems do not support folder replication without help. SureSync, by Software Pursuits (http://www.spursuits.com/), is a third-party software program that supports Windows 9x-to-Windows NT folder replication.

Using folder replication as a method of workstation backup has the following advantages:

No user intervention required: All that users have to do is save their data to their folders on their workstations. The replication software copies the data to the server automatically.

Redundancy: The users' data exists in two places: on the workstation and on the server. If one or the other device fails, the data will still be available.

Can be used with other workstation backup methods: This backup method can be used at the same time as other workstation backup methods, to provide an additional level of protection for the workstation data.

Folder replication also has its share of disadvantages:

Complex setup: Folder replication usually requires additional workstation software.

Synchronization: Unfortunately, because the data exists in two places at the same time, the data files on the server could be slightly out of sync with the files on the workstations. If the workstation crashes, and data needs to be restored, the user may lose whatever changes he or she made since the last replication.

High cost: The additional software required for the workstation is somewhat costly, especially for hundreds of workstations. This disadvantage is the main reason why folder replication is not a popular backup method.

Multigeneration Tape Rotations

Multigeneration tape rotations are a backup strategy in which multiple backups are made as normal during the week, but weekly and monthly tapes are kept for archival purposes. Multigeneration tape rotations are used in case someone needs to refer to older data. Almost all types of backups (tape, CD-ROMs, and other removable media) can implement multigeneration rotational schemes.

Multigeneration tape rotation is also known as the *grandfather, father, and son* (GFS) method. In a GFS multigeneration rotation scheme, daily, weekly, and monthly backups are kept. The daily (son) backups are differential, incremental, or full. A full backup is performed at the end of the week (the father backup). Because the daily tapes are reused after a week, they age only five days. The weekly tapes stay around for a month and are reused during the following month. The last full backup of the month is known as the monthly backup, or the grandfather. The grandfather tapes become the oldest, and you retain them for a year before reusing them. Figure 11.1 shows an example of a GFS tape scheme.

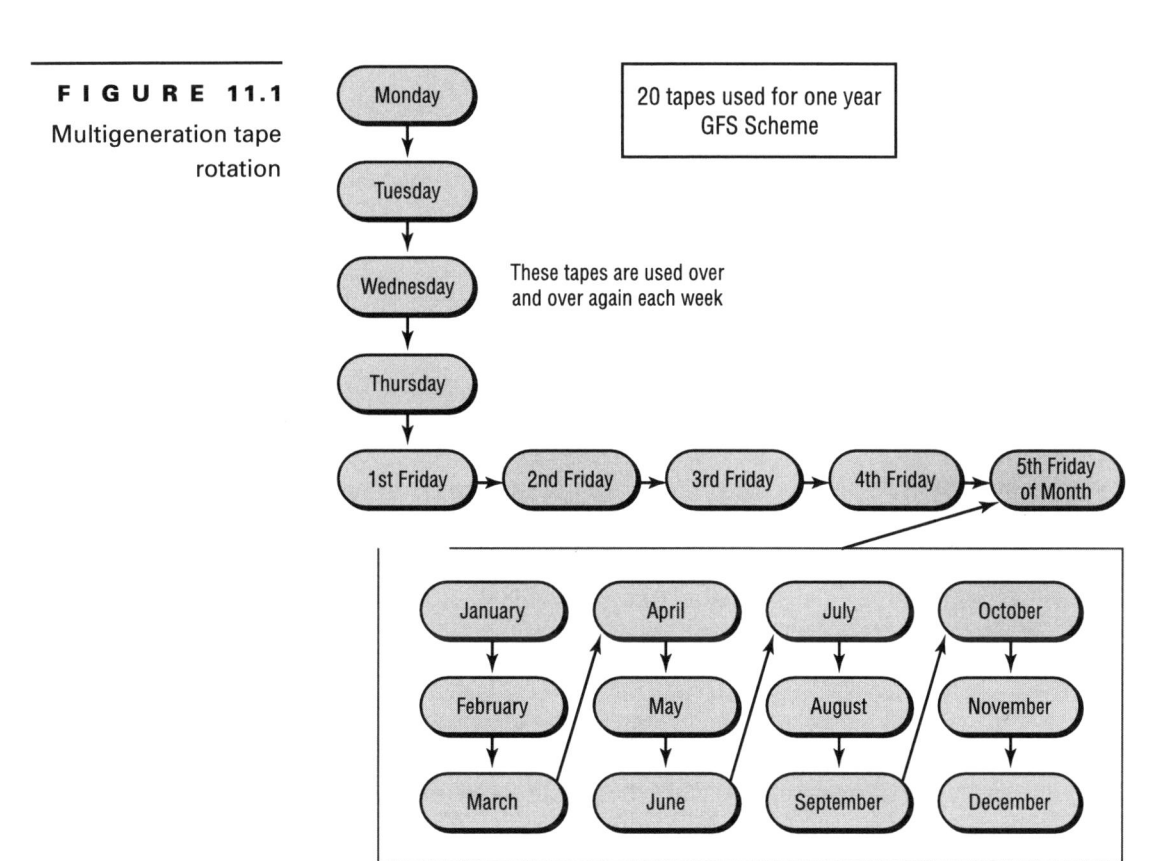

FIGURE 11.1
Multigeneration tape rotation

Removing Unnecessary Software Components

After you install new applications, it is a good idea to clean up a workstation. You should remove all unnecessary files, drivers, and protocols to prevent software conflicts later. These components can conflict with the loading of a new application.

When you upgrade old software or install new software, the hard drive will contain files for that application that are no longer needed. These unneeded application and data files take up disk space and should be removed. Unneeded files that are left on a workstation can take up drive space that could be used for other applications or data.

Unneeded drivers can cause a workstation to slow or to lock up. In one case, a workstation had an Iomega Jaz drive installed. That drive was removed, but the drivers for the Jaz drive were left installed in the machine. When the Jaz drive was removed, the workstation began to lock up when the Jaz drivers were loading, because the device could not be found.

Unneeded network protocols can also slow a workstation and cause intermittent application errors. Any time you upgrade a network and change the protocols, you should remove the old protocols, after you thoroughly test the network with the new protocols.

Understanding Local Changes That Cause Adverse Network Effects

This section applies mainly to Windows 9*x* or NT computers acting as servers on peer-to-peer networks. The Network+ exam wants you to understand that any changes that you make on the computer that acts as a server locally (installing software, and so on) can affect the computer's capability to be a server, if you make those changes incorrectly. Following are some examples of local changes that might affect a network:

- Version conflicts
- Overwritten DLLs (Dynamic Link Libraries)
- Local-resource use

These problems may be serious enough to prevent the computer from responding to network requests, which is an even more serious problem.

Version Conflicts

Shared files are pieces of software code that are designed to be shared among applications, so that a programmer doesn't have to write the same program routines for multiple applications. The Windows DLLs are examples of shared files that are widely used.

Shared files are the source of many Windows and application problems that can affect the network. The first problem—version conflicts—occurs when you install some piece of software that requires one version of a specific shared file. That piece of software may require version 1 of a shared file, so it installs that version in its own directory. Another application may require version 2 of the same shared file, so that application installs version 2 in its directory. The main problem is that, generally speaking, only one version of any shared file can be loaded into memory at any time. If the first application loads first, it loads the version 1 shared file into memory. If you later try to start the second program, which requires version 2 of the shared file, you will more than likely get an error; the system can't find version 2, because version 1 is already loaded into memory. In most programs today, the current version includes all the operational characteristics of the earlier version.

> **Note:** The Visual Basic Runtime library (VBRUN*xxx*.DLL, in which *xxx* is the version) is a good example of a shared file that experiences version conflicts.

How does this situation affect the network? If you load a local application that uses the same shared file as a network service (a Web server, SQL database server, or mail server, for example), you could prevent that service from loading, which could affect the entire network's capability to use the service.

The main symptoms of version conflicts include network services that work or don't work, depending on the program load order. Fortunately, with DLLs and shared files that have multiple versions, the older programs generally work with the newer versions of the shared file. Solving these problems usually involves changing the load order of the network services until they all load.

Overwritten DLLs

Some shared files (such as DLLs) are stored in a central location (such as the Windows directory, C:\WINDOWS or C:\WINNT). In this setup, an installation program may simply overwrite the newer version of the shared file with a different version, thereby disabling the capability of the newer network program to load properly. This situation would affect all users who need the network service that won't load properly.

Unfortunately, the solution to this problem usually involves reinstalling the newer program after the program that contains the older shared files, so that the newer version of the DLL or shared file can be installed. If you know the name and version of the DLL that has been overwritten, you may be able to copy the new DLL version to the Windows directory (or to the newer program's installation directory), thereby solving the problem without reinstalling the application.

Local-Resource Use

In addition to software version conflicts and overwritten DLLs, other local changes on a machine that acts as a server can affect the network. If a user starts using a processor- or disk-intensive program (such as a graphics or page-layout program) on the server, server-to-network data transfers will be slower, because the processor is busy working on that large graphic or page layout. Generally speaking, anything a user does that can slow the server will slow network-response time for users who are accessing that server.

Performing Drive Mapping

Servers share files, which are located in directories. How do you access those directories in a client-server environment? Client computers based on Window 95/98 share the history of stand-alone–DOS-based computers. These computers were limited and emphasized proper operation of the hardware; they also ran a limited number of applications, including BASIC. How can modern computers, with legacy designs, access network resources? DOS machines and their Windows 95/98 replacements access hard and floppy drives by assigning a drive letter to each drive. The process of assigning a drive letter to a network disk device is called *mapping*.

Each network disk resource is mapped to a local drive letter via a process known as *network redirection*. Requests by applications for local resources are redirected to network resources by the network client software. In the case of drive mapping, the redirector takes requests and reroutes them from the local file system to a server on the network. All disk accesses, regardless of type, end up looking like disk accesses on the local PC.

Drive Mapping in Windows 95/98 and NT

To access network resources provided by either Windows 95/98 or Windows NT computers, you access a directory that the administrator has shared. Such directories are called *shares*. Network shares are identified on Windows networks by the *Universal Naming Convention* (UNC). The Client for

Microsoft Networks uses this format to connect to network shares. The UNC path specifies the name of the server hosting the share, along with the name of the share. Following is the format of a UNC name:

`\\servername\sharename`

This format provides a universal network name that refers to any network resource.

You map to a share by using the `net use` command. The format is `net use`, followed by a space, the drive letter that you want to map, a colon, another space, and the UNC name of the resource that you want to access, as follows:

`net use g: \\servername\sharename`

> **Tip:** If you are using Windows 95/98 or NT workstations on a Windows network, and if you have the Windows client software for that platform installed, you can use Explorer and Network Neighborhood to map drives. Simply browse to the network directory (share), right-click the directory, and choose Map Network Drive from the shortcut menu to open the Map Network Drive dialog box. Select the drive letter that you want to map to the device, and indicate whether you want the drive mapping to be permanent (meaning that it is reconnected every time you start up). Then click OK to map the drive.

Drive Mapping in NetWare

In NetWare, a slightly different naming convention is used for the directory structure on a NetWare server. The terms used are *server name* and *volume name* (or *volume object name*, if you're using NDS), *directory*, and *subdirectory*. A user can map to any directory on the network in which he or she has rights. Directories in which a user does not have rights are not visible if the user browses the directory structure.

To map a drive, you can use the `MAP` command. The syntax is map, followed by a space, drive letter, colon, equal sign, server name with a backslash, the volume name (or the name of the volume object), colon, directory, subdirectory, subdirectory, and so on. Following are two examples.

Using server and volume names:

`MAP F:=SERVER\VOLUME:DIRECTORY\SUBDIRECTORY`

Using the volume object name:

`MAP F:=VOLUMEOBJECTNAME:DIRECTORY\SUBDIR`

> **TIP**
> If you are using Windows 95/98 or NT workstations on a NetWare network, and if you have the Windows client software for that platform installed, you can use Explorer and Network Neighborhood to map drives. Simply browse to the network device, right-click the device, and choose Map Network Drive from the shortcut menu to open the Map Network Drive dialog box. Select the drive letter that you want to map to the device, and indicate whether you want the drive mapping to be permanent (meaning that it is reconnected every time you start up). Then click OK to map the drive. If you have the Novell Client installed, you can also use Novell Map Network Drive (after right-clicking the Network device), which gives you the additional choices of mapping a drive as a root and mapping a drive as a search drive.

Mapping Drives in Unix

Unix shares use the same terminology as NetWare, but they are reversed. A colon separates the server name, and forward slashes are used for directory and subdirectory divisions. Also, case is important in Unix. The names *Data* and *data* denote the same directory in Windows NT and NetWare, but they are in different locations in a Unix file system. The command used is mount, and it has the following syntax: mount, space, server name, colon, forward slash, directory, forward slash, subdirectory, space, forward slash, and the local directory to which the remote share will be mapped. Following is an example:

```
mount server:/directory/subdirectory /localDirectory
```

This command mounts the /directory/subdirectory NFS share to the /localDirectory directory mount point.

Capturing Printer Ports

Just as shared network directories need to be mapped to a local equivalent, so do remote shared printers. A Windows 95/98 workstation can have as many as three locally configured printers: LPT1, LPT2, and LPT3. Windows 95/98 allows far more than three printers for remote printing. For DOS programs or non-network-aware applications, you need to grab data sent to the local LPT port and redirect it to a printer on the network. This process is called *capturing* the printer port. The three clients—Microsoft, NetWare, and Unix —use different syntax to capture printer ports.

Capturing a Printer Port in Windows 95/98 and NT

To capture a local port and redirect a print job sent to the port to a Microsoft shared printer, the Client for Microsoft Networks uses the net use command. (This command is also used to map drives, as discussed earlier in this unit.) This time, instead of a drive letter, you use an LPT (parallel) port. The syntax is net use parallel port number, colon, space, and the UNC name of the shared printer. Following is an example:

```
net use LPT1: \\server\printer
```

> **TIP** You can also use Explorer and Network Neighborhood to capture printer ports. Simply choose the printer in Network Neighborhood, right-click the printer, and choose Capture Printer Port from the shortcut menu. Select the port, and click OK.

Capturing a Printer Port in NetWare

In NetWare, you use the CAPTURE command to capture printer ports. Using switches, you can define many options, such as the local port number, server name, printer name, queue name, banner page, and form feed. The syntax of the command is CAPTURE, space, L, equal sign, LPT port number, space, Q, equal sign, queue name, space, P, equal sign, printer name, space, option, space, option, and so on. Following is an example:

```
CAPTURE L=# Q=QueueName P=PrinterName nb nff
```

To see a list of all available switches, type **capture /?** at the command prompt.

In NetWare 4.*x* or later, with the Novell Client for Windows installed, you can also perform capturing by browsing to a network printer with Windows Explorer, right-clicking the queue or printer, and choosing Capture Print Port. From then on, the process is the same as it is for Windows NT.

Capturing a Printer Port in Unix

To print directly to a remote Unix-managed printer from a workstation, you use the `lpr` command. You do not need to map a network printer to your desktop Unix box, because Unix was created from the ground up to be a networked operating system. (A Windows 95/98 client requires a Unix server to have special print-job-management software to handle Windows 95/98 requests.) To print from one Unix box to another, use `lpr`, space, minus sign (also called a dash), P, printer name, space, and the filename. Following is an example:

`lpr -Pprinter filename`

Drive and printer mappings are two features of a network that you should know. These two types of mappings are commonly used with UNC names.

> **NOTE:** Keep in mind that you need proper rights to add, modify, or delete mappings in user accounts.

Verifying Network and Critical-Application Functionality

When you are moving or changing a network, there is always the chance that something can go wrong (at least, according to Murphy's Law). For this reason, the Network+ exam requires you to be able to verify network and critical-application functionality after network equipment has been moved or changed.

> **TIP:** Before you move a server or other network component to its new location, you should test the new location's facilities, including power quality and availability as well as the new network connection.

To test network-component and critical-application functionality after a move or network change, you simply try using the network as you normally would—logging in, uploading and downloading files, and so on. If all network features and functions perform normally in the new location (according to the baseline information that you gathered, as discussed earlier in this unit), the network is functioning correctly. The same holds true for network and local applications. Simply perform several normal operations in these applications in their new location. If the applications function normally, the move or change did not affect them.

If the network or the applications don't function properly after a move or change, you must use troubleshooting techniques to find the source of the problem. Troubleshooting is discussed in Unit 14.

Verifying Equipment Functionality

In addition to network and critical-application functionality, you should test the individual components of a network for functionality after a move or network change. These components can include servers, workstations, printers, scanners, copiers, and telecommunications equipment (NICs, cables, hubs, and so on). Before moving equipment, you should test all connections to ensure that the move will be as problem-free as possible. After equipment has been transferred to the new location, you should install it component by component, if possible. When you use this method, you can find and diagnose most problems faster.

Using Permissions for Administration

Every network operating system (NOS) requires you to have the appropriate network security permissions to administrate the network. You must have rights to add users, delete users, and modify settings and properties. If you are trying to add, delete, or modify a user's properties, and the system indicates that it can't perform the operation, you probably don't have the appropriate rights.

Rights are the capabilities you have on the network, according to the way that the NOS handles security. The terms *permissions* and *rights* are often used synonymously in this book, unless otherwise mentioned. In Windows NT, however, these terms mean different things. *Rights* are the kinds of activities that you can perform on the network (back up the server, log on locally, and so on). *Permissions*, on the other hand, are what you can and can't do to files and network shares.

Generally speaking, all NOSes have an administrative account that you can use to administrate the network. This account has all the appropriate rights and allows you to add, delete, and modify all user-account properties. Most NOSes also have the capability to grant these rights to other users as well.

Table 11.1 lists the rights that you must have to add, delete, and modify users in Windows NT 4 and NetWare 5.

TABLE 11.1: Administration rights required for Windows NT 4 and NetWare 5

Function	NetWare Rights Required	NT Rights Required
Add user	The Create Object right for the new Novell Directory Services (NDS) object's parent container	Member of the Account Operators or Administrators group
Delete user	The Delete Object right for the object that you want to delete	Member of the Account Operators group
Modify user	The Write Property right for the properties that you want to change	Member of the Account Operators group

Understanding Network-Administration Concepts

Aside from obtaining the correct permissions, you must understand a few basic concepts before you can administrate the network. These concepts include some of the basic items that you administrate within the change-control system. Following are some of the elements that are involved in the change-control system:

- Login accounts
- Administrative utilities
- Profiles

- Rights
- Procedures/policies

Each of these items has a different purpose and function, as described in the following sections.

Login Accounts

A *login account* (also called a *username* or *user account*) is the network operating system's logical representation of an individual user. Login accounts are required for all users. These accounts give users access to the network and differentiate one user from another. To gain access to a network, a user must have an individual login account.

Each login account contains individual properties for the user, including identification information, security settings, group memberships, and password. Aside from a login account, the only item that you must have to log in is a password on your login account. That way, no one else can log in, pretending to be you, and usurp your network access.

Administrative Utilities

Administrative utilities are programs that control and manipulate all aspects of a network, including user accounts, passwords, user groups, file security, application security, and network communications. Most network operating systems are bundled with several administrative utilities. Table 11.2 details the major administrative utilities used for user-account administration in several popular NOSes.

TABLE 11.2 Major NOSes' user-administration utilities	NOS	User Administration Utility
	NetWare 3.x	SYSCON
	NetWare 4.x and later	NetWare Administrator
	Windows NT 3.51 and later	User Manager (NT Workstation) and User Manager for Domains (NT Server)
	Unix	Varies by flavor—most use command-line utilities such as useradd, although some can use graphical alternatives

Profiles

A *network profile* is a compilation of a user's workstation settings. You can use profiles in a networking environment to allow users to retain individual settings: color schemes, fonts, icons, backgrounds, screen savers, and so on. Often, user profiles are stored on the network, so when a user logs in from a different workstation on the network, his or her personal workstation settings appear on the new workstation.

Rights

Rights control whether a particular user can access a particular network resource. *Rights* (also called *permissions*; see the note in "Using Permissions for Administration" earlier in this unit) are assigned for individual users or groups of users with regard to a particular network resource or service. Users can be assigned rights to various network entities, including applications, printers, files, and other network services. A user (or group of users) can be assigned rights to view a file and see it in a directory listing, but not change it.

Policies and Procedures

Policies are network mechanisms that help enforce different types of network security. Policies can specify what applications can be executed on a workstation, remove certain desktop-access capabilities, specify what items appear in the Start menu (for Windows 9x and NT 4), and specify whether desktop settings can be changed.

Procedures, on the other hand, are the standard ways of doing things on the network, according to the standard operating procedures (SOPs). Procedures must be followed on a network whenever any kind of administrative procedures are performed (such as adding, deleting, or modifying users), so that the changes are made consistently.

> **NOTE** Unit 10 provides a more detailed discussion of standard operating procedures.

STUDY QUESTIONS

Documenting a Workstation Baseline

1. Documentation can give an administrator vital information for _____ workstation and network errors.

2. Documentation should be _____ before any changes take place on a workstation or network level.

3. Documentation can include hardware specifications and settings, installed applications, and network and _____.

4. Documentation can help expedite troubleshooting bugs in new upgrades, patches, or _____ conflicts.

5. You can find standard operating procedures in your network's _____.

6. Documentation of statistics should include average transfer rates, average _____ rates, and average boot time.

Returning a System to Its Original State

7. The capability to restore a workstation to its _____ state with little trouble can greatly reduce the time required to get a workstation up and running.

8. You can restore a workstation to its original state quickly and efficiently by creating an _____ of a workstation after its initial build.

Unit 11 • The Change-Control System

STUDY QUESTIONS

9. Restoring a workstation manually involves loading the workstation with the appropriate operating system, installing any _____, and modifying the user interface.

10. When a workstation needs to be rebuilt manually or by an image, what is the result?
_____

Performing Workstation Backups

11. Jaz drives, Zip drives, LS-120 drives, and standard floppy disks are examples of _____ disk media.

12. _____ copy all user data on a workstation.

13. What removable medium most commonly has a capacity of 1,000MB?
_____

14. What removable medium most commonly has a capacity of 100MB?
_____

15. What removable medium most commonly has a capacity of 120MB?
_____

16. What removable medium most commonly has a capacity of 1.44MB?
_____

17. What removable medium most commonly has a capacity of 720KB?
_____

STUDY QUESTIONS

18. LS-120 disks require a special drive to _____.

19. A removable hard drive has been installed in a _____ for easy replacement.

20. You can use a backup system tape to back up _____.

21. Folder replication takes advantage of _____.

22. An LS –120 drive can read _____, _____, and _____ disks.

23. Removable hard drives are an excellent choice for _____ and transportation.

24. A removable hard drive operates as the primary drive or as a secondary drive used only for _____ storage.

Removing Unnecessary Software Components

25. _____ can be used to back up large amounts of data (up to 650MB) and can be read, but not written to, by most CD-ROM readers.

Understanding Local Changes That Cause Adverse Network Effects

26. Unneeded protocols can _____ a workstation.

STUDY QUESTIONS

27. When a new application has been installed on a workstation, it's a good idea to _____.

28. Unneeded _____ that are left on a workstation can take up drive space that could be used for other applications.

29. Unneeded drivers can cause a workstation to _____ or _____.

30. _____ can overwrite files that are necessary to run other critical applications, network connections, or the operating system itself.

Performing Drive Mapping

31. The _____ is the standard for network path listings.

32. _____ connect a drive letter to shared disk space on a server.

33. In most cases, replication is the process of _____ files from a local drive to a network server.

34. True or false: One advantage of replicating to a file server is that the files that are replicated are backed up along with the files stored on the server.

35. A UNC path consists of _____ and _____, preceded by _____ and separated by _____.

STUDY QUESTIONS

36. In a network environment, using _____ can simplify finding, running, and managing applications on networks.

Capturing Printer Ports

37. _____ is the process in which a local parallel port is connected to a network printer.

38. _____ applications need a port to be captured for printing.

39. What does UNC stand for? _____

40. _____ applications cannot use the UNC naming convention.

Verifying Network and Critical-Application Functionality

41. Before moving equipment, you should _____ all connections to ensure that the move will be as smooth as possible.

42. You should test applications with a _____ account.

43. True or false: When a network has been moved, it is important to test users' e-mail accounts.

44. True or false: When a network has been moved, it is important to test all Internet connections.

Unit 11 • The Change-Control System

STUDY QUESTIONS

45. True or false: When a network has been moved, it is important to test the capability to transfer files.

46. True or false: When a network has been moved, it is important to test the users' games.

Verifying Equipment Functionality

47. True or false: When a network has been moved, it is important to test all modems.

48. True or false: When a network has been moved, it is important to test all NICs.

49. True or false: When a network has been moved, it is important to test the positions of all mice.

50. True or false: When a network has been moved, it is important to test all network connections.

51. True or false: When a network has been moved, it is important to test the elevation of all the keyboards.

52. True or false: When a network has been moved, it is important to test all tape backup units.

Using Permissions for Administration

53. Proper rights are required to _____ user accounts.

54. Which Windows NT group must you be a member of to administrate user accounts?

STUDY QUESTIONS

Understanding Network-Administration Concepts

55. _____ can be used in a networking environment to allow users to retain individual desktop settings.

56. _____ are required to access and modify resources on a network.

57. A _____ and a _____ are required to access to network services.

58. What networking-administration concept discussed in this unit includes user settings such as color schemes and fonts? _____

59. What networking-administration concept discussed in this unit includes the capability to remove the Run command from the Windows 9x Start menu? _____

60. What networking-administration concept discussed in this unit includes the capability to manage user accounts and files? _____

SAMPLE TEST

11-1 When you clean a workstation's file system, what types of files could you remove?

   A. Unneeded drivers

   B. Unneeded protocols

   C. Unneeded files

   D. Unneeded operating systems

11-2 How could you confirm the speed performance of a workstation as being normal?

   A. Use a protocol analyzer

   B. Check the cabling

   C. Verify the user account

   D. Refer to the workstation's baseline information

11-3 Which of the following are advantages of folder replication?

   A. It provides more fault tolerance.

   B. Used in smaller networks, it can be simple.

   C. It can scale to hundreds of workstations.

   D. Files are also backed up from the server.

11-4 In the event of a server crash, what is the easiest way to return the system to its original state?

   A. Buy a new server

   B. Restore from a backup

   C. Reinstall all applications on the server

   D. Replace the server with a workstation

SAMPLE TEST

11-5 What should you do to maximize network performance if more protocols are running than are needed?

    A. Install a second server

    B. Change to a wireless medium

    C. Remove the unnecessary protocols

    D. Remove all protocols

11-6 What must you do to ensure that a DOS application can print to a network printer?

    A. Configure infrared printing

    B. Use a wireless serial cable

    C. Purchase a Windows application

    D. Capture a local printer port to a network printer

11-7 What is the first thing you should do if you cannot create a user on a Microsoft Windows NT server?

    A. Load the newest patch

    B. Load the UserMkr utility

    C. Determine whether you have insufficient rights

    D. Determine whether you are on the wrong workstation

11-8 What types of disks can an LS-120 drive read?

    A. 1.44MB

    B. 720KB

    C. 120MB

    D. 144MB

SAMPLE TEST

11-9 What components should you test after moving a network?

   A. Physical equipment

   B. Users' chairs

   C. Applications

   D. Position of a user's mouse

11-10 Which of the following can help determine whether the server is functioning properly after being moved?

   A. Determining whether users can log in

   B. Running a self-test

   C. Running a protocol analyzer

   D. Determining whether error lights are displayed

11-11 On average, what is the capacity of a Zip drive?

   A. 100MB

   B. 1,000MB

   C. 120MB

   D. 1.44 MB

11-12 You have installed a new network application on a workstation. Now the workstation can't connect to the network. What is the most likely cause of this problem?

   A. The NIC settings were changed.

   B. The net.ini was changed.

   C. Some DLLs were overwritten with a different version.

   D. The password was changed.

SAMPLE TEST

11-13 On average, what is the capacity of a Jaz drive?

    A. 100MB

    B. 1,000MB

    C. 120MB

    D. 1.44MB

11-14 What should you do before a network move to ensure that the transition is smooth?

    A. Test all connections at the destination

    B. Upgrade the server

    C. Install more memory in the server

    D. Change the network settings

11-15 On average, what is the capacity of an LS-120 drive?

    A. 100MB

    B. 1,000MB

    C. 120MB

    D. 1.44MB

11-16 Which of the following is the proper syntax of a UNC name?

    A. *//servername/sharename*

    B. *//sharename /servername*

    C. *\\servername\sharename*

    D. *\\sharename \servername*

SAMPLE TEST

11-17 How often should documentation (baseline) be updated?

    A. Every day

    B. Once a month

    C. When the year 2000 date changes

    D. When network configuration changes

11-18 What controls access to resources on a network?

    A. The network interface

    B. User rights

    C. NIC

    D. The type of network

11-19 Which of the following items should be documented in a baseline report?

    A. Processor type

    B. Memory

    C. General statistics

    D. Computer brand

    E. Client version

11-20 The application GOCART.EXE needs to be run from the CART share on the TOYS server. Which of the following UNC paths refers to this executable?

    A. TOYS:GOCART.EXE

    B. TOYS/CART:GOCART.EXE

    C. \\GOCART.EXE/CART:TOYS

    D. \\TOYS\CART\GOCART.EXE

SAMPLE TEST

11-21 Which of the following items does a user need to access network services?

    A. Login account

    B. Color monitor

    C. Password

    D. Printer

UNIT 12

Maintaining and Supporting the Network

Test Objectives: Maintaining and Supporting the Network

- **Identify the kinds of test documentation that are usually available regarding a vendor's patches, fixes, upgrades, etc.**

- **Given a network-maintenance scenario, demonstrate awareness of the following issues:**
    - Standard backup procedures and backup-media storage practices
    - The need for periodic application of software patches and other fixes to the network
    - The need to install antivirus software on the server and workstations
    - The need to frequently update virus signatures

Exam objectives are subject to change at any time without notice and at CompTIA's sole discretion. Please visit CompTIA's Web site (www.comptia.org) for the most current exam-objectives listing.

Network maintenance and support means the set of tasks that an administrator must perform to keep the network operating at peak efficiency. A network can experience problems, and if left unattended, it can eventually experience a serious failure. For this reason, the Network+ exam tests you on the concepts involved in keeping a network running.

Network maintenance and support falls into two major categories:

- Support documentation
- Network-maintenance issues

Together, procedures in these two categories take up the largest portion of a network support person's time.

Support Documentation

Support documentation is technical-support files and information about a particular hardware or software product. Support documentation can consist of support CD-ROMs, support Web sites, mailings, group forums, and readme files. In most cases, current technical information and software is available on a manufacturer's support Web site; you can find the address in the documentation or in the help files. Group support forums are excellent sources of current software fixes and information about known incompatibilities. If a manufacturer has a support forum, you can find the URL on the manufacturer's Web site or in its documentation. Readme files included on software installation disks or CD-ROMs contain last-minute changes or updates to the product documentation. For this reason, reading these files before installing new software is a good idea.

These support-documentation sources offer three kinds of software:

- Patches
- Fixes
- Upgrades

Patches, fixes, and upgrades differ primarily in terms of what they are used for on a network. The following sections examine these three types of support-documentation software.

Patches

A *patch* is a large set of files made to replace out-of-date files for a specific piece of software. Patches are designed to bring a particular portion of a specific piece of software—typically, an NOS—up to date. Software patches typically fix several known problems and may also add a few features to the software. You apply patches to software by running an installation program, which updates all the files that need to be patched.

Patches are available from any of the vendor-support sources mentioned earlier in this unit.

> **TIP** NOSes should be patched, generally speaking, as soon as a new patch is available. You should try the patch on a test system, however, to ensure that the software differences don't cause a problem on your network.

Fixes

A software *fix* is a small set of files (or a single file) that corrects a particular problem in a piece of software. A manufacturer issues a fix to solve a known problem with software. Fixes may have their own installation programs. If a fix consists of a single file, however, you may only need to copy it over the existing file of the same name in the software's installation directory.

Upgrades

An *upgrade* is a software or hardware component that adds features to existing hardware or software. Upgrades are performed to increase the functionality of hardware or software. Upgrades are support items that cost money, because with an upgrade, you usually aren't fixing problems but adding new features.

Network-Maintenance Issues

Network *maintenance* is the category of tasks that you must perform on your network on a regular basis, either daily or weekly. These tasks protect the overall health of your network. Generally speaking, these tasks ensure that your network stays functional and at peak performance.

Network-maintenance tasks can be broken into the following categories:

- Network backup
- Network patches and fixes
- Antivirus procedures

Together, these three maintenance tasks take up most of a network administrator's time. The following sections briefly discuss these tasks.

Network Backup

An important part of any network, *disaster recovery* is the set of procedures used to recover network data after a major network failure. Disaster recovery includes reparations for hardware repair, software repair, and data replacement. The most common data-replacement method is network backup. *Network backup* (*backup*, for short) is the process in which the data stored on servers is archived on another storage medium (most often, magnetic tape). This process ensures that the data will be available after a total system failure. After a failure, the hardware can be fixed or replaced, and the data can be restored (copied back) from the backup medium—the most common type of disaster recovery.

The Network+ exam includes two items that relate to network backup:

- Standard backup procedures
- Media-storage practices

Standard Backup Procedures

Standard backup procedures are the procedures that you follow to ensure that all data is protected. These procedures include what type of backup you are going to run. Backup types vary by how much data they back up each time and how many tapes it takes to restore data after a complete system crash. The three backup types are:

- Full backup
- Differential backup
- Incremental backup

Full Backup   A *full backup* makes a copy of all the server data without skipping any files. This type of backup is simple, because you simply tell the software which server to back up and where to back it up to, and then start the backup. If you have to do a restore after a crash, you have only one set of tapes to restore from (as many tapes as it took to back up the entire server). Simply insert the most recent full backup into the drive, and start the restore.

Figure 12.1 shows the amount of data backed up each day in a full-backup scheme. If you are working with 20GB of data, approximately 20GB is stored on a new tape each night, along with any additional data from that day. Of all the backup types, full backups take the longest time to complete.

FIGURE 12.1

Amount of data backed up in a full backup

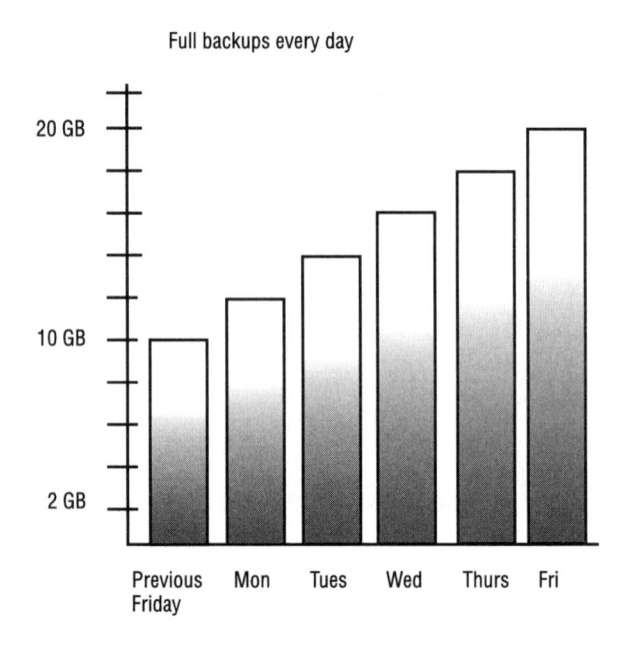

Differential Backup *Differential backup* allows you to use a maximum of two backup sessions to restore a file or group of files. In a differential-backup strategy, a single full backup typically is done once per week. Every night for six nights during the week, the backup utility backs up all files that have changed since the last full backup (the actual differential backup). After differential backups have been performed for a week, another full backup is done, starting the cycle over.

The backup utility keeps track of which files have been backed up, through the use of the archive attribute. The *archive attribute* is an attribute that each file contains that is used by the operating system to indicate the file's status with relation to the current backup type.

The archive attribute is cleared for each file backed up during the full backup to denote that each file was backed up. Thereafter, any time that a workstation program opens and makes changes in a file, the NOS sets the archive attribute, indicating that the file has changed and needs to be backed up. Then, each night, in a differential backup, the backup program copies every item that has its archive attribute set, indicating that the file has changed since the last full backup. The archive bit is not modified during each nightly differential backup.

When you restore a server after a complete server failure, you must restore two sets of tapes: the last full backup and the most current differential backup. A full restoration may take longer, but the nightly backup takes much less time than a full backup. You use this type of backup when the amount of time you have each day to perform a system backup—a period called the *backup window*—is smaller during the week and larger on the weekend.

Figure 12.2 shows the amount of data being backed up each day in a differential backup. Notice that the amount of data becomes larger every day as the files that need to be backed up each day get larger. Remember that the archive attribute doesn't get cleared each day, so by the end of the week, the files that changed at the beginning of the week may have been backed up several times, even though they haven't changed since the first part of the week.

Incremental Backup In an *incremental backup*, a full backup is used in conjunction with daily partial backups to back up the entire server, which reduces the amount of time that a complete backup takes. This method provides the fastest daily backups for networks that have an extremely small daily backup window. The network administrator pays a price for shortened

FIGURE 12.2

Amount of data backed up in an differential backup

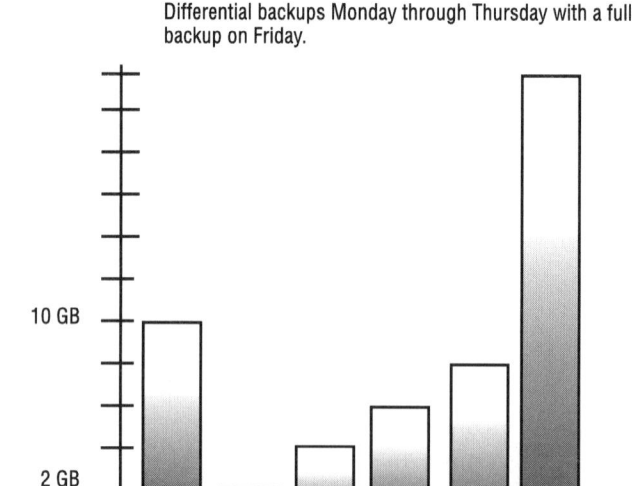

Differential backups Monday through Thursday with a full backup on Friday.

backup sessions, however: The restores after a server failure take more time than in either of the other two methods. The full backup set is restored, along with every tape from the day of the failure back to the preceding full backup.

The weekly full backup works as it does during a differential backup, and the archive attribute is cleared during the full backup. The incremental daily backups copy only the data that has changed since the last backup performed (*not* the last full backup). The archive attribute is cleared each time a backup occurs.

In this method, only files that change since the previous night's backup are copied. Each night's backup is a different size, because a different number of files is modified each day.

Figure 12.3 shows the incremental-backup scenario. The amount of data backed up each day differs, but it is much smaller than the amount backed up in a differential or full backup.

Each backup type is used for a different purpose. Full backups are used when restore time is at a premium. Incremental backups are used when backup time is at a premium. Differential backups are a compromise between the two methods. Table 12.1 summarizes the different backup types.

FIGURE 12.3

Amount of data backed up in an incremental backup

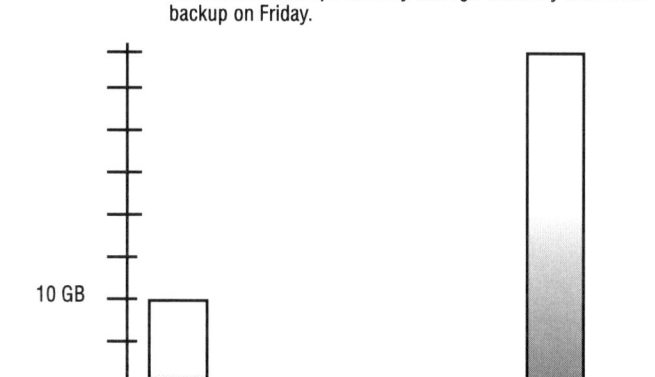

Incremental backups Monday through Thursday with a full backup on Friday.

TABLE 12.1: Backup-type summary

Name	What Is Backed Up	Archive Attribute Cleared?	Number of Sets to Restore after Server Crash:
Full	All data on server	Yes	Full only
Differential	Data since last full backup	No	Full plus last differential
Incremental	Data since last backup	Yes	Full plus every daily tape since last full backup

Media-Storage Practices

Media-storage practices are the procedures you must follow in storing the tape or other backup medium to ensure that the medium remains valid. These practices include determining where and how you store the backup medium. Backup media can be stored onsite or offsite. The safest method is to store the most current tape offsite, which helps prevent theft of the tape and keeps the tape available if something happens to the main site (fire, flood, and so on).

> **NOTE** If you are using backup tapes, you have one particular backup-maintenance procedure to perform. In addition to storing the backup medium in a safe place, you must maintain the tape drive by cleaning it to ensure backup integrity. Cleaning tapes rid the tape-drive mechanism of foreign matter and ensure that the read/write head of the tape drive is clean. Tape drives should be cleaned periodically or whenever errors occur. An example of when the tape drive needs to be cleaned is when a tape drive is reporting read errors on multiple tapes that are known to be good. Running a cleaning tape through the drive may fix it.

Network Patches and Fixes

Keeping a network up to date is one of the most important maintenance items for a network. As discussed earlier in this unit, patches, and software upgrades are applied to the network to ensure that the network is always up to date. This procedure can cause problems, however. When the patch or upgrade overwrites DLLs or other software components that another program requires to function, a patch or upgrade can cause problems with other software and could disable your entire network.

To ensure that the impact of applying patches and fixes is the correct one (adding features and fixing problems), you should try installing a patch on a test network before applying it to your entire network. This procedure allows you to examine the possible impact of the patch or upgrade on your network without disabling your entire network.

Antivirus Procedures

A *virus* is a small piece of software that enters a computer system through improper methods and causes that computer to malfunction. With the continued growth of the Internet, viruses are fast becoming a big problem. The best way to protect a network from viruses is to install a virus-protection utility. *Antivirus software* is a software program (or set of programs) that examines computer activity and prevents viruses from invading a system and doing damage. The utility must be installed on the workstations as well as on the server; otherwise, one of the network devices could be left vulnerable to a virus. You should use only a virus-protection utility that is approved for use with your operating system.

Scanning for Viruses

All antivirus tools have the capability of automatically searching for viruses on a computer or server. This capability is known as *virus scanning*. During this process, the antivirus utility searches all the files on the system and examines them for suspicious patterns of programming code. These patterns are known as *virus signatures*. Every antivirus utility comes with a list of these virus signatures, which should be updated monthly.

Updating Virus Signatures

Antivirus software programs contain lists of commonly known viruses and their behaviors, called *virus lists* (or *virus-definition files*). These files give the antivirus software the tools it needs to combat the various viruses that exist. Unfortunately, an antivirus program is only as good as its virus list, so the list should be updated periodically—monthly, at the very least.

When a system displays errors that are commonly associated with a virus, but the virus utility does not find a virus, the next step is to update the virus-list files. After you update the list, rescan the device. To update a virus list, download the current version and install it according to the manufacturer's specifications.

STUDY QUESTIONS

Support Documentation

1. Support documentation is available from support CD-ROMs, Web sites, mailings, group forums, and _____ files.

2. You can find a manufacturer's Web-site URL in a product's _____.

3. _____ files, which are sent with the product, include the last-minute changes in a product's documentation.

4. You can find the most current technical information on the manufacturer's _____.

5. Why is it a good idea to read all readme files before installing an application?
   _____

Network-Maintenance Issues

6. True or false: You should always install the most current patches on your production network as soon as they become available.

7. _____ is the most common disaster-recovery method.

8. Storing tapes _____ is the safest storage method.

9. If a tape drive is receiving intermittent read errors, what should you do first to try to resolve the problem?
   _____

STUDY QUESTIONS

11. _____ and software upgrades are two common types of upgrades.

12. Patches are available from software and hardware _____.

13. Where should you install a new patch or upgrade when a network is receiving no errors?

_____

14. True or false: All patches are error-free and do not conflict with other currently installed applications.

15. Which software items are generally available to software owners for free: patches or software upgrades? _____

16. The best way to protect a network from viruses is to install an _____ utility.

17. When you install antivirus software, you should install it on the server as well as on the _____.

18. To keep antivirus software effective, you must periodically update the _____ by downloading the most current version.

19. The _____ is a large factor in the rapid spread of viruses.

20. A _____ is a suspicious pattern of programming code that often indicates the presence of a virus.

21. Which backup type backs up the most data every day? _____

SAMPLE TEST

12-1 Where is the most current technical information located?

    A. Manufacturer product documentation

    B. Manufacturer support CD-ROM

    C. Manufacturer support Web site

    D. Manufacturer readme files

12-2 A company plans to connect to the Internet. What utility should the company first consider purchasing?

    A. A Mac utility

    B. An antivirus utility

    C. A Y2K utility

    D. An Internet utility

12-3 Which of the following should you read for product information and installation tips before performing an installation or an upgrade?

    A. Manufacturer product documentation

    B. Manufacturer support CD-ROM

    C. Manufacturer support Web site

    D. Manufacturer readme files

12-4 If a network is connected to the Internet, and the users transfer hundreds of files per day, what precaution could you take to prevent viruses?

    A. Install a firewall

    B. Install a network antivirus suite

    C. Install an antivirus utility on the workstations

    D. Install an Internet backup

SAMPLE TEST

12-5 You can install a patch or upgrade immediately if what condition exists?

    A. It fixes a critical error.

    B. It has cool new options.

    C. A user requests it.

    D. An Internet group recommends it.

12-6 A tape drive keeps reporting errors, and you have tried multiple tapes. What is the next thing that you should try to resolve the problem?

    A. Replace the tape drive

    B. Replace the SCSI cable

    C. Use a cleaning tape

    D. Replace the SCSI interface

12-7 How often should you update a virus list?

    A. Daily

    B. Monthly

    C. Yearly

    D. Never

12-8 A network has begun to generate miscellaneous errors. You have added a new patch to the NOS, added 10 new users to the network, and installed a new printer. What is the first thing that you should do?

    A. Reinstall the NOS

    B. Remove the users

    C. Remove the printer

    D. Remove the patch

SAMPLE TEST

12-9 A manufacturer has just released a patch for its operating system, but you are not having any problem with the operating system. What should you do?

    A. Install the patch on your servers

    B. Don't install the patch

    C. Install the patch in a test environment

    D. Install the patch on a single workstation

12-10 If a workstation is experiencing problems that may be related to a virus, but the virus scanner can't find a virus, what is your next step?

    A. Run VREPAIR

    B. Update the virus list

    C. Run the antivirus program again

    D. Run VSCAN /A /*.*

12-11 Before you install a patch on your network, what should you do?

    A. Install all older versions of the application, for backward compatibility

    B. Update all the drivers

    C. Test the patch on a test system

    D. Copy all the data from the server

12-12 All servers on a network are experiencing the same intermittent crashes, and all of them are configured the same way. What could you do to fix the problem if you know that the crashes are related to the software?

    A. Replace the server

    B. Check to see whether a patch or update is available for the software

SAMPLE TEST

    C. Check the network cable for interference

    D. Check the hard-drive rotation speed

12-13 On which two of the following network devices should you install antivirus software to ensure that the entire network is protected?

    A. Server

    B. Workstation

    C. Hubs

    D. Repeater

12-14 What is the best way to protect backup tapes from theft?

    A. Destroy the tapes after every use

    B. Don't back up at all

    C. Hide the tapes in a back room

    D. Store tapes in an offsite location

12-15 An error occurs on a server. You cannot find a reference to the specific error code in the documentation, and the documentation does not include a technical-support telephone number. What other locations could provide valuable information?

    A. Support forum

    B. Web site

    C. A and B

    D. None of the above

UNIT 13

Identifying, Assessing, and Responding to Problems

Test Objectives: Identifying, Assessing, and Responding to Problems

- Given an apparent network problem, determine the nature of the action required (i.e., information transfer vs. handholding vs. technical service).

- Given a scenario involving several network problems, prioritize them based on their seriousness.

Exam objectives are subject to change at any time without notice and at CompTIA's sole discretion. Please visit CompTIA's Web site (www.comptia.org) for the most current exam-objectives listing.

When you work in a large-enough organization, you are bound to encounter many network problems. It is important to be able to identify the seriousness of a problem, assess its priority, and choose an appropriate response. Not all network problems require an immediate response. Some problems, although they need attention, require less immediate attention than do other, more serious problems. The Network+ exam tests your knowledge of the following:

- Determining the nature of network problems
- Prioritizing network problems

Determining the Nature of an Apparent Network Problem

An *apparent network problem* is a problem someone reports that on the surface appears to be a network problem, but in reality may result from a different cause. When apparent network errors begin to surface in a networking environment, you must determine what solution each apparent network problem requires, so that you can prepare an appropriate response. You can fix some workstation problems by using network tools, for example, and never have to visit the workstation. Other problems require you to go to the workstation that is having the problem and show the user how to perform a specific operation.

Solutions to apparent network problems fall into three main categories:

- Information transfer
- User training (or handholding)
- Technical service

Each method puts increasing demands on the person who responds to the problem (a network administrator or a help-desk person). The following sections examine these three categories.

Information Transfer

Information transfer means giving the person who reports the problem some information that allows that person to solve the problem himself, without further interaction with network-maintenance personnel. Generally speaking, this problem-solving method requires the person who will fix the problem to be capable of fixing that problem, given some direction. You simply transfer some information to the person who responds to the problem (in some cases, the person who actually reported the problem).

The information that you provide depends on the type of problem being reported and on the user's level of experience. If a user calls you to report that her workstation has "hung up," for example, you understand that this person is not very skilled in network maintenance—but the solution doesn't require much network-maintenance skill. You can solve this problem through information transfer by saying, "Turn off your computer. Wait 10 seconds. Then turn your computer on again."

Information transfer requires the smallest amount of time spent by network-maintenance personnel.

User Training (Handholding)

Handholding is the category of network solution that you use when the problem isn't a problem at all, but a lack of knowledge on the part of a user. This category of solution requires a network-maintenance person to slowly walk a user through the solution to the problem, thus training the user so that he doesn't have the problem again. Because the network-maintenance person is, in effect, holding the user's hand as they walk through the steps, this method is called handholding.

Although handholding takes more time than information transfer, it often takes less time than an average technical-support call. This method has never been popular with network-maintenance people, however, because many of them don't have the patience to walk a user through an operation.

Technical Service

Technical service is the category of network solution that is used when the problem can't be solved over the phone and requires a network-maintenance person to visit the affected portion of the network. This category of solution often takes the most time, because it involves researching the problem, determining its source, and implementing the solution. Each step can take anywhere from several minutes to several days.

This category of solution is used to solve most network problems, because many problems do not have immediate solutions. For this reason, when many problems are reported simultaneously, and all the problems require attention, you must prioritize them so that you can solve them in the most effective manner. This type of prioritization is the topic of the following section.

Prioritizing Multiple Network Problems

You must prioritize network problems because you want to assign the most troubleshooting resources to the problem that affects the greatest number of users. Problems fall into two categories: critical errors and noncritical errors. *Critical errors* are errors that take down the entire network or major portions of the network or that affect the largest number of people. *Noncritical errors* affect only a single workstation or user.

The most critical errors (those that affect the most people) should be repaired first, and the least serious problems (those that affect only one or two users) should be repaired last. Generally speaking, problems that affect the entire network (or a large portion of it) should be high on the priority list. Following are some examples of conditions that would be high on the priority list:

- Down server (NetWare ABEND or Windows NT "Blue Screen of Death")
- Users unable to connect
- Users cannot access any of their documents
- Power outages
- Important applications do not open

STUDY QUESTIONS

Determining the Nature of an Apparent Network Problem

1. Name the three categories of solutions to network problems. _____, _____, and _____

2. True or false: Information transfer is the category of network-problem resolution that takes the most time for a network-maintenance person.

3. Several users have called, indicating that they can't access the S2 server. Which problem-resolution method would you use? _____

4. True or false: Technical service is the best way to solve all problems.

5. A user can't print to the local printer. After asking a few questions, you determine that the user simply needs to turn the printer off and reset it. The user seems to be reluctant to do so, however, and has indicated that he isn't sure where to find the power switch. Which category of network-problem resolution would you use to solve this problem? _____

6. True or false: It's sometimes better to show users how to fix a particular problem themselves than to fix the problem without telling them the details, to avoid taking up too much of your time.

7. True or false: A server has experienced a critical error. Which category of problem resolution would this situation generally fall into? _____

8. A user's workstation has experienced a critical error and hung. Which category of network-problem resolution would you use to resolve this situation? _____

STUDY QUESTIONS

9. Which problem-resolution category requires technical maintenance personnel to visit the affected portion of the network? _____

Prioritizing Multiple Network Problems

10. Which errors should be prioritized as those that should be repaired first?
_____

11. Which errors should be prioritized as those that aren't as serious and don't need to be repaired first? _____

12. Is a Microsoft Windows NT server with a "Blue Screen of Death" a critical or a noncritical error? _____

13. A user cannot print to his local printer but can print to the printer in the office next door. Is this error critical or noncritical? _____

14. None of the users on a network can print to any printer. Is this error critical or noncritical?
_____

15. An accounting company cannot launch its main database, which houses all account statistics. Is this error critical or noncritical? _____

16. A user cannot change the color of her toolbar. Is this error critical or noncritical?
_____

STUDY QUESTIONS

17. All the users on the 23rd floor of an office building cannot connect to the network, but the users on the 24th floor report no problem. Is this error critical or noncritical?

_____

18. On payday, the accountant's printer is not working correctly, and she is unable to print the checks. Is this error critical or noncritical? _____

SAMPLE TEST

13-1 As a networking engineer, you are called out to a remote site that is having a problem. The user reports that he is having an intermittent problem with locking up. When you arrive, the user says that he was running only a word processing application. What is the first question that you should ask?

  A. What other application was running?

  B. Has the application been updated or patched lately?

  C. What is the error message?

  D. Has the application ever worked?

13-2 The users on a small network are complaining that they have not been able to change printers for about a week. They applied the newest patch to their server about a month ago and upgraded their network client four days ago. What is most likely to be the source of the problem?

  A. Too many users logged in at the same time

  B. The network client

  C. Too many printers

  D. The server patch

13-3 A network server has an ABEND message on the screen. A remote user cannot dial in to send an e-mail message, and the accountant can't print her Christmas letters in color. In what order do you rank these problems?

  A. ABEND first, printing second, e-mail third

  B. Printing first, e-mail second, ABEND third

  C. E-mail first, ABEND second, printing third

  D. ABEND first, e-mail second, printing third

SAMPLE TEST

13-4 A user's workstation has crashed after running a word processing application. Nothing has changed on the network or the workstation. The other users, who have the same configuration and applications, are not having any problems. What question should you ask?

    A. What other application was running at that time?

    B. Where is the workstation placed on the desk?

    C. What type of monitor does the user have?

    D. None of the above

13-5 As a networking engineer, you are called out to a remote site that is having a problem. The user reports that he is having an intermittent problem with locking up. When you arrive, the user says that he was running only a word processing application and that it used to work well. What is the first question that you should ask?

    A. What other application was running?

    B. Has the application been updated or patched lately?

    C. What is the error message?

    D. Has the application ever worked?

13-6 Which of the following errors is the most critical?

    A. A user cannot load a shareware game.

    B. The color printer is jammed.

    C. None of the users can connect to the network.

    D. An Internet connection is running a little slower than normal.

13-7 A user is complaining that her monitor is too dim. At the same time, the server needs to have a software patch applied to fix an error. In what order do you rank these problems?

    A. Monitor first, server patch second

    B. Server patch first, monitor second

SAMPLE TEST

    C. Server patch only

    D. Monitor only

13-8 Which of the following questions does not pertain to an application lockup?

    A. What other applications are running?

    B. What is the specific error message (if any)?

    C. What is the user's name?

    D. Has this error occurred before?

13-9 As a networking engineer, you are called out to a remote site that is having a problem. The user reports that she is having an intermittent problem with locking up. What is the first question that you should ask?

    A. What other application was running when this problem occurred?

    B. Has the application been updated or patched lately?

    C. What is the error message?

    D. Has the application ever worked?

13-10 Critical errors are classified on a case-by-case basis for which of the following reasons?

    A. Every network is different.

    B. Special circumstances may change the severity of problems.

    C. Both of the above

    D. Neither of the above

13-11 After you diagnose multiple network errors, what is the next step?

    A. Hire more people and fix all the errors at the same time

    B. Repair the errors as fast as possible with quick fixes

SAMPLE TEST

C. Repair the errors in order of who complains the most

D. Prioritize the errors in order of their seriousness and then repair them

13-12 As a networking engineer, you are called out to a remote site that is having a problem. The user reports that an intermittent error message is appearing on his screen. What is the first question that you should ask?

A. What other application was running?

B. Has the application been updated or patched lately?

C. What is the error message?

D. Has the application ever worked?

13-13 You arrive at work one morning and have four voice-mail messages waiting, all flagged urgent. The first message states that the user cannot print a memo about the new policy on phone calls. The second message states that the user, along with all the other users on that floor, cannot log on to the network. The third voice mail is from the accounting department, where a user cannot change his screen saver. The last voice mail is from a user who has a stuck key on her keyboard. In what order should you attend to these problems?

A. Printing the memo

B. Users not able to log on

C. Unable to change screen saver

D. Stuck key on keyboard

A. A, B, C, D

B. B, A, D, C

C. C, A, B, D

D. D, A, C, B

UNIT 14

Troubleshooting the Network

Test Objectives: Troubleshooting the Network

- **Identify the following steps as a systematic approach to identifying the extent of a network problem, and, given a problem scenario, select the appropriate next step based on this approach:**
  - Determine whether the problem exists across the network
  - Determine whether the problem is workstation, workgroup, LAN, or WAN
  - Determine whether the problem is consistent and replicable
  - Use standard troubleshooting methods

- **Identify the following steps as a systematic approach for troubleshooting network problems, and, given a problem scenario, select the appropriate next step based on this approach:**
  1. Identify the exact issue.
  2. Re-create the problem.
  3. Isolate the cause.
  4. Formulate a correction.
  5. Implement the correction.
  6. Test.
  7. Document the problem and the solution.
  8. Give feedback.

- **Identify the following steps as a systematic approach to determining whether a problem is attributable to the operator or the system, and, given a problem scenario, select the appropriate next step based on this approach:**
  1. Have a second operator perform the same task on an equivalent workstation.
  2. Have a second operator perform the same task on the original operator's workstation.
  3. See whether operators are following standard operating procedure.

- **Given a network troubleshooting scenario, demonstrate awareness of the need to check for physical and logical indicators of trouble, including:**
  - Link lights
  - Power lights
  - Error displays
  - Error logs and displays
  - Performance monitors

- **Identify common network troubleshooting resources, including:**
  - Knowledge bases on the World Wide Web
  - Telephone technical support
  - Vendor CDs

- **Given a network problem scenario, including symptoms, determine the most likely cause or causes of the problem based on the available information. Select the most appropriate course of action based on this inference. Issues that may be covered include:**
  - Recognizing abnormal physical conditions
  - Isolating and correcting problems in cases where there is a fault in the physical medium (patch cable)
  - Checking the status of servers
  - Checking for configuration problems with DNS, WINS, HOST file
  - Checking for viruses
  - Checking the validity of the account name and password
  - Rechecking operator logon procedures
  - Selecting and running appropriate diagnostics

- **Specify the tools that are commonly used to resolve network equipment problems. Identify the purpose and function of common network tools, including:**
  - Crossover cable
  - Hardware loopback
  - Tone generator
  - Tone locator (fox and hound)

- **Given a network problem scenario, select appropriate tools to help resolve the problem.**

Exam objectives are subject to change at any time without notice and at CompTIA's sole discretion. Please visit CompTIA's Web site (www.comptia.org) for the most current exam-objectives listing.

*N*etwork *troubleshooting* is the process of determining the source of a network problem. Networks, like computers, require periodic attention when they experience problems. This unit introduces some items to keep in mind when you troubleshoot networks and also discusses the troubleshooting topics covered in the Network+ exam. This unit examines the following troubleshooting topics:

- Narrowing down the problem
- Troubleshooting a network systematically
- Recognizing physical and logical trouble indicators
- Using common network troubleshooting resources
- Determining the most likely cause of the problem
- Using common network tools
- Selecting the appropriate troubleshooting tools

As you can see, troubleshooting a network is a complex procedure, and you have many concepts to keep in mind. The following section discusses the questions that you could ask to try to narrow down the problem.

Identifying the Problem

When you troubleshoot network problems, it is always best to try to narrow the scope of the problem, so that you know which direction to take with your troubleshooting efforts. When you narrow the problem down to a few possible areas, you have somewhere to start troubleshooting. Otherwise, you may just blindly stab at a problem.

The best way to narrow down a problem is to ask yourself some questions. Three of the most common are:

- Does the problem exist across the network?
- Is the problem limited to a particular workstation or workgroup, or to the LAN or WAN?
- Is the problem consistent or replicable?

The answers to these three questions will direct your troubleshooting efforts.

> **NOTE** When you are trying to troubleshoot any kind of problem, using some kind of standard troubleshooting method is very important. Having a standard method allows you to retrace your steps if you run into a problem and need to reassess the troubleshooting that you have done so far. Generally speaking, standard troubleshooting methods are troubleshooting methods that are agreed upon by the general networking community. For an example of a standard troubleshooting method, see "Troubleshooting a Network Problem Systematically" later in this unit.

Determining Whether the Problem Exists Across the Network

One question you must ask yourself when you try to narrow down a problem is "Does everyone on the network experience this problem?" The answer to this question helps you discover which item(s) on your network you must troubleshoot. If the answer is yes, the problem may be related to a server or network cabling. If the answer is no, the problem may be related to a particular segment or workstation.

Determining Whether the Problem Is a Workstation, Workgroup, LAN, or WAN

After you decide how far-reaching a problem is, you must narrow it down even further. You must ask yourself whether the problem is limited to a particular workstation or workgroup, or whether it is limited to the LAN or the WAN. If the problem is limited to a particular workstation, you would focus your troubleshooting efforts on that workstation. If the problem is related to a single workgroup of computers, the cause may be either the cabling system for that workgroup (including any patch cables and hubs) or the server that services that workgroup. If a problem affects only a WAN link, the problem could be related to the router for the WAN or to the telephone company that provides that WAN telephone line. On the other hand, if the problem affects only one segment of the LAN, the problem may be due to cabling or network infrastructure problems.

Determining Whether the Problem Is Consistent or Replicable

Determining whether a problem is consistent or replicable is probably the most important question to ask yourself when you try to determine the scope of a problem. If a problem is consistent and can be replicated, you can fix the problem much more easily, because you have a known problem and can find the source with less difficulty. Try a solution, and see whether the problem goes away; if it does, you've fixed the problem.

Problems that pop up now and again are more difficult to troubleshoot, because they aren't consistent. The only way to detect whether a solution has affected the problem is to track how often the problem occurs. If you try a solution, and the problem occurs less frequently, the change probably is due to the solution, and you are on the right track. Because the problem is non-consistent, however, it may be only a coincidence that the problem is occurring less frequently.

Troubleshooting a Network Problem Systematically

Troubleshooting a problem in a networking environment is simpler when you use a logical, systematic method. Such a method makes troubleshooting a network problem simpler, because you aren't just trying any possible solution. The following systematic method is the one used in the Network+ exam. The steps are as follows:

1. Identify the exact issue.
2. Re-create the problem.
3. Isolate the cause.
4. Formulate a correction.
5. Implement the correction.
6. Test the solution.
7. Document the problem and the solution.
8. Give feedback.

These eight steps make troubleshooting network problems easier if you use them consistently from one network problem to the next.

Identify the Issue

Identifying the issue means discovering exactly what the problem is, where the problem is, and who is having the problem. You can't solve a problem if you can't identify it. The more details that you can obtain, the faster you can diagnose and resolve the problem. In some cases, such as when a problem occurs intermittently, you can't do anything until the user records what was happening at the time of the problem. You may have to ask a user questions to find out exactly what the problem is, such as "What were you doing when this happened?" and "What exactly are you having problems doing?"

Re-Create the Problem

After you identify a problem, you can attempt to re-create the problem. This practice is helpful, because when the problem is re-created, you can eliminate individual variables one at a time until you find the cause of the problem. If you can re-create the problem, generally speaking, you know the steps that caused the failure. Then you can work on isolating each step to determine which step is causing the problem.

Isolate the Cause

Now that you understand the problem, you can work on finding a cause. What causes a problem isn't always clear, but causes usually fall into two categories: hardware failures and software failures. If a piece of hardware fails, some device on the computer is not functioning correctly, and usually, the solution is fairly obvious. If you can't see anything on the computer screen, chances are that either the monitor or video card has failed. If a hard drive fails, the computer's operating system usually detects that failure and produces an error message to that effect.

Software failures, on the other hand, aren't always obvious. When software fails, a particular program functions normally most of the time, but it occasionally produces a strange, cryptic error such as "Bit overrun in memory segment F400Ah." Additionally, software problems are not always reproducible.

The most important things to remember in isolating a problem are that you should make only one change at a time and then document all changes. If you make several changes and don't document those changes, you have no way of knowing which of the changes is the true solution to the problem. Documenting all changes is helpful when making many changes, or making changes in a specific order, is required to resolve a problem.

Formulate a Correction

When you have isolated the problem, you must find a correction for the problem. If the problem is hardware-related, most often, you need to replace some component. If the problem is software-related, you may need to reinstall an application, install a patch for the specific problem, or do something in between.

If the correction includes installing an upgrade or a patch, it is vital to confirm that the upgrade or patch will not conflict with any other applications running on the network. If an upgrade for the network client is needed, for example, you must first confirm that all the other applications on the network will function correctly with the new network client. The correction for each problem is problem-specific and varies as much as the types of problems that exist. Through experience, you will gain knowledge of the types of correction methods for different types of problems.

Implement the Correction

When you know what is needed to correct a problem, you need to implement the correction. Implementing the correction simply means installing whatever hardware or software will fix the problem. Implementations of a correction, or fix, can vary, depending on the problem.

Following are some questions that you need to ask when you are planning to implement a correction:

- How long will the correction take?
- Will there be any down time?
- Will every workstation on the network need to be fixed on an individual basis, or can the fix be rolled out all at once?

Sometimes, a correction is critical, so the answers to these questions are irrelevant, and you must roll out the fix immediately.

Test the Solution

After you implement a solution, you must test the functionality of the component(s) that are experiencing the problem, so that you can see whether the correction solved the problem or made it worse. If the correction solved the problem, it is important to do a complete test of the affected system to determine whether the correction had any side effects. What good would a solution be if it created three more problems? If the solution fixes the problem and has no ill effects, move on to the next step in the troubleshooting process.

If the solution has ill effects, or if the solution does not solve the problem, you must back up to the "formulate a correction" step in the troubleshooting model and start the process again.

Document the Problem and Solution

You should document any network problem that occurs, as well as its solution, so that you have a reference for future use. If the same problem or a similar problem occurs in the future, you may not remember what you did to correct the problem. You can refer to this documentation to recall what you did to resolve the problem.

Give Feedback

When you find a solution on the World Wide Web or from a telephone support center, you should tell the manufacturer whether you solved the problem and, if so, how you solved it. This information allows a support center to assign troubleshooting resources to the issue, if it was not resolved, or to note the solution for use with other networks.

Determining Whether the Problem Is the Operator or the System

This troubleshooting topic is a favorite among network technicians, because it results in many jokes about users who don't know how to perform "simple" operations on their computers. Often, someone reports a problem to a technician, but the "problem" turns out to be the user's lack of knowledge about the procedure that he or she is trying to perform.

You can determine whether a problem is related to the operator or the system by having a different user try the same operation on the same machine. If the other user can perform the operation, there's a good chance that the problem lies with the operator, not the machine. If the second operator can't perform the same function, however, the problem may be the machine or the application.

Recognizing Physical and Logical Trouble Indicators

Network systems have different warning systems that indicate when they are experiencing problems and that warn you of potential loss of network use. These warning systems are known as *physical and logical trouble indicators*. The indicators that the Network+ exam tests you on are:

- Link lights
- Power lights

- Error logs and displays
- Performance monitors

These indicators can be useful for detecting when a problem occurs, as well as for preventing problems by tracking any abnormal activity.

Checking Link Lights

Link lights are small light-emitting diodes (LEDs), located on most NICs and on most hubs and switches, that indicate a successful basic network connection. When lighted, these lights indicate that that the network device is successfully linked to another network entity. :Link lights are most commonly used on NICs and hubs. When you connect a workstation to a hub, the link lights on both the hub and the workstation's NIC should illuminate. If not, a cabling problem may have occurred somewhere between the two devices or the NIC may have failed.

Link lights are very useful for troubleshooting a connection problem. If a workstation is connected to the network with a known-good NIC, but the link lights don't illuminate when you attempt to connect, the problem could be a faulty cable run, patch cables, hub, switch port, or NIC port.

Checking Power Lights

A *power light* or indicator is the small LED that illuminates when a particular network component has power. Almost every major computer and network component has a power light. These lights vary in color but are most often green or red.

Power lights are useful for troubleshooting, because they indicate whether a device is powered up. Many network devices, such as routers or bridges, have no display system, however. Sometimes, the only way that you can tell whether a router or bridge is functioning is to see whether the power light is on.

If the power light is not on, the device may have a faulty power supply or power cord, or the device may be plugged in to a bad power outlet. Replacing the power cord and power outlet eliminates those two variables and leaves only the power supply.

> **TIP** An additional test for proper power-supply functionality is to see whether the power supply's fan spins when the power to the unit is turned on.

Checking Error Logs and Displays

An *error log* or *error display* is a text file or program that records every error that occurs on the system. Error logs generally are kept on servers, but a few are kept on the workstation. Each NOS has its own format and use for log files. Table 14.1 shows the common log files used for NetWare, their locations, and the information that they contain. Table 14.2 shows the same information for Windows NT.

TABLE 14.1: NetWare error logs, locations, and descriptions

Log File	Location	Description
CONSOLE.LOG	SYS:ETC	Keeps a history of all errors and information displayed on the server's console
ABEND.LOG	SYS:SYSTEM	Records all ABENDs that have occurred on that server and the conditions surrounding those errors
SYS$LOG.ERR	SYS:SYSTEM	Lists any errors that occur on the server, including ABENDs and NDS errors, and the times and dates of their occurrence

TABLE 14.2: Windows NT error logs, locations, and descriptions

Log File	Location	Description
System Log	Event Viewer utility	Tracks just about every event that occurs on that computer
Security Log	Event Viewer utility	Tracks security events specified by the domain's audit policy
Application Log	Event Viewer utility	Tracks events for network services and applications

Error logs and displays are useful for troubleshooting network and local problems on both workstations and servers. The errors that these logs and displays contain indicate the general health of a server and the network, and you can use this information to track down the source of a problem. If a server is not loading a network service at boot time, for example, the various log files will indicate whether a problem exists and show a possible source of the problem.

Running Performance Monitors

If server, workstation, or network performance seems to be sluggish, running a performance monitor can help you track and diagnose the problem. Some of the most common components that a performance monitor tracks are processor use, memory access, hard-drive read/writes, and network idle time. Reviewing performance monitors can also help you diagnose and locate any bottlenecks that are affecting network performance.

Two examples of performance monitors are the NetWare MONITOR .NLM and the Windows NT Performance Monitor.

> **NOTE**
>
> To start the MONITOR.NLM utility in NetWare, simply type **LOAD MONITOR** at the console prompt. To start the Performance Monitor program in Windows NT, you must first be logged in as Administrator (or as a member of the Server Operators group). When you are logged in, choose Start ➢ Programs ➢ Administrative Tools ➢ Performance Monitor.

Using Common Network Troubleshooting Resources

Because not everyone can know every error code and troubleshooting tip, manufacturers of network hardware and software provide troubleshooting resources to help their customers troubleshoot particular problems. Knowing what resources are available and where they are located is very important in troubleshooting a network or workstation problem.

Knowledge Bases on the World Wide Web

As the popularity of the World Wide Web grows, so does its usefulness as a research tool. A large number of corporations and small businesses have published Web pages. Up-to-date drivers, patches, and documentation are placed on these Web sites by most hardware and software manufacturers. Many manufacturers are also encouraging the use of technical-support databases located on their Web pages. These searchable support databases, known as *knowledge bases*, are updated on an ongoing basis with the latest known issues and problems related to the product. These knowledge bases generally are free to use, are the most current sources of technical-support information available, and are the best sources of troubleshooting information.

Other Web sites offer discussion forums. Anybody can register in these forums and join open technical chat sessions or post problems on a bulletin board, so that other users can respond with a possible resolution. The Internet and the Web are good resources to help resolve many problems in the world of networking.

Telephone Technical Support

Telephone technical support means dialing a telephone number and speaking to a manufacturer technician for the product for which you need support. This one-on-one interface can be helpful when you are trying to examine a problem and determine a solution.

When you call a telephone support center, make sure that you have all vital information handy, and if possible, you should be at the workstation that is having the problem. Some manufacturers, including Novell and Microsoft, use the same database for telephone support as the one that is available on the company's Web page.

Vendor Support CDs

Vendor support CDs are another technical-support option to use when a telephone line is busy or unavailable. (Both of the resources discussed in the preceding sections require a telephone line.) *Vendor support CDs* are CD-ROMs that contain technical-support information, including a knowledge base, patches, drivers, and readme files. Unfortunately, these CD-ROMs are only as current as their last release, and even the most current support CD-ROM may be weeks (or even months) behind. These items are useful mainly as a compact troubleshooting resource when a telephone line is unavailable. Two examples of vendor support CDs are Novell's Support Connection and Microsoft's TechNet.

Determining the Most Likely Cause of a Problem

A few problems are common occurrences on many networks, and if you cannot figure out the cause of a problem, it may not be a bad idea to check the following items:

- Abnormal physical conditions
- Patch-cable faults
- Server status
- Configuration problems
- Viruses
- User-account validity
- Login procedures

Recognizing Abnormal Physical Conditions

As discussed briefly in Unit 10, the proper physical environment is extremely important to a computer's operational efficiency. If heat, humidity, and power are not set to the proper levels, malfunctions can result. Of all environment-related problems, electrostatic discharge (ESD) is by far the most common.

ESD is the discharge of static between two charged entities. You can give an ESD to a computer component without realizing that you have done so. The voltages imparted through an ESD are so low that humans can't detect them, but they are significant enough to damage electronic components.

ESD is prevalent in areas that have low humidity, especially in northern climates in winter, where humidity levels approach zero. Symptoms of ESD include the following:

- High incidence of dead-on-arrival (DOA) components

- Spontaneous reboots for no apparent reason
- Random errors with no apparent pattern

You can prevent ESD damage to components by taking a few simple precautions:

- Wear an antistatic strap (also called an ESD strap) when you work on computer equipment
- Ensure that environmental controls are set to prevent ESD (40 percent humidity and 68°F to 70°F temperature)

Isolating Patch-Cable Faults

Another source of frustrating network problems is patch-cable faults. Patch-cable-fault problems have two main symptoms: a workstation that won't connect to the rest of the network and an NIC that passes all diagnostics but has no link light. A different workstation plugged into the same connection will experience the same problem.

The most common patch-cable fault is a broken wire inside the patch cable, which could be caused by repeated, severe bending or movement of a patch cable. An example of this kind of fault is when a patch cable is run over a high-traffic area without a protector of some kind. People can (and do) trip over these cables, often putting undue strain on the connector or the internal wires. Typically, the workstation-to-wall-plate patch cable experiences cable faults more often than the patch-panel-to-hub patch cable, because the latter doesn't move or change much, if at all. If this patch cable has problems, those problems usually are due to a manufacturing fault, not strain due to movement.

To solve patch-cable faults, you have to replace either of two patch cables: the workstation-to-wall-plate patch cable or the hub-to-patch-panel patch cable.

Checking Server Status

Another likely cause of an apparent network problem is server status. A server's status is either up or down. *Up status* means that the server is powered up and responding to network requests. *Down status* means that the server can no longer respond to network requests. If a server is down, no one can receive responses to their network requests, and users will report that the network is having a problem, when in fact, the server is actually the network entity that has the problem.

A few situations indicate that a server is down. In one common situation, the server is not responding to any requests. To test whether a server is down, try to log in and transfer files to and from the suspect server. If you cannot send or receive messages, more than likely, that server is down. You can also test whether a server is functional by going to the server console and checking for user connections.

Identifying Configuration Problems

Name-resolution problems can be hard to locate, because they may not always appear to be name-resolution problems. A server may appear to be down when the client simply cannot resolve its name to a network address. Most often, name-resolution problems are caused by misconfigured name-resolution software.

The Network+ exam tests you on three name-resolution methods:

- Domain Name Service (DNS)
- Windows Internet Naming Service (WINS)
- `hosts` file

All the preceding items are TCP/IP name-resolution methods. Although other name-resolution methods are used on networks, the Network+ exam tests you on only these three methods.

Domain Name Service (DNS)

DNS is a network service that maps Internet host names to TCP/IP addresses. DNS must be configured at a client to resolve Internet domain names into TCP/IP host addresses through the use of a DNS server. If DNS is misconfigured, a client cannot access a server by its DNS name (such as www.myserver.com) but *can* access the server by its IP address (such as 10.22.108.37). To fix this problem, you must enter the correct IP address for the DNS server in the client's DNS configuration utility.

Windows Internet Naming Service (WINS)

WINS maps the NetBIOS names of Windows hosts to TCP/IP addresses so that you can access a Windows server over a TCP/IP-only network (such as the Internet). If WINS is misconfigured, you won't be able to find a Windows NT server over a TCP/IP-only network by using the Network Neighborhood icon or the Find utility, but you will still be able to ping the machine.

To fix this problem, make sure that the WINS server on your network is configured correctly and that all Windows clients that need to use it are configured with the TCP/IP addresses of the primary and, if necessary, backup WINS servers.

hosts File

The hosts file, which is a text file that resides on each TCP/IP host, is used to resolve host names to TCP/IP addresses manually (without the need for a DNS server). If this file is not formatted correctly, you may be able to access some TCP/IP hosts by name, but only those that are configured correctly. You cannot access by name those hosts that have incorrect entries in the hosts file.

To fix this problem, you must ensure that all TCP/IP hosts have the same hosts file and that the hosts file is formatted correctly. The proper format for an entry in the hosts file is:

<IP address>   <host name>

You replace <IP address> with the actual host's TCP/IP address and <host name> with the name of the host.

> **NOTE** Remember that the pound sign (#) is the comment symbol for the hosts file. Any line that begins with a pound sign is interpreted as a comment, not as a proper name-resolution entry.

Checking for Viruses

Another likely cause of problems on a network, and a frequently overlooked one, is viruses. As discussed in Unit 12, a *virus* is a malicious software program that can cause unexpected problems with computers and networks. When you encounter a problem that is random and seems to change slightly with each occurrence, the problem may be caused by a virus. An example of a virus-related problem is an intermittent hard-drive-failure error. Although this error may be an actual hard-drive failure, it never hurts to try a virus scan before spending money for a new hard drive. Some boot-sector viruses can cause this problem, which can be solved by a simple antivirus scan-and-clean cycle. Even though both methods would solve the problem, the antivirus scan is the faster and cheaper of the two.

Validating User Accounts

When a user is using the network and its resources, he must be logged in as a valid user with appropriate rights. Even though that requirement seems to be a simple one, many users don't understand that network security must be enforced, and they don't understand the concepts of restricted logon hours or user-account and password expiration.

When a user reports a problem logging in, you may want to ask whether the system generated any error messages. When a login problem is related to the validity of the account, the system generally issues a message such as "This user account has been disabled. Please contact your network administrator." This message indicates that the user account has been disabled and that the user can't use it to log in. All you have to do to fix the problem is to use the network-administration utilities to reenable that account. A similar message appears when the user's password has expired. When a user's password has expired, the user generally is forced to change it. If the user fails to change her password, she is denied access to the network, and the administrator must change the password manually to give the user access to the network.

Verifying Login Procedures

The problem that network administrators most commonly hear is "I can't log in." Incorrect login procedures usually are the result of an incorrectly entered username or password. The user may be entering an old password or misspelling the password. More often than not, however, the user may be trying to log in with the Caps Lock key activated, so that usernames and passwords are entered in capital letters. This situation causes the system to reject the user, because most login systems for the various NOSes use case-sensitive passwords.

Running Appropriate Diagnostics

The final procedure that you can use to determine the most likely cause of a network problem is to run network diagnostics. These diagnostics take the form of protocol analyzers, which analyze individual packets on the network for possible problems, and performance-monitoring utilities (discussed earlier in this unit). Although the results of these diagnostics take time to interpret, they often provide the most detailed information about the types of traffic that cross your network and any problems that result from that traffic.

Using Common Network Tools

In addition to manufacturer-provided troubleshooting tools, you can use a few hardware devices to troubleshoot a network. Some devices have easily recognizable functions; the functions of others are more obscure. Following are four of the most popular hardware troubleshooting tools:

- Crossover cable
- Hardware loopback
- Tone generator
- Tone locator

The Network+ exam tests you on all these tools.

Crossover Cable

Sometimes also called a *cross cable*, a *crossover cable* typically is used to connect two hubs, but it can also be used to test communications between two stations directly, bypassing the hub. A crossover cable is used only in Ethernet UTP installations. You can connect two workstations' NICs (or a workstation and a server NIC) directly by using a crossover cable.

A normal Ethernet (10BaseT) UTP cable uses four wires: two to transmit and two to receive. Figure 14.1 shows this wiring, with all wires going from pins on one side directly to the same pins on the other side.

FIGURE 14.1
A standard Ethernet 10BaseT cable

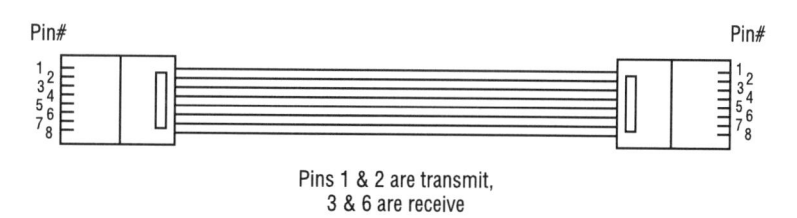

Pins 1 & 2 are transmit, 3 & 6 are receive

The standard Ethernet UTP crossover cable used in both situations has its transmit and receive wire pairs crossed, so that the transmit set on one side (hooked to pins 1 and 2) is connected to the receive set (pins 3 and 6) on the other side. Figure 14.2 shows this arrangement. Notice that four of the wires are crossed, compared with the straight-through wiring of the standard 10BaseT UTP cable shown in Figure 14.1.

FIGURE 14.2

A standard Ethernet 10BaseT crossover cable

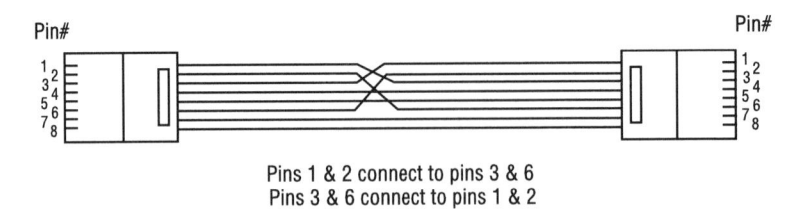

Pins 1 & 2 connect to pins 3 & 6
Pins 3 & 6 connect to pins 1 & 2

> **WARNING** Be sure to label a crossover cable as such, to ensure that no one tries to use it as a workstation patch cable. If a crossover cable is used as a patch cable, the workstation won't be able to communicate with the hub and the rest of the network.

You can carry a crossover cable in your tool bag along with your laptop. If you want to ensure that a server's NIC is functioning correctly, you can connect your laptop directly to the server's NIC by using the crossover cable. You should be able to log in to the server (assuming that both NICs are configured correctly).

Hardware Loopback

A *hardware loopback* is a special connector for Ethernet 10BaseT NICs. This device functions similarly to a crossover cable, except that it connects the transmit pins directly to the receive pins (as shown in Figure 14.3). The NIC's software diagnostics use a hardware loopback to test transmission and reception capabilities. You cannot completely test NICs without one of these devices.

FIGURE 14.3

A hardware loopback and its connections

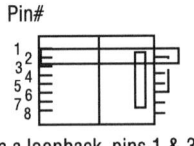

In a loopback, pins 1 & 3, 2 & 6 are connected

Usually, the hardware loopback is no bigger than a single RJ-45 connector with a few small wires on the back of the connector. If the NIC has hardware diagnostics that can use the loopback, the hardware loopback plug is included with the NIC. To use the loopback, simply plug it into the RJ-45 connector on the back of the NIC and then start the diagnostic software. Select the option in your NIC's diagnostic software that requires the loopback, and start the diagnostic routine. You can tell whether the NIC can send and receive data by using these diagnostics.

Tone Generator and Tone Locator

Tone generators and tone locators are used most often on telephone systems to locate cables. Because telephone systems use multiple pairs of UTP cable, it is nearly impossible to determine which set of wires goes where. Network documentation would be extremely helpful in making this determination, but if no documentation is available, you can use a tone generator and a tone locator.

A *tone generator* is a small electronic device that sends an electrical signal down one set of UTP wires. A *tone locator* is a device that is designed to emit a tone when it detects the signal in a particular set of wires. When you need to trace a cable, hook the generator (often called the *fox*) to the copper ends of the wire pair that you want to find. Then move the locator (often called the *hound*, because it chases the fox) over multiple sets of cables until you hear the tone. (You don't have to touch the copper part of the wire pairs; this tool works by induction.) A soft tone indicates that you are close to the right set of wires. Keep moving the tool until the tone gets the loudest. Bingo—you have found the wire set. Figure 14.4 shows a tone generator and locator.

> **NOTE** Don't confuse these tools with a cable tester, which tests cable quality. You use the tone generator and locator only to determine which UTP cable is which.

FIGURE 14.4

Use of a common tone generator and locator

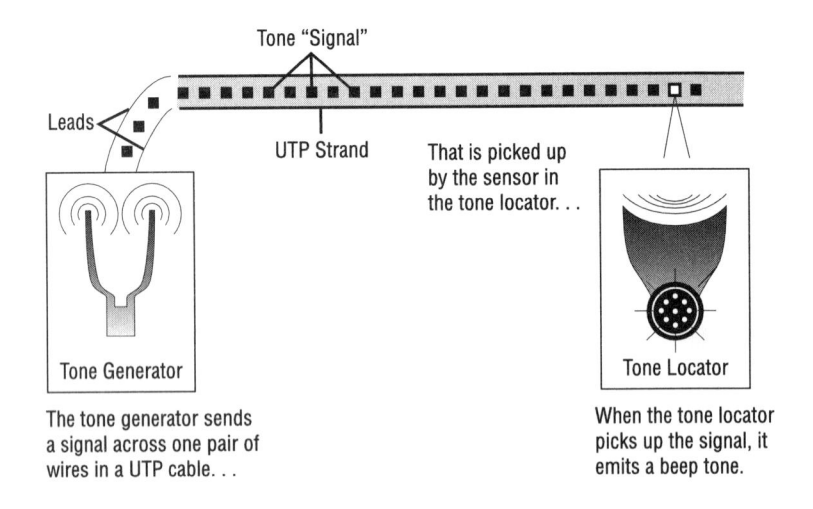

Tone "Signal"

Leads

UTF Strand

That is picked up by the sensor in the tone locator...

Tone Generator

The tone generator sends a signal across one pair of wires in a UTP cable...

Tone Locator

When the tone locator picks up the signal, it emits a beep tone.

WARNING

Never hook a tone generator to a cable that is hooked up to either an NIC or a hub. Because the tone generator sends electrical signals down the wire, it can blow an NIC or a hub—which is why tone generators usually are not used on networks.

Selecting the Appropriate Troubleshooting Tools

After reading about all these troubleshooting tips and tools, you should have a fairly good idea of how to approach almost any network problem. Remember, however, to select the right troubleshooting tool for the right job. This knowledge comes from experience. After a time, you will be able to decide whether a particular problem warrants a quick fix or whether you must dive deep into the inner workings of the network or server with tools such as protocol analyzers. Generally speaking, the less complex the problem you are trying to solve, the less complex the tools you need to solve it.

STUDY QUESTIONS

Identifying the Problem

1. The first thing to do when a problem occurs is to see whether the problem is affecting the _____.

2. When a network error occurs, you should determine whether other users on the _____ are having the same problem and whether users on a different segment are having the same problem.

3. When a network problem has been isolated, you can determine whether the problem is consistent and can be replicated or whether it is an _____ problem that occurs sporadically.

4. If a problem is _____, it is easier to troubleshoot than a problem that occurs randomly.

5. True or false: If the a problem is limited to one workstation, you should need to fix only that workstation.

6. Problems that pop up now and again are _____ difficult to troubleshoot, because they aren't consistent.

Troubleshooting a Network Problem Systematically

7. _____ is the systematic troubleshooting step in which you determine the cause of an actual network problem.

Unit 14 • Troubleshooting the Network

STUDY QUESTIONS

8. _____ is the systematic troubleshooting step in which you actually fix the problem.

9. _____ is the systematic troubleshooting step in which you try to replicate the error condition to determine the source of the problem.

10. _____ is the systematic troubleshooting step in which you communicate your findings to the manufacturer of the defective product to ensure that other people don't have the problem.

11. _____ is the systematic troubleshooting step in which you note the problem and its associated solution so that you have a reference for future use.

12. _____ is the systematic troubleshooting step in which you come up with a possible solution to the apparent network problem.

13. _____ is the systematic troubleshooting step in which you try to determine what the problem is.

Determining Whether the Problem Is the Operator or the System

14. What should you do to determine whether the problem is operator error? _____

15. If you determine that the problem is a user's lack of knowledge about a procedure, what is the solution? _____

STUDY QUESTIONS

16. True or false: Network problems are always related to network hardware or software failure.

17. True or false: A motherboard failure is a system failure, not an operator error.

18. True or false: A hard-drive failure is a system failure, not an operator error.

Recognizing Physical and Logical Trouble Indicators

19. _____ are small LEDs that indicate the presence or absence of a basic network connection.

20. Link lights are most commonly used on _____ and _____.

21. _____ indicate whether power is applied to a network component.

22. _____ keep track of all network errors.

23. _____, _____, and _____ are the three primary error logs on a NetWare server

24. _____, _____, and _____ are the three primary error logs for Windows NT.

25. Where can you find the error logs on a Windows NT server? _____

26. What utility can you use to view performance statistics on a NetWare server? _____

STUDY QUESTIONS

27. What utility can you use to view performance statistics in Windows NT?
_____

28. The ABEND.LOG file for NetWare is located in the _____ directory.

29. The CONSOLE.LOG file for NetWare is located in the _____ directory.

30. Which category of physical and logical trouble indicator can display statistics on network packets transmitted and server-processor use? _____

31. Which Windows NT log file is used to track the majority of all errors for Windows NT?
_____

32. Which NetWare log file records everything displayed on the system console?
_____

33. Which Windows NT log file tracks events for network services and applications?
_____

34. Which Windows NT log file is used to track login violations and other items in the Windows NT security policy? _____

Using Common Network Troubleshooting Resources

35. Up-to-date drivers, patches, and documentation are placed on _____ by most hardware and software manufacturers.

STUDY QUESTIONS

36. Manufacturer-supplied _____ typically contain the most outdated support information.

37. A _____ is a collection of technical-support problems and their solutions in a searchable database.

38. Which two network troubleshooting resources require the use of a telephone line?_____ / _____

39. Which network troubleshooting resource requires access to the Internet?
_____

40. Which troubleshooting resource allows you to talk to a company's technical representative? _____

41. Which network troubleshooting resource typically is the least current?
_____

Determining the Most Likely Cause of a Problem

42. _____ is a possible cause of network problems, producing strange symptoms such as large instances of DOA replacement components and spontaneous reboots.

43. A workstation that can't connect to the network with a known-good NIC and properly configured client software more than likely has a _____.

44. A common patch-cable fault is _____.

STUDY QUESTIONS

45. A _____ server is one that can't respond to user requests.

46. When a user is having problems logging in to a network, you should confirm that the user is using the correct login account and _____.

47. If a user cannot access a Web site, but you can ping its TCP/IP address, check the _____ configuration.

48. If a user cannot access a Windows machine by name over a TCP/IP-only network, check the _____ configuration.

49. If a user can access some DNS hosts but not others, check the _____.

50. A _____ is a piece of software that may cause unexplained reboots or disk problems on a computer or network.

51. If you suspect a server of having a problem responding to clients' requests, _____ can confirm that the server is responding correctly.

52. If a user cannot log in, you should first check _____.

53. _____ is required to configure a DNS client properly.

54. Which physical conditions minimize the effects of ESD?
_____   _____

STUDY QUESTIONS

55. If a user's account is disabled, what is he unable to do? _____

56. True or false: If a server is down, it cannot respond to network requests.

57. True or false: If your DNS is misconfigured, you can still access a Web server through a TCP/IP address.

58. The proper comment character for a hosts file is the _____.

59. What does ESD stand for? _____

60. Any time that multiple errors occur without warning, or when unpredictable errors occur on a network, always scan for _____.

Using Common Network Tools

61. A _____ cable differs from a standard patch cable in the way that the cable is wired.

62. In addition to testing network connections, crossover cables _____.

63. A hardware loopback plug physically loops the sending channels of a cable back into the _____ channels on the same connector.

64. You can use a hardware loopback plug to test a workstation's capability to send and receive packets without using a _____ or a _____.

STUDY QUESTIONS

65. You can use a _____ to find the location of a network cable.

66. A _____ sends a tone through a network cable, and a _____ picks up the tone.

67. True or false: You should hook a tone generator to a network while workstations are plugged in.

68. True or false: Tone generators and locators should be used only on coaxial cable.

69. True or false: You can hook a UTP patch cable between two workstations to form a mini-LAN.

70. True or false: You can use a tone generator and tone locator to test cable quality.

Selecting the Appropriate Troubleshooting Tools

71. True or false: You should use a protocol analyzer to check whether a user can log in correctly.

72. True or false: You should use a quick fix when a problem is simple.

73. What is the best source you can use to you determine which troubleshooting tool to use? _____.

74. Generally speaking, the less complex the problem is, the _____ complex the tool that you use to solve it.

SAMPLE TEST

14-1 Which components do you need to make an Ethernet crossover cable?

   A. RJ-45 connectors

   B. Twisted-pair cabling

   C. BNC connectors

   D. AUI connectors

14-2 A user has a problem connecting to a Web page. You try the link and receive the same error. What could the problem be?

   A. The Web server is down.

   B. The user needs help.

   C. The network is down.

   D. The user doesn't have the proper rights.

14-3 What tests can you use to determine whether a server is responding to client requests?

   A. Power light

   B. Disk-drive activity light

   C. Capability to log in and transfer files

   D. Protocol analyzer

14-4 Users are complaining that they can't log in to the server. How can you find out whether the problem is related to the server, the network, or the workstations?

   A. Run NBTSTAT on the workstation

   B. Run NETSTAT on the workstation

   C. Go to the server console and check for user connections

   D. Run network diagnostics on the server

SAMPLE TEST

14-5 A user is having problems accessing a Web site (the corporate intranet). How can you find out whether the problem is related to the user's workstation or the network?

    A. Run tracert to InterNIC from the workstation

    B. Try pinging the intranet from the workstation

    C. Try accessing the intranet from another workstation

    D. Run winipcfg

14-6 You were downloading files yesterday, and now you are receiving many weird errors. What is the most likely cause of this problem?

    A. Bad power supply

    B. Misconfigured NIC

    C. Hard-drive virus

    D. Serial-port conflict

14-7 Management services will not load on a server after a recent reboot. Where should you look for a possible problem?

    A. Server-connection monitor

    B. Server-performance monitors

    C. Protocol analyzers

    D. Server Log file

14-8 A workstation can't communicate with the rest of the network. All protocols, the NIC, and the network client have been installed, configured, and tested. What else should you check?

    A. The router

    B. The server

SAMPLE TEST

    C. The patch cable

    D. The processor in the workstation

14-9 You cannot access the Web site http://www.sybex.com, but you can ping the TCP/IP address. What could be the problem?

    A. Web server

    B. Internet router

    C. Network card

    D. DNS

14-10 What network tools can help you find a cable fault?

    A. Network cable tester

    B. Crossover cable

    C. Hardware loopback

    D. Ethernet terminator

14-11 A user cannot log in to the network one morning. The day before, everything was fine, and no other users are having problems. What could be the possible causes of this problem?

    A. Login time restriction on that user

    B. Login station restriction

    C. Expired password

    D. Expired user account

14-12 What network troubleshooting tool can you use to connect two PCs through their NICs without using a hub?

    A. Serial cable

    B. Parallel cable

SAMPLE TEST

   C. SCSI cable

   D. Crossover cable

14-13 What do you need to perform the full suite of network-card diagnostics without a second workstation?

   A. Protocol analyzer

   B. Router

   C. Hardware loopback

   D. Additional NIC

14-14 What could you check to determine the source of a bottleneck in a server?

   A. NIC's link light

   B. Server's error logs

   C. Network hub's link lights

   D. Performance-monitoring tools

14-15 A new eight-port hub has just been installed, and known-good cables are connected to the workstations, but none of the workstations can see the network. The hub is connected to the backbone with a standard patch cable in a port labeled MDI-X. What should you replace to solve the problem?

   A. Workstation patch cables

   B. Server patch cable

   C. Network cable

   D. Hub patch cable

SAMPLE TEST

14-16 When you boot your workstation one morning, you receive a "missing operating system" error. Yesterday, you were downloading files from the Internet. What is the most likely cause of this problem?

   A. Hard-drive virus

   B. Bad NIC

   C. Misconfigured serial port

   D. Bad power supply

14-17 A user complains that she can't log into the network. Which of the following actions will *not* help you determine the scope of the problem?

   A. Checking the server status

   B. Asking users on other segments whether they are having similar problems

   C. Asking users on the same segment as that user's workstation whether they are having similar problems

   D. Changing the NIC in that user's workstation

14-18 Printing services will not load on one of your Windows NT servers after a recent reboot. Where could you look to determine the source of the problem?

   A. Application Log file

   B. System Log file

   C. Security Log file

   D. ABEND.LOG file

14-19 Your server has just experienced an ABEND. After rebooting the server, where could you find information about the ABEND?

   A. Security Log file

   B. ABEND.LOG

SAMPLE TEST

    C. CONSOLE.LOG

    D. System Log file

14-20 A user calls the help desk, reporting a problem in connecting to the sales department's Web page link on the sales Web server after logging into the corporate Web site. You are the sales-department administrator. You try the link from your Web browser and receive the same error. What is the most likely cause of the problem?

    A. The corporate Web server is down.

    B. The sales-department Web server is down.

    C. You don't have rights to administrate the corporate Web server.

    D. You don't have rights to administrate the sales Web server.

14-21 You have a server that crashes regularly. You have tried rebooting the problem several times, and the problem still exists. You have determined that the cause of the problem is corrupted Web server software. What is your next troubleshooting step?

    A. Implement the correction

    B. Isolate the cause

    C. Identify the issue

    D. Formulate a correction

14-22 A user calls the help desk, reporting a problem in logging in to the corporate intranet. You can access the Web site with the user's username and password. The user has tried logging in from other workstations unsuccessfully. What is the most likely cause of the problem?

    A. The Web server is down.

    B. The user doesn't have login rights.

    C. The user is not using the correct login procedure.

    D. The entire network is down.

SAMPLE TEST

14-23 You can use a crossover cable to connect which components?

    A. An NIC and a hub

    B. Two workstations' NICs

    C. A hub and a router

    D. Two hubs

14-24 Several users in the accounting department call the help desk, complaining that they can't log in to the network. Other users in the sales department aren't reporting any problems. You suspect that a cabling problem exists for the accounting-department users' connection, so you go into the cabling closet. What is the first thing on the hub that you should check?

    A. Server-connection link light

    B. Station link lights

    C. Internet gateway

    D. Collision activity on that segment

14-25 Your Web server is slow in responding to requests. You have just upgraded the memory in your main Web server in an attempt to solve the problem. The memory upgrade caused only a slight improvement. What would you check to determine the source of the bottleneck in your server?

    A. Hub link light for the Web server's connection

    B. Web server's NIC link light

    C. Performance-monitoring tools

    D. Web server's error logs

SAMPLE TEST

14-26 Your company is moving into a new building. You are installing all the workstations for your company. When you plug a workstation into a jack and plug in the patch cable from the patch panel to the hub, you don't get a link light on either the NIC or the hub. You have tried replacing both patch cables with known-good patch cables. The workstation still won't connect. What do you try next?

　　A. Power-cycle the hub

　　B. Use performance-monitoring tools

　　C. Reinstall the workstation's NIC drivers

　　D. Test the drop cable from the wall jack to the patch panel

14-27 The office that you work in is located in a northern climate. You frequently experience spontaneous reboots on your servers and workstations for no apparent reason. To solve the problem, you have tried replacing some of the motherboards, but the new motherboards don't solve the problem. The hardware and software are not from the same vendor, and the problem follows no recognizable pattern. What is the most likely cause of the problem?

　　A. Electrostatic discharge (ESD)

　　B. Bad power cables

　　C. Ground-shipping-related damage

　　D. Faulty network cable

14-28 A user calls you, complaining that she can't log in to the network. You try logging in from her workstation, but cannot do so. The client software is configured correctly, but you get no link light on either the workstation's NIC or the hub. You notice that the user works in a high-traffic area. Which component is most likely at fault?

　　A. Hub patch cable

　　B. Workstation patch cable

　　C. Hub

　　D. NIC

SAMPLE TEST

14-29 What can you use to determine whether a server is operational and responding to client requests?

    A. Capability to log in and transfer files

    B. NIC link light

    C. Power lights

    D. Protocol analyzer (to determine response time)

UNIT 15

Final Exam

15-1 What OSI-model layer is responsible for establishing and maintaining logical connections?

   A. Transport

   B. Session

   C. Network

   D. Application

15-2 What OSI-model layer is responsible for the physical aspects of the network, including the connections, the media, and the conversion of upper-layer data into electrical impulses?

   A. Data Link

   B. Physical

   C. Network

   D. Application

15-3 What are the specifications for the 100BaseT standard?

   A. 100 meters maximum, 0.6 meter minimum, 100Mbps speed

   B. 330 meters maximum, 3 meters minimum, 100Mbps speed

   C. 150 meters maximum, 0.6 meter minimum, 100Mbps speed

   D. 300 meters maximum, 0.6 meter minimum, 100Mbps speed

15-4 Why is striping with parity (RAID 5) the most fault-tolerant storage method?

   A. Data is stored offline.

   B. Data is striped across all the drives, along with its parity information.

   C. Data is copied in sections on each drive, with parity information being copied to a single drive.

   D. Data stored on the first drive is duplicated on every other drive on the server.

15-5 A company is rebuilding its network infrastructure and is looking at different topologies, trying to find the one that best suits it. The most important item that the company is looking for is fault tolerance; price is not a factor. The future addition of workstations is not a factor. Which type of topology would you recommend?

    A. Star

    B. Ring

    C. Star and bus

    D. Mesh

15-6 What is the primary purpose of using a repeater?

    A. Extending the maximum segment length of a network

    B. Connecting multiple, dissimilar network topologies

    C. Reducing total traffic on a single network segment

    D. Connecting Token Ring networks to 100Mbps Ethernet

15-7 Which of the following statements is a drawback of an active hub?

    A. It regenerates all incoming signals, including noise.

    B. It cannot be programmed on a per-port basis.

    C. It has no management capability.

    D. It boosts only data signals.

15-8 A known-good workstation is moved into a newly cabled office. The NIC is known to have a good connection to 100BaseT. The workstation will not connect. What is the first thing to check?

    A. The wall-plate-to-patch-panel cable

    B. The NIC

C. The patch-panel-to-hub cable

D. The patch panel

15-9 An NIC has been installed in a workstation. There are no hardware conflicts, and the cabling is known to be good, but the NIC will not connect. What is the next thing that you should do?

A. Use the NIC's external diagnostics to test the NIC's components

B. Use the NIC's internal diagnostics to test the NIC's components

C. Replace the NIC

D. None of the above

15-10 You have just installed an NIC in a new Microsoft Windows 95 system, but the system cannot find the card. You followed these steps: turned off the power, installed the card, and powered on the system. What is the next thing that you should do?

A. Reboot

B. Try a different NIC

C. Confirm that the NIC is Plug-and-Play-compliant

D. Try the NIC in a different computer

15-11 Which 802 standard uses a 4Mbps and 16Mbps data rate and a token-passing media-access method?

A. 802.3

B. 802.4

C. 802.5

D. 802.10

15-12 What are the specifications for the 10Base2 standard?

A. 185 meters, 10Mbps, thin coaxial, bus topology

B. 100 meters, 10Mbps, fiber-optic, star topology

C. 1,800 meters, 10Mbps, 75-ohm coaxial, bus topology

D. 200 meters, 10Mbps, twisted-pair, star topology

15-13 What are the specifications for the 10BaseT standard?

A. 185 meters, 10Mbps, thin coaxial, bus topology

B. 200 meters, 10Mbps, fiber-optic, star topology

C. 1,800 meters, 10Mbps, 75-ohm coaxial, bus topology

D. 100 meters, 10Mbps, twisted-pair, star topology

15-14 You are the administrator of a network. The network has two segments and is plagued by large amounts of traffic that originates from one segment. What network device could you place between the segments to restrict the heavy traffic to one segment?

A. Hub

B. Transceiver

C. Bridge

D. Modulator/demodulator

15-15 What are the specifications for the 100BaseT standard?

A. 185 meters, 100Mbps, thin coaxial, bus topology

B. 200 meters, 100Mbps, fiber-optic, star topology

C. 1,800 meters, 100Mbps, 75-ohm coaxial, bus topology

D. 100 meters, 100Mbps, twisted-pair, star topology

15-16 A customer has both Ethernet and Token Ring networks. He asks you what device he could use to connect the networks. What would you suggest?

A. Hub

B. Filter

C. Media converter

D. Gateway

15-17 Which route-selection technology requires the most administrative overhead?

A. Static

B. Dynamic

15-18 Which of the following protocols are connectionless transport methods?

A. UDP

B. TCP

C. SPX

D. IPX

15-19 What is the name for the process of mapping an alphanumeric name to a network address?

A. Number mapping

B. Name resolution

C. Alpha devices

D. Name assigning

15-20 Which layer of the OSI model is responsible for connection services (reliable end-to-end communications)?

A. Physical

B. Transport

C. Session

D. Presentation

15-21 What are the minimum steps required for configuring WINS on a Microsoft Windows 95/98 workstation?

    A. Enable WINS resolution

    B. Disable WINS resolution

    C. Enter primary WINS server

    D. Enter secondary WINS server

15-22 What is the default TCP/IP port for NNTP?

    A. 80

    B. 110

    C. 117

    D. 119

15-23 What is the subnet mask for a Class C TCP/IP address?

    A. 255.255.255.0

    B. 255.255.0.0

    C. 255.255.255.255

    D. 255.0.0.0

15-24 What TCP/IP protocol is used to transfer files or requests from a Web server to a Web browser?

    A. SMTP

    B. HTTP

    C. ICMP

    D. OSPF

15-25 What is one disadvantage of using a bus topology on a 100-workstation network?

    A. Complex software problems

    B. Isolating cable faults

    C. Expensive cabling

    D. Required termination on each node

15-26 Which of the following NOSes can have a graphical user interface?

    A. Unix

    B. Windows NT

    C. OS/400

    D. OS/2

    E. NetWare

15-27 Which network topology provides multiple, redundant links between networked devices?

    A. Star

    B. Bus

    C. Ring

    D. Mesh

15-28 If you have been assigned an IP address of 223.123.75.142, what is the default subnet mask?

    A. 255.255.255.220

    B. 255.255.255.255

    C. 223.123.75.142

    D. 255.255.255.0

15-29 To test whether a mail server is ready to receive mail and respond to SMTP communications, what TCP/IP utility could you use?

    A. tracert

    B. Telnet

    C. Ping

    D. NETSTAT

15-30 You are having trouble connecting to Internet servers from your Windows 9*x* workstation. What utility could you use to check your workstation's current TCP/IP configuration?

    A. NETSTAT

    B. ipconfig

    C. winipcfg

    D. tracert

15-31 Which TCP/IP utility displays all the current connections for a workstation?

    A. NETSTAT

    B. NetBIOS

    C. NBTSTAT

    D. Ping

15-32 Which Microsoft Windows TCP/IP utility allows an administrator to view statistics on NetBIOS running over TCP/IP?

    A. NETSTAT

    B. NetBIOS

    C. NBTSTAT

    D. Ping

15-33 Which protocol maps TCP/IP addresses to Data Link layer addresses?

    A. AFP

    B. MAP

    C. ARP

    D. NBT

15-34 Which of the following `ping` command switches verify that a local TCP/IP interface is working properly?

    A. `ping host`

    B. `ping localhost`

    C. `ping 127.0.0.1`

    D. `ping address-server`

15-35 What must you do so that the following modems work simultaneously when installed in a single server? Both modems are known to be good. The first modem is set to COM3, IRQ 4, I/O 2F8h. The second modem is set to COM4, IRQ 3, I/O 2F8h.

    A. Change the IRQ of modem 1

    B. Change the I/O address of modem 1

    C. Change the IRQ of modem 2

    D. Change the COM port of modem 2

15-36 Which transport protocol does PPTP use?

    A. IPX/SPX

    B. TCP/IP

    C. AppleTalk

    D. SNA

15-37 Which TCP/IP protocol resides at both the Physical layer and the Data Link layer of the OSI model?

   A. PPP

   B. SLIP

   C. PPTP

   D. PSTN

15-38 Which of the following is the most secure type of password?

   A. A password that never expires

   B. A password that is based on a user's phone number

   C. A password on a shared resource

   D. A password that is always changed

15-39 What can you do to ensure that sensitive data remains secure during a transmission?

   A. Reformat the data to include unnecessary information that will confuse unauthorized users

   B. Use removable media to transfer data

   C. Set share-level security on the data before transmission

   D. Encrypt the data before transmission

15-40 What security benefit can a firewall offer?

   A. Authenticate all remote-access users

   B. Ensure that file and print resources are used by WAN users but not by LAN users

   C. Prevent local-network users from creating unauthorized user accounts

   D. Prevent unauthorized network users from accessing sensitive data

15-41 A tape drive keeps generating errors, and you have tried multiple tapes. What is the next thing you should do?

    A. Replace the tape drive

    B. Replace the SCSI cable

    C. Use a cleaning tape

    D. Replace the SCSI interface

15-42 Which of the following should you read for product information and installation tips before performing an installation or an upgrade?

    A. Manufacturer product documentation

    B. Manufacturer support CD-ROM

    C. Manufacturer support Web site

    D. Manufacturer readme files

15-43 Which of the following errors would you classify as being the most critical error, and thereby needing attention first?

    A. A user cannot load a shareware game.

    B. The color printer is jammed.

    C. None of the users can connect to the network.

    D. An Internet connection is running a little slower than normal.

15-44 The users on a small network are complaining that they have not been able to print for about a week. The newest patch was applied to the server about a month ago, and the network client was upgraded four days ago. What is likely to be the problem?

    A. Too many users logging in at the same time

    B. The network client

C. Too many printers

D. The server's patch

15-45 Routing occurs at which layer of the OSI model?

A. Routing

B. Network

C. Transport

D. Application

15-46 If you are implementing disk striping with parity on your server, what is the minimum number of hard drives required?

A. 2

B. 3

C. 4

D. 5

15-47 You are installing a Windows 9x-based TCP/IP network. You accidentally set workstation B to the same IP address as workstation Which workstation has a valid IP address?

A. A

B. B

C. Neither

D. Both

15-48 You are troubleshooting a workstation that can't send data to the Internet. Upon checking the TCP/IP configuration, you notice that the IP address and the DNS server are configured correctly. The workstation can access IP hosts on the local segment. Which of the following items could be misconfigured?

    A. WINS server

    B. Default gateway

    C. IPX address

    D. Default NDS context

15-49 Which of the following 802.x specifications is *not* commonly used on PC-based LANs?

    A. 802.2

    B. 802.3

    C. 802.4

    D. 802.5

15-50 What network-cable components do you need to make a 10BaseT Ethernet crossover cable?

    A. F connectors

    B. Twisted-pair cabling

    C. BNC connectors

    D. AUI connectors

    E. RJ-11 connectors

    F. Coax cabling

    G. DB-25 connectors

    H. RJ-45 connectors

    I. Fiber-optic cabling

15-51 Which backup method has the shortest daily backup time?

  A. Full

  B. Differential

  C. Incremental

  D. Multigenerational

15-52 Which directory service does NetWare 4.*x* use, by default?

  A. DNS

  B. NDS

  C. NTDS

  D. ABS

15-53 Which backup method backs up the entire server in one operation?

  A. Full

  B. Differential

  C. Incremental

  D. Multigenerational

15-54 The required result is to connect to the headquarters server. The first optional result is to allow the server to call back the workstation. The second optional result is to ensure that all communications are encrypted.
Proposed solution:
You have installed a POTS telephone line, modem cable, and modem on a workstation. NetBEUI is installed and configured on the workstation. TCP/IP and IPX are installed and configured on the office server. You configure the software settings on the modem. Then you dial

in to your headquarters. The appropriate modem lights turn on, and a connection tone issues from the speaker of the workstation's modem. The office network is set up to allow the entire network to be accessed via a dial-in connection.

   A. The proposed solution produces the required results.

   B. The proposed solution produces the required results and one of the optional results.

   C. The proposed solution produces the required results and both of the optional results.

   D. The proposed solution does not produce the required or the optional results.

15-55 Which of the following connects two or more components for the purpose of sharing resources?

   A. Modem

   B. Computer

   C. Dumb terminal

   D. Network

15-56 What is the maximum distance for a 10Base5 segment?

   A. 200 meters

   B. 500 meters

   C. 1,000 meters

   D. 2,000 meters

15-57 IPX was designed for use with which NOS?

   A. Windows NT

   B. Unix

   C. NetWare

   D. All of the above

15-58 Plenum-rated cable has which of the following features?

   A. Lower cost than polyvinyl chloride (PVC) cable

   B. Won't emit toxic gases when burned

   C. Transmits data faster

   D. All of the above

15-59 You have a Windows-based network that runs NetBEUI and TCP/IP. WINS has not been implemented, and you have a great deal of traffic on one segment from broadcasts. Which network device could you implement to isolate these broadcasts and still allow node–to-node communication?

   A. Transceiver

   B. Bridge

   C. Repeater

   D. Switch

15-60 Which number in the following graphic corresponds to a star network topology?

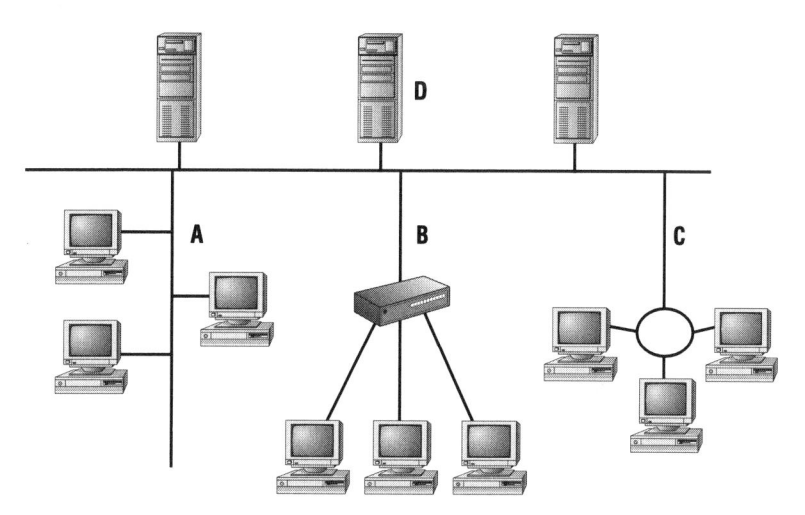

15-61 Which letter in the following graphic corresponds to the backbone?

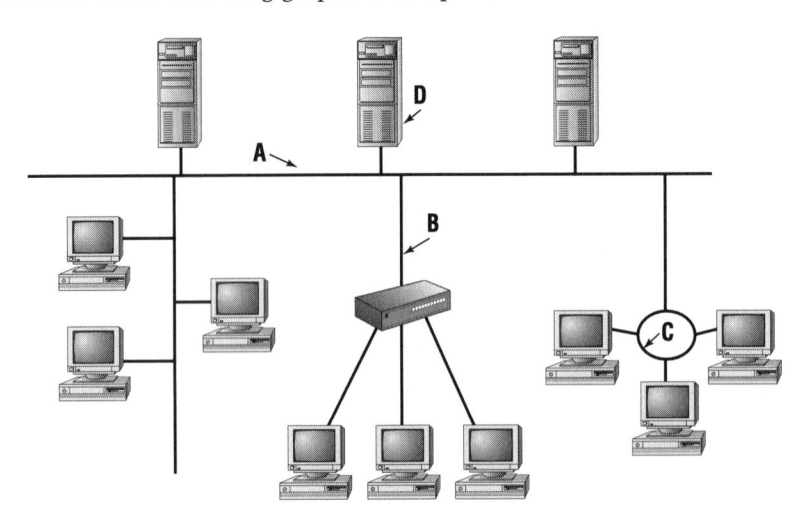

15-62 Which of the following NOS directory services is based on X.500?

    A. Windows NT Directory Services (NTDS)

    B. Novell Directory Services (NDS)

    C. US West Yellow Pages (USWY)

    D. Windows 98 Directory Services (W98DS)

15-63 What is a benefit of using an HTTP (Web) proxy server on your network?

    A. Managing SMTP traffic

    B. Managing a Web server

    C. Managing Web-browser settings

    D. Managing Web ports

15-64 Your network has been set up with the appropriate devices (such as routers and CSUs/DSUs) to make Internet connection possible, and these devices have been installed and configured properly. Now you must configure all Windows 9*x* workstations with the appropriate parameters. What are the minimum settings you must have in the Network Control Panel applet before this station can communicate with the Internet via TCP/IP?

- **A.** TCP/IP protocol
- **B.** IPX/SPX-compatible protocol
- **C.** NetBEUI protocol
- **D.** Network adapter driver
- **E.** Client for Microsoft Networks
- **F.** Client for NetWare Networks

15-65 Which Windows TCP/IP utility generates the following type of output?

```
Interface: 199.162.8.120
  Internet Address      Physical Address        Type
  199.162.8.120         a8-e1-78-ac-09-11       dynamic
```

- **A.** NBTSTAT
- **B.** ARP
- **C.** NETSTAT
- **D.** Ping

15-66 Which of the following NOS directory services uses domains and domain controllers?

- **A.** Windows NT Directory Services (NTDS)
- **B.** Novell Directory Services (NDS)
- **C.** US West Yellow Pages (USWY)
- **D.** Windows 98 Directory Services (W98DS)

15-67 Which NBTSTAT switch lists all the NetBIOS over TCP/IP names that your computer has resolved recently and their associated IP addresses?

    A. -r

    B. /r

    C. -R

    D. /R

15-68 Which NBTSTAT switch purges and reloads the entire NetBIOS name cache?

    A. -r

    B. /r

    C. -R

    D. /R

15-69 You are setting up a workstation for remote access to the office. The office has a modem pool configured and is working correctly. The following results are required:
1. The workstation and modem bank must establish a connection.
2. The server at the office must authenticate the workstation.

The following results are desirable but optional:
1. The workstation and office must be able to communicate by using a single protocol.
2. The workstation must be able to access all network devices at the office.

Following is the proposed solution:
Install a POTS telephone line, modem cable, and modem connected to the workstation. TCP/IP is installed and configured to have a DHCP server assign an IP address automatically. TCP/IP and IP forwarding are installed and configured on the office server. You configure the software settings on the modem. Then you dial in to your headquarters. The appropriate modem lights turn on, and a connection tone issues from the speaker of the workstation

modem. The office network is set up to allow the entire network to be viewed via dial-in. Dial-in permissions have been granted to the users, and user-level security has been enabled.

   A. The proposed solution provides the required results.

   B. The proposed solution provides the required results and one of the optional results.

   C. The proposed solution provides the required results and both of the optional results.

   D. The proposed solution does not provide the required results.

15-70 The UART in your PC is an 8250. You have installed an external ISDN terminal adapter (ISDN modem) on your computer. You are not getting the full speed of an ISDN line. With which chipset must you must replace the UART?

   A. 85*xx*

   B. 115*xx*

   C. 125*xx*

   D. 16550

15-71 Which of the following is the dotted-decimal equivalent of this binary representation of a subnet mask?

   11111111.11111111.11111111.10000000

   A. 255.255.255.255

   B. 255.255.255.0

   C. 255.255.255.196

   D. 255.255.255.128

15-72 What does the acronym DHCP stand for?

   A. Dynamic Host Carrier Protocol

   B. Dynamic Host Configuration Protocol

   C. Dynamic Host Client Protocol

   D. Dynamic Host Control Protocol

15-73 Which of the following ipconfig switches displays the most complete list of IP configuration information for that station?

  A. `/All`

  B. `/Renew`

  C. `/Release`

  D. `/?`

15-74 You are running UTP cable in an Ethernet network from a workstation to a hub. Which of the following items are included in the total-length measurement of the cable?

  A. Workstation patch cable

  B. Main cable run

  C. Hub internal network

  D. Hub patch cable

15-75 Which Windows 9*x* utility do you use to administrate NetWare 4.*x* and later networks?

  A. User Configuration

  B. SYSCON

  C. User Manager

  D. NetWare Administrator

15-76 When you boot your workstation, you receive a "missing operating system" error message. You try rebooting, but you get the same error message. After rebooting several times, you remember that you were downloading files from the Internet yesterday. What is the most likely cause of this problem?

  A. A misconfigured NIC

  B. A virus infection

  C. A parallel-port IRQ conflict

  D. A blown power supply

APPENDIX

Study Questions and
Sample Tests Answers

Unit 1 Answers

Study Questions

1. two

2. first, last

3. False

4. False

5. star

6. every other device

7. backbone

8. Segment

9. False

10. False

11. hub

12. physical topology

13. 32-

14. Novell NetWare

15. Novell NetWare

16. Microsoft Windows NT

Unit 1 Answers

17. Unix

18. False

19. Unix

20. the X.500 recommendation

21. NTFS

22. Novell Client for Windows 9*x*

23. NetBEUI

24. TCP/IP

25. IPX

26. SPX

27. octet

28. TCP/IP

29. IPX/SPX

    Explanation: Although versions since 3.1*x* support TCP/IP, IPX/SPX is the default protocol for NetWare and is required for versions up to NetWare 5. NetWare 5 is the first version in which IPX/SPX is an optional protocol.

30. False

    Explanation: Although TCP/IP addresses *can* be assigned dynamically (through DHCP), they can also be assigned manually by an administrator.

31. Transmission Control Protocol/Internet Protocol

32. NetBEUI

33. IPX/SPX

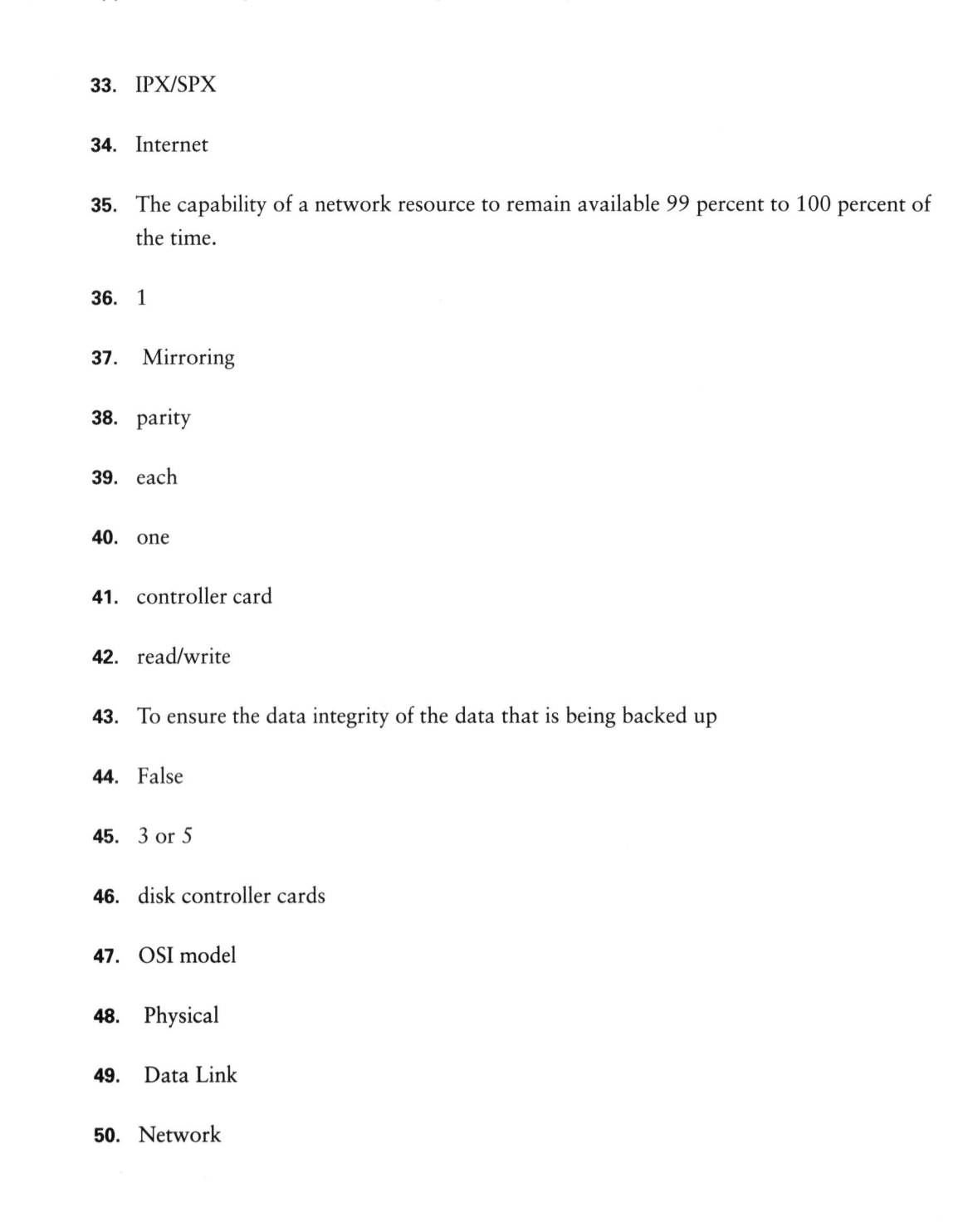

34. Internet

35. The capability of a network resource to remain available 99 percent to 100 percent of the time.

36. 1

37. Mirroring

38. parity

39. each

40. one

41. controller card

42. read/write

43. To ensure the data integrity of the data that is being backed up

44. False

45. 3 or 5

46. disk controller cards

47. OSI model

48. Physical

49. Data Link

50. Network

51. Network
52. Transport
53. Session
54. Presentation
55. Application
56. Transport
57. Network
58. Data Link
59. Session
60. Presentation
61. Open Systems Interconnect
62. Transport
63. Physical
64. Presentation
65. Application
66. False
67. Unshielded twisted-pair (UTP)
68. 100
69. 100

70. 0.6

71. cable

72. 185

73. RJ-45

74. Fiber-optic

75. BNC

76. Registered Jack

77. 100BaseT4 and 100BaseVG

78. 00BaseFX

79. False

80. True

81. False

82. send and receive

83. Local area network (LAN), metropolitan area network (MAN), and wide area network (WAN)

84. server

85. One another

86. Connects a device to the network medium and allows it to communicate with other devices

87. A router

88. Baseband

89. gateway

90. Broadband

Sample Test

1-1   A

1-2   D

1-3   C

1-4   A

1-5   D

1-6   B

1-7   B

1-8   B

1-9   C

1-10 B

1-11 D

1-12 B

1-13 B

1-14 A

1-15 B

1-16 B

1-17 C

1-18 B

1-19 D

1-20 C

1-21 A

1-22 A

1-23 B

1-24 A

1-25 B

1-26 A

Unit 2 Answers

Study Questions

1. The operating system

2. False

3. IRQ

4. jumpers

5. software application

6. physically

7. Internal, external

8. Internal

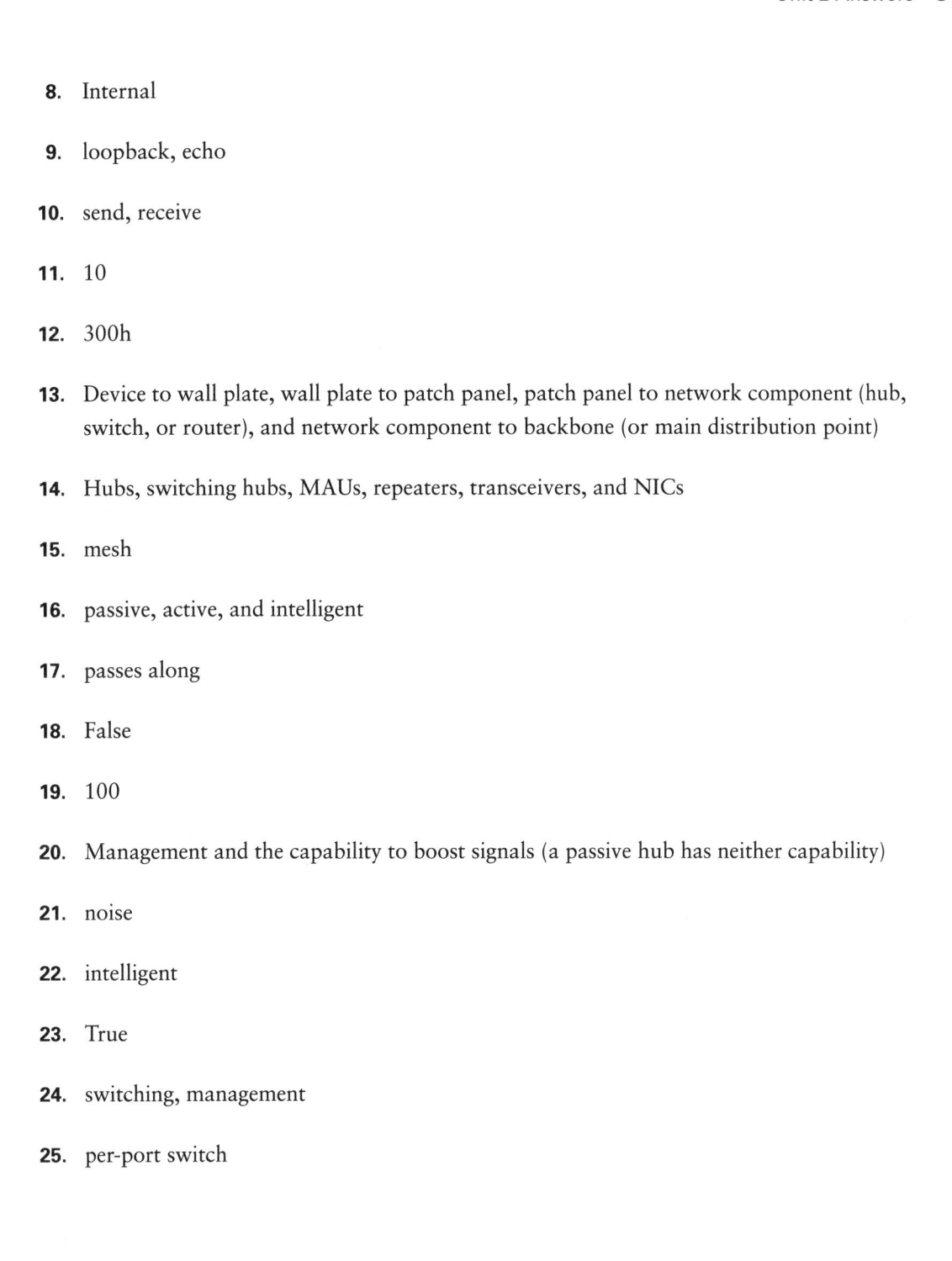

9. loopback, echo

10. send, receive

11. 10

12. 300h

13. Device to wall plate, wall plate to patch panel, patch panel to network component (hub, switch, or router), and network component to backbone (or main distribution point)

14. Hubs, switching hubs, MAUs, repeaters, transceivers, and NICs

15. mesh

16. passive, active, and intelligent

17. passes along

18. False

19. 100

20. Management and the capability to boost signals (a passive hub has neither capability)

21. noise

22. intelligent

23. True

24. switching, management

25. per-port switch

26. programmed

27. disable

28. Token Ring

29. False

30. repeater

31. False

32. NICs

33. convert

Sample Test

2-1   A

2-2   B

2-3   A, D

2-4   D

2-5   D

2-6   C

2-7   C

2-8   B

2-9   A

2-10 A

2-11 B

2-12 C

2-13 A

2-14 A

2-15 B

2-16 A

2-17 B

Unit 3 Answers

Study Questions

1. Logical Link Control (LLC), Media Access Control (MAC)

2. rejects (does not forward)

3. False

4. True

5. 802.3

6. 802.2

7. Token Ring

8. 802.4

9. Token Ring

10. 100 meters

11. False

12. False

13. True

Sample Test

3-1   C

3-2   B

3-3   B

3-4   D

3-5   D

3-6   C

3-7   A

3-8   B

3-9   B

3-10   C

3-11   D

3-12   C

Unit 4 Answers

Study Questions

1. Routers

2. path

3. Network and Data Link

4. False

5. Dynamic

6. Static

7. path

8. static

9. gateway

10. subnetwork

11. False

    Explanation: With the use of a routing protocol, a smaller subnetwork running a single protocol can connect to a larger network.

Sample Test

4-1	C
4-2	D
4-3	D
4-4	A
4-5	C, D
4-6	A
4-7	D
4-8	A
4-9	B

4-10 D

Explanation: You compare the IP address of the workstation with the destination IP address by using the subnetmask. If the comparison is equal, the packet is forwarded on the local network. If the comparison is not equal, the packet is forwarded to the default gateway.

4-11 A

Explanation: An incorrect IP address affects communications with all workstations. The default gateway affects only communications outside the local area. An incorrect subnetmask could still allow communications within the local network.

Unit 5 Answers

Study Questions

1. The middle

2. Network, Session

3. connection-oriented

4. False

5. Connection-oriented

6. True

7. random

8. Connection-oriented

9. Connectionless

10. an alphanumeric name

11. Service-requester-initiated, service-provider-initiated

12. numeric

13. service-requester-initiated name resolution

14. network address

15. The provider

Sample Test

5-1   C

5-2   B

5-3   D

5-4   B

5-5   A

5-6   A

5-7   B

5-8   A

5-9   B

5-10 D

5-11 B

5-12 C

5-13 A

Unit 6 Answers

Study Questions

1. Microsoft Windows 95/98, Microsoft Windows NT, IBM OS/2, Apple Macintosh, Unix

2. DHCP

3. Static

4. Dynamic

5. Automatic

6. WINS

7. DNS

8. organizational

9. com, edu, gov, int, mil, net, org

10. Geographical

11. False

12. us

13. False

14. IP

15. hosts

16. lmhosts

17. UDP

18. SNMP

19. Application

20. FTP

21. HTTP

22. Port numbering

23. 23

24. 110

25. 119

26. 80

27. 25

28. 255.255.255.0

29. 255.0.0.0

30. 255.255.0.0

31. 16,777,214

32. 8

33. 255.0.0.0

34. 1 to 127

35. 255.255.0.0

36. 128 to 191

37. 255.255.255.0

38. 192 to 223

39. 16,384

40. 65,534

41. C

42. TCP/IP

43. IP address, DNS, default gateway, host name, Internet domain name

44. IP proxy

45. Server address, host name, Internet domain name

46. Subnet mask

47. Choose Start ➤ Settings ➤ Control Panel ➤ Network ➤ TCP/IP ➤ Properties ➤ WINS Configuration

48. Default gateway

49. The server's IP address

50. Answers: DHCP, WINS, and IP proxy

Sample Test

6-1   B

6-2   A, B

6-3   B

6-4	C
6-5	A, B, C
6-6	A
6-7	A, C, D
6-8	B
6-9	B
6-10	A
6-11	C
6-12	B
6-13	C
6-14	A
6-15	C
6-16	D
6-17	B
6-18	A
6-19	A, B, D
6-20	D
6-21	D
6-22	B
6-23	D
6-24	A, C

6-25   A, C

6-26   D

6-27   A, B

Unit 7 Answers

Study Questions

1. Network

2. ARP

3. -a

4. Deletes the host address specified by `inet_addr`

5. NBTSTAT

6. Purges and reloads the locally cached name table

    Explanation: The -R must be capitalized to perform this specific action. A lowercase r lists resolved NetBIOS names.

7. -S

    Explanation: The S must be capitalized.

8. NETSTAT

9. -a

10. Displays the contents of the routing table

11. FTP

12. TCP

13. FTP

14. Ping

15. Resolve addresses to host names

16. -t

17. ipconfig

18. winipcfg

19. tracert

20. Traces the route, but responds with TCP/IP addresses instead of host names (the default)

21. Telnet

22. Session, Presentation, and Application

Sample Test

7-1   D

7-2   B

7-3   B

7-4   B, C

7-5   C

7-6   C

7-7 C

7-8 B

7-9 C

7-10 C

7-11 D

7-12 A

7-13 A

7-14 B

7-15 B

7-16 C

7-17 A

7-18 C

7-19 B

Unit 8 Answers

Study Questions

1. remote

2. PPP, SLIP, and PPTP

3. ISDN, PSTN

4. PPP

5. Physical and Data Link

6. TCP/IP

7. PPTP

8. False

9. data

10. PSTN

    Explanation: Although ISDN is easy for some people to configure, PSTN is considered to be easy enough for almost anyone to use for a remote connection.

11. True

12. analog, digital

13. PSTN

14. COM port

    Explanation: Although you can configure IRQ and I/O addresses, selecting the COM port automatically chooses the default IRQ and I/O addresses associated with the selected COM port.

15. Device Manager

16. 165xx

17. An account created for the remote user, with the proper dial-in privileges; the capability to accept incoming connections; and the capability to allow incoming connections to browse the network or access specific applications

18. A modem

19. 3F8

20. 2F8

Sample Test

8-1	A
8-2	B
8-3	B
8-4	B
8-5	B
8-6	A
8-7	C
8-8	D
8-9	A, B, C, D, E, F
8-10	C
8-11	A, B, D
8-12	B
8-13	B
8-14	A, B, C
8-15	A

Unit 9 Answers

Study Questions

1. share

2. encrypt

3. protect

4. user-level

5. client-server

6. Share-level security

7. Share-level security

8. True

9. letters, numbers, and symbols

10. passwords

11. Encryption is the process by which sensitive network data is encoded for transmission over an insecure network.

12. key

13. Rivest, Shamir, and Adleman

14. unauthorized users

15. False

16. Packet filtering, application filtering, and circuit filtering

17. The firewall examines each packet as it passes through the firewall and then passes or rejects packets based on the information in the firewall's ACL.

    Explanation: The ACL information is based on the TCP or UDP port address and the direction (inbound or outbound) of the packet.

18. The firewall examines the source and destination address and then views the path that each packet took. If a packet took a route other than one of the routes specified in the firewall's ACL, the packet is rejected.

Sample Test

9-1   B

9-2   D

9-3   A

9-4   C

9-5   D

9-6   D

9-7   B

9-8   D

9-9   A, D

9-10 B

Unit 10 Answers

Study Questions

1. protocol scheme

2. Administrative

3. What class addresses to use, what subnet masks to use, how to assign TCP/IP addresses, what range of addresses are blocked for static addressing, and what range of addresses are blocked for dynamic addressing

4. admin

5. administrator

6. addresses

7. range

8. locations

9. True

10. False

11. fluorescent

12. False

13. False

14. True

15. False

16. False

17. moisture, heat

18. True

19. software

20. UPS

21. battery True or false: A patch panel needs power to operate.

22. False

23. Token Ring

24. shielded

25. 25-, 50-, 68-

26. Analog

27. False

28. server

29. power outlets

30. eliminate

31. True

32. Fiber-optic

33. False

34. RJ-45

35. Analog

36. False

Sample Test

10-1   B, C, D

10-1   A

10-2   C

10-3   C

10-4   B

10-5	D
10-6	A
10-7	A, B, C
10-8	A, C, D
10-9	D
10-10	A
10-11	A, C, D
10-12	B
10-13	D
10-14	A, B, D
10-15	B
10-16	D
10-17	B
10-18	A
10-19	D

Unit 11 Answers

Study Questions

1. troubleshooting

2. updated

3. performance statistics

4. Answers: application

5. documentation

6. request

7. original

8. image

9. applications

10. A clean workstation, but any user data files that were not backed up and any applications loaded on that machine after the image was created will be lost.

11. removable

12. Workstation backups

13. Jaz drive

14. Zip drive

15. LS-120 disk

16. High-density floppy disk

17. Low-density floppy disk

18. read and write to them

19. hot-pluggable case

20. data files and applications

21. the server's storage capability

22. 720 KB, 1.44MB, and 120MB
23. security
24. file
25. CD-ROM writers/rewriters
26. slow
27. remove any unnecessary files, drivers, and protocols
28. files
29. slow, lock up
30. Installing a new application
31. UNC
32. Drive mappings
33. duplicating
34. True
35. the server name, the share name, a double backslash (\\), single backslashes (\).
36. drive mappings
37. Capturing a printer port
38. DOS
39. Universal Naming Convention
40. DOS

41. test
42. user
43. True
44. True
45. True
46. False
47. True
48. True
49. False
50. True
51. False
52. True
53. add, modify, or delete
54. Account Operators or Administrators
55. Profiles
56. Rights
57. login account, password
58. Profiles
59. Policies

60. Administrative utilities

Sample Test

- **11-1** A, B, C
- **11-2** D
- **11-3** B, D
- **11-4** B
- **11-5** C
- **11-6** D
- **11-7** C
- **11-8** A, B, C
- **11-9** A, C
- **11-10** A
- **11-11** A
- **11-12** C
- **11-13** B
- **11-14** A
- **11-15** C
- **11-16** C
- **11-17** D
- **11-18** B
- **11-19** A, B, C, E

11-20 D

11-21 A, C, D

Unit 12 Answers

Study Questions

1. readme

2. documentation

3. Readme

4. Web site

5. The files contain information on software issues discovered immediately before shipment.

6. False

7. Tape backup

8. offsite

9. Use a cleaning tape.

10. Patches

11. manufacturers

12. On a test network

13. False

14. Patches

15. antivirus

16. workstations

17. virus list

18. Internet

19. virus signature

20. Full backup

Sample Test

12-1 C

12-2 B

12-3 A, D

12-4 B

12-5 A

12-6 C

12-7 B

12-8 D

12-9 C

12-10 B

12-11 C

12-12 B

12-13 A, B

12-14 D

12-15 C

Unit 13 Answers

Study Questions

1. Information transfer, handholding, and technical service

2. False

3. Technical service

4. False

5. Handholding

6. True

7. Technical service

8. Information transfer

9. Technical service

10. Critical errors

11. Noncritical errors

12. Critical

13. Noncritical

14. Critical

15. Critical

16. Noncritical

17. Critical

18. Critical

Sample Test

13-1   D

13-2   B

13-3   D

13-4   A

13-5   B

13-6   C

13-7   B

13-8   C

13-9   A

13-10 C

13-11 D

13-12 C

13-13 B

Unit 14 Answers

Study Questions

1. entire network
2. same segment
3. intermittent
4. replicable
5. True
6. very
7. Isolating the cause
8. Implementing the correction
9. Re-creating the problem
10. Giving feedback
11. Documenting the problem and the solution
12. Formulating a correction
13. Identifying the issue
14. Have a different user try the same operation on the same machine
15. Train the user

16. False

    Explanation: Network problems can be related to a user's lack of knowledge about a specific procedure.

17. True

18. True

19. Link lights

20. NICs, hubs

21. Power lights

22. Error logs

23. ABEND.LOG, SYS$LOG.ERR, CONSOLE.LOG

24. System Log, Security Log, Application Log

25. Windows NT Event Viewer

26. MONITOR.NLM

27. Windows NT Performance Monitor

28. Answer SYS:SYSTEM

29. SYS:ETC

30. Performance monitors

31. System Log

32. CONSOLE.LOG

33. Application Log

34. Security Log

35. support Web sites

36. vendor support CDs

37. knowledge base

38. Knowledge bases on the Web and telephone technical support

39. Knowledge base

40. Telephone technical support

41. Vendor support CDs

42. ESD

43. faulty patch cable

44. broken wires inside the patch cable

45. down

46. password

47. DNS

48. WINS

49. configuration of the `hosts` file

50. virus

51. logging in and transferring files

52. his or her login procedures

53. The IP address of the local DNS server

54. 40 percent humidity and temperature around 70°F

55. Log in to the network

56. True

57. True

58. pound sign (#)

59. Electrostatic discharge

60. viruses

61. crossover

62. connect hubs

63. receiving

64. hub, crossover cable

65. tone generator and locator

66. tone generator, tone locator

67. False

68. False

69. False
    Explanation: You would need a crossover cable for this purpose.

70. False

71. False

72. True

73. Personal experience

74. less

Sample Test

14-1   A, B

14-2   A

14-3   C

14-4   C

14-5   C

14-6   C

14-7   D

14-8   C

14-9   D

14-10 A

14-11 C, D

14-12 D

14-13 C

14-14 D

14-15 D

14-16 A

14-17 D

14-18 B

14-19 B, C

14-20 B

14-21 D

14-22 C

14-23 B, D

14-24 A

14-25 C

14-26 D

14-27 A

14-28 B

14-29 A

Unit 15 Answers

Final Test

15-1 B

15-2 B

15-3 A

15-4 B

15-5	D
15-6	A
15-7	A
15-8	C
15-9	B
15-10	C
15-11	C
15-12	A
15-13	D
15-14	C
15-15	D
15-16	D
15-17	A
15-18	A, D
15-19	B
15-20	B
15-21	A, C
15-22	D
15-23	A
15-24	B
15-25	B

15-26 A, B, C, D, E

15-27 D

15-28 D

15-29 B

15-30 C

15-31 A

15-32 C

15-33 C

15-34 B, C

15-35 B

15-36 B

15-37 B

15-38 D

15-39 D

15-40 D

15-41 C

15-42 A, D

15-43 C

15-44 B

15-45 B

15-46 B

15-47 A

15-48 B

15-49 C

15-50 B, H

15-51 C

15-52 B

15-53 A

15-54 D

15-55 D

15-56 B

15-57 C

15-58 B

15-59 B

15-60 B

15-61 A

15-62 B

15-63 D

15-64 A, D

15-65 B

15-66 A

15-67 A

15-68 C

15-69 C

15-70 D

15-71 D

15-72 B

15-73 A

15-74 A, B, D

15-75 D

15-76 B

Glossary

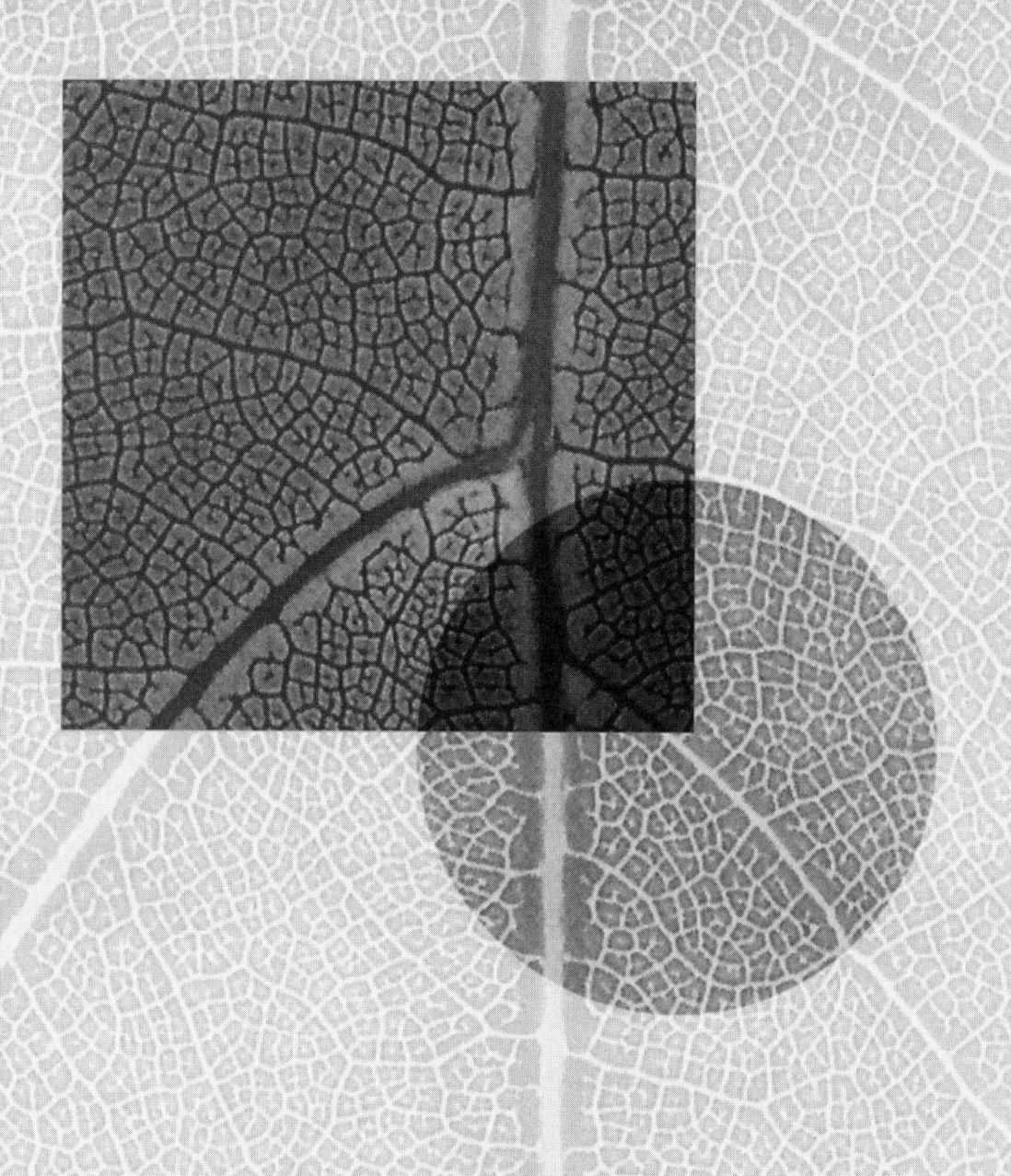

10Base2 Ethernet   An implementation of Ethernet that specifies a 10Mbps signaling rate, baseband signaling, and coaxial cable with a maximum segment length of 185 meters (607 feet).

ABEND   Short for *abnormal end,* Novell's term for a server crash.

ABEND.LOG   The log file in the SYS:\SYSTEM directory on a NetWare 4.11 or later server that records all ABENDs that have occurred on a NetWare server, including detailed information about the ABEND.

Access Control List (ACL)   A list of rights that an object has to resources on the network. Also a type of firewall. In this case, the lists reside on a router, and determine which machines can use the router and in what direction.

ACK   See *acknowledgment.*

acknowledgment (ACK)   A message confirming that the data packet was received. Acknowledgment occurs at the Transport layer of the OSI model.

ACL   See *Access Control List.*

active detection   A type of intruder detection that constantly scans the network for possible break-ins.

active monitor   Used in Token Ring networks, a process that prevents data frames from roaming the ring unchecked. If the frame passes the active monitor too many times, it is removed from the ring. An active monitor also ensures that a token is always circulating the ring.

Address Resolution Protocol (ARP)   The protocol within the TCP/IP suite that resolves IP addresses to physical (MAC) addresses.

antivirus   A category of software that uses various methods to eliminate viruses from a computer. The software typically protects against future infection as well. See also *virus.*

Application layer   Layer 7 of the OSI model, which deals with how applications access the network and describes application functionality (file transfer, messaging, and so on). See also *Open Systems Inter-connect (OSI) model.*

Application log Windows NT Log file, viewable in Event Viewer, that is used to keep track of events for network services and applications.

application server Any server that hosts a network application.

ARCNet Acronym for Attached Resource Computer Network, which was developed by Datapoint Corporation in the late 1970s as one of the first baseband networks. ARCNet can use either a physical star or bus topology.

ARP See *Address Resolution Protocol.*

ARP table A table used by the ARP protocol, containing a list of known TCP/IP addresses and their associated MAC addresses. The table is cached in memory so that ARP lookups do not have to be performed for frequently accessed TCP/IP and MAC addresses. See also *Address Resolution Protocol, media-access control,* and *Transmission Control Protocol/Internet Protocol.*

Asynchronous Transfer Mode (ATM) A connection-oriented network architecture based on broadband ISDN technology that uses constant-size 53-byte cells instead of packets. Because cells don't change size, they are switched much faster and more efficiently than packets across a network.

ATM See *Asynchronous Transfer Mode.*

Attachment Unit Interface (AUI) port Port on some NICs that allows the NIC to be connected to different media types by means of an external transceiver.

B Channel See *Bearer Channel.*

Backup Domain Controller (BDC) Computer on a Windows NT network that has a copy of the SAM database for fault-tolerance and performance-enhancement purposes. See also *Security Accounts Manager.*

bandwidth In network communications, the amount of data that can be sent across a wire in a given time. Each communication that passes along the wire decreases the available bandwidth.

baseband A transmission technique in which the signal uses the entire bandwidth of a transmission medium.

baseline A category of network documentation that indicates how the network normally runs. A baseline report includes such information as network statistics, server-use trends, and processor-performance statistics.

Bearer Channel The channels in an ISDN line that carry data. Each Bearer Channel typically has a bandwidth of 64Kbps.

bindery Flat database used in NetWare 3.*x* and earlier servers to store network-resource information (such as user, group, and security information). Each server on the network has its own bindery database.

Bit Fiddler A virus that changes random bits in files.

BNC connector A type of tubular connector most commonly used with coaxial cable.

boot-sector virus A virus that overrides the boot sector, therefore making it appear as though no pointer to your operating system exists. When this virus is active, you see a "missing operating system" or "hard disk not found" error message on power-up.

bounded medium A network medium used at the Physical layer. The signal travels over a cable of some kind.

bridge A network device, operating at the Data Link layer, that logically separates a single network into segments, but makes the two segments appear to higher-layer protocols to be one network.

broadband A network transmission method in which a single transmission medium is divided so that multiple signals can travel across the same medium simultaneously.

brouter A device that combines the functionality of a bridge and a router, but can't be distinctly classified as being either device.

brownout See *power brownout*.

browser A computer program that uses HTTP and is used to access hosts on the World Wide Web.

burst mode   An addition to NCP that allows the sending of multiple data frames without waiting for an acknowledgment on the preceding data frame. See also *NetWare Core Protocol*.

cable   A physical transmission medium that consists of a central conductor of wire or fiber surrounded by a plastic jacket.

cable map   General network documentation indicating each cable's source and destination, as well as where each network cable runs.

cable tester   See *time-domain reflectometer*.

CAD program   Any program that is used during the computer-aided design (CAD) process; typically used by engineers.

Carrier Sense Multiple Access/Collision Avoidance (CSMA/CA)   A media-access method that sends a request-to-send (RTS) packet and waits to receive a clear-to-send (CTS) packet before sending. When the CTS is received, the sender transmits the packet of information.

Carrier Sense Multiple Access/Collision Detection (CSMA/CD)   A media-access method that first senses whether a signal is on the wire, indicating that a device is transmitting. If no other device is transmitting, CSMA/CD attempts a transmission and listens to hear whether another device tries to transmit at the same time. In such a case, both senders back off and don't transmit again until a random period of time has passed.

centralized WAN   A WAN with a computer that connects other computers and dumb terminals to a central site. See also *wide area network*.

CIR   See *Committed Information Rate*.

client-server network   A server-centric network in which all resources are stored on a file server; processing power is distributed among workstations and the file server.

Client Services for NetWare (CSNW)   Software that allows Windows NT computers to access NetWare resources.

clipper chip   A hardware implementation of the skipjack encryption algorithm.

coaxial cable Often referred to as coax; a type of cable used in network wiring. Typical coaxial-cable types include RG-58 and RG-62. 10Base2 Ethernet networks use coaxial cable. Coaxial cable usually is shielded.

cold site backup system A backup system that does not run continuously. Therefore, before you can restore data, you must repair the computer and reload the software on the server.

collision The error condition that occurs when two stations on a CSMA/CD network transmit data (at the Data Link layer) at the same time. See also *Carrier Sense Multiple Access/Collision Detection*.

Committed Information Rate (CIR) A commitment from your Internet Service Provider, stating the minimum bandwidth that you get on a frame-relay network.

concentrator See *hub*.

connectionless protocol A transport protocol, such as UDP, that does not create a virtual connection between sending and receiving stations. See also *User Datagram Protocol*.

connection-oriented protocol A transport protocol that uses acknowledgments and responses to establish a virtual connection between sending and receiving stations. TCP is a connection-oriented protocol. See also *Transmission Control Protocol*.

CONSOLE.LOG A NetWare server log file that keeps a history of all errors and information that have been displayed on the server's console since the CONLOG.NLM file was loaded.

contention A media-access method that allows any computer to transmit whenever it has data. Every station has an equal opportunity to transmit.

country codes The two-letter abbreviations for countries used in the DNS hierarchy. See also *Domain Name Service*.

CRC See *cyclical redundancy check*.

crossover cable The troubleshooting tool used in Ethernet UTP installations to test communications between two stations, bypassing the hub. See also *unshielded twisted-pair cable*.

CSMA/CA See *Carrier Sense Multiple Access/Collision Avoidance.*

CSMA/CD See *Carrier Sense Multiple Access/Collision Detection.*

CSNW See *Client Services for NetWare.*

cyclical redundancy check (CRC) An error-checking method in data communications that runs a formula against data before transmissions occur. The sending station appends the resulting value (called a *checksum*) to the data and then sends it. The receiving station uses the same formula on the data. If the receiving station doesn't get the same checksum result for the calculation, it considers the transmission to be invalid, rejects the frame, and asks for a retransmission.

Data Encryption Standard (DES) A government standard for private-key systems that has lookup-table functions and fast encryption. A 64-bit private key is used. See also *private key* and *public key.*

datagram A unit of data smaller than a packet.

Data Link layer The second layer of the OSI model, which describes the logical topology of a network—the way that packets move throughout a network—as well as the method of media access. See also *Open Systems Interconnect (OSI) model.*

data packet A unit of data sent over a network. A packet includes a header, addressing information, and the data itself. A packet is treated as a single unit as it is sent from device to device.

default gateway The router to which all packets are sent when the workstation doesn't know where the destination station is or when it can't find the destination station on the local segment.

Delta Channel A channel on an ISDN line used for link management. See also *Integrated Services Digital Network.*

demilitarized zone (DMZ) The special area defined by a firewall in which all public-access servers are located, protected from outside attack yet available to users on both sides of the firewall.

Denial of Service (DoS) A type of hack that prevents users—even legitimate users—from using the system.

Department of Defense (DoD) The government agency responsible for defending the United States from any kind of attack (including computer attacks).

DES See *Data Encryption Standard*.

DHCP See *Dynamic Host Configuration Protocol*.

differential backup A backup method that copies only data that has changed since the last full backup.

digital Any signal that has discrete values over time. A digital signal has no transition between values; it has one value in one instant (that is, a specific number, such as 1) and a different value the next (that is, a second number, such as 0).

Digital Subscriber Line (DSL) A digital WAN technology that brings high-speed digital networking to homes and businesses over POTS. Types of DSLs include HDSL (High-Speed DSL) and VDSL (Very High Bit-Rate DSL). See also *Public Switched Telephone Network*.

directory A network database that contains a list of all network resources, such as users, printers, and groups.

directory services A network service that provides access to a central database of information that contains detailed information about the resources available on a network.

disk-drive subsystem The entire set of hard drives, controllers, and software that makes up the storage component of a workstation or a server.

disk drivers NLMs that give NetWare access to the disk channel. See also *NetWare Loadable Module*.

disk striping Technology that enables the writing of data to multiple disks simultaneously, in small portions called *stripes*. These stripes maximize use by having all the read/write heads working constantly. Different data is stored on each disk and is not duplicated automatically, which means that disk striping does not provide fault tolerance.

distance vector   A route-discovery method in which each router, using broadcasts, tells every other router what networks and routes it knows about and the distances to them.

DLL   See *Dynamic Link Library*.

DNNS   See *Dynamic DNS*.

DNS resolver   Client software that makes requests of the DNS server to resolve DNS host names into IP addresses. See also *Domain Name Service* and *Internet Protocol*.

DNS server   Any server that performs DNS-host-name-to-IP-address resolution. See also *Domain Name Service* and *Internet Protocol*.

DNS zone   An area in the DNS hierarchy that is managed as a single unit. See also *Domain Name Service*.

DoD   See *Department of Defense*.

DoD networking model   A four-layer conceptual model that describes how communications between computer systems should take place. The four layers are Process/Application, Host-to-Host, Internet, and Network Access.

domain   A group of networked Windows computers that share a single SAM database. See also *Security Accounts Manager*.

Domain Name Service (DNS)   The network service used in TCP/IP networks that translates host names into IP addresses. See also *Transmission Control Protocol/Internet Protocol*.

drive mapping   The process of assigning a drive letter at the client workstation to a directory or folder on the server.

DSL   See *Digital Subscriber Line*.

D-type connector   A type of network connector that connects computer peripherals. The connector contains rows of pins or sockets arranged in a sideways D.

dumb terminal A keyboard and monitor that send keystrokes to a central-processing computer (typically, a mainframe or minicomputer) and return screen displays to the monitor. The unit has no processing power of its own—hence, the name *dumb*.

duplexed hard drives Two hard drives to which identical information is written simultaneously. A dedicated controller card controls each drive. Used to provide disk fault tolerance for servers.

Dynamic DNS (DNNS) A proposed feature of Windows 2000 that would dynamically assign a DNS host name for network workstations as they are brought online. See also *Domain Name Service*.

dynamic entry An entry made in the ARP table whenever an ARP request is made by the Windows TCP/IP stack and the MAC address is not found in the ARP table. The ARP request is broadcast on the local segment. When the MAC address of the requested IP address is found, that information is added to the ARP table. See also *Address Resolution Protocol, Internet Protocol, media-access control,* and *Transmission Control Protocol/Internet Protocol*.

Dynamic Host Configuration Protocol (DHCP) A protocol used on a TCP/IP-based network to send client configuration data (including TCP/IP address, default gateway, subnet mask, WINS configuration, and DNS configuration) to clients. See also *Domain Name Service, default gateway, subnet mask,* and *Transmission Control Protocol/Internet Protocol*.

Dynamic Link Library (DLL) Small pieces of executable Windows code that Windows programmers use so that they don't have to write commonly used routines into each program.

dynamic packet filtering A type of firewall filtering that accepts or rejects packets.

dynamic routing The use of route-discovery protocols to talk to other routers and find out what networks they are attached to. Routers that use dynamic routing send out special packets to request updates of the other routers on the network, as well as to send their own updates.

dynamic state list A list held on a firewall that changes as communication sessions are added and deleted. Only computers that are in a current communication session are allowed to send information back and forth.

EEPROM   See *Electrically Erasable Programmable Read-Only Memory.*

Electrically Erasable Programmable Read-Only Memory (EEPROM)
A special integrated circuit on expansion cards that allows data to be stored on the chip. If necessary, the data can be erased by a special configuration program. EEPROM typically is used to store hardware-configuration data for expansion cards.

electromagnetic interference (EMI)   The interference that can occur during transmissions over copper cable because of electromagnetic energy outside the cable. The result is degradation of the signal.

electronic mail   An application that allows people to send messages via their computers on the same network or over the Internet.

electrostatic discharge (ESD)   A problem that occurs when two devices that have dissimilar static-electrical charges are brought together. The static-electrical charges jump to the device that has fewer electrical charges, causing ESD, which can damage computer components.

emergency scan   A scan (with an emergency antivirus boot disk) that is made after a virus has taken control of a computer.

EMI   See *electromagnetic interference.*

encoding   The process of translating data into signals that can be transmitted over a transmission medium.

ENS   See *Event Notification Services.*

ESD   See *electrostatic discharge.*

Ethernet   A shared-media network architecture that operates at the Physical and Data Link layers of the OSI model. Ethernet uses baseband signaling over either a bus or a star topology, using CSMA/CD as the media-access method. The cabling used in Ethernet networks can be coax, twisted-pair, or fiber-optic. See also *Carrier Sense Multiple Access/Collision Detection* and *Open Systems Interconnect.*

Event Notification Services (ENS)   A component of Novell Distributed Print Services (NDPS) broker that notifies users and administrators of network-printing events. See also *Novell Distributed Print Services.*

expansion slot A slot on the computer's bus. Expansion cards are plugged into these slots to expand the functionality of the computer. An NIC card, for example, enables the computer to interface a network. See also *network interface card*.

failover server A hot site backup system in which a second, redundant server (the *failover server*) is connected to the primary server. A heartbeat is sent from the primary server to the backup server. If the heartbeat stops, the failover system starts and takes over. Thus, the system doesn't go down, although the primary server is not running.

fault-resistant network A network that is up and running at least 99 percent of the time or that is down fewer than eight hours a year.

fault-tolerant network A network that can recover from minor errors.

fax server A computer with a special fax board that sends and receives faxes without the need for paper. The device delivers and receives faxes for the entire network.

FDDI See *Fiber Distributed Data Interface*.

FDM See *frequency-division multiplexing*.

Fiber Distributed Data Interface (FDDI) A network topology that uses fiber-optic cable as a transmission medium and dual, counter-rotating rings to provide data delivery and fault tolerance.

fiber-optic A type of network cable that uses a central glass or plastic core surrounded by a plastic coating.

Fiber Channel A type of server-to-storage system connection that uses fiber-optic connectors.

File and Print Services for NetWare (FPNW) A method of providing files and printers hosted by Windows NT to Novell clients. When installed and configured on a Windows NT server, this service makes a Windows NT server look like a NetWare server to Novell clients.

file server A server that specializes in storing and distributing files.

File Transfer Protocol (FTP)   A TCP/IP protocol and software that permit the transfer of files between computer systems. Because FTP has been implemented on numerous types of computer systems, files can be transferred between disparate computer systems (such as a personal computer and a minicomputer). See also *Transmission Control Protocol/Internet Protocol*.

firewall   A combination of hardware and software that protects a network from attack by hackers who could gain access through public networks, including the Internet.

FPNW   See *File and Print Services for NetWare*.

FQDN   See *Fully Qualified Domain Name*.

frame relay   A WAN technology that transmits packets over a WAN by means of packet switching. See also *packet switching*.

frequency-division multiplexing (FDM)   The division of a single transmission medium into multiple channels so that multiple signals can be carried on the medium simultaneously, each using a different frequency.

FTP   See *File Transfer Protocol*.

FTP proxy   A server that uploads and downloads files from a server on behalf of a workstation.

full backup   A backup that copies all the data to the archive medium.

Fully Qualified Domain Name (FQDN)   An address that uses both the host name (workstation name) and the domain name.

gateway   The hardware and software needed to connect two disparate network environments so that communications can occur.

Gateway Services for NetWare   Software installed as a service on a Windows NT server that translates requests for Windows NT resources into NetWare requests. The software also translates Server Message Block (SMB) protocol requests into NCP requests. The software allows multiple Windows NT clients to connect through a Windows NT server to NetWare servers by using only Windows NT client software and protocols. See also *NetWare Core Protocol*.

global group A type of group in Windows NT that is used throughout a network. Members can be anywhere on the network, and rights can be assigned to any resource on the network.

grandfather-father-son (GFS) backup method A standard rotation scheme for backup tapes. Daily backups are the son, the last full backup of the week is the father, and the last full backup of the month is the grandfather.

ground loop A condition that occurs when a signal cycles through a common ground connection between two devices, causing EMI. See also *electromagnetic interference*.

grouping A method of organizing users that eases network administration. Groups can include administrator groups, printer groups, and so on.

HAL See *Hardware Abstraction Layer*.

HAM See *Host Adapter Module*.

Hardware Abstraction Layer (HAL) The layer in the Windows NT architecture that makes Windows NT platform-independent. Running Windows NT on a platform other than the commonly accepted choices (Intel, MIPS, and Alpha) requires a new HAL.

hardware address A Data Link layer address assigned to every NIC at the MAC sublayer. The address is in the format *xx:xx:xx:xx:xx:xx*. Each xx represents a two-digit hexadecimal number. See also *network interface card* and *media-access control*.

Hardware Compatibility List (HCL) The list of Microsoft-recommended hardware for running Windows operating-system software. Hardware must be on this list to be truly compatible with Windows operating systems.

hardware loopback A method that connects the transmission pins directly to the receiving pins, allowing diagnostic software to test whether an NIC can successfully transmit and receive. See also *network interface card*.

HCL See *Hardware Compatibility List*.

header The section of a packet in which the source and destination addresses reside.

hop   One pass through a router. See also *router*.

host   Any network device that has a TCP/IP network address. See also *Transmission Control Protocol/Internet Protocol*.

Host Adapter Module (HAM)   A feature of the NetWare Peripheral Architecture that provides communication with the host adapter.

Host-to-Host layer   A layer in the DoD model that corresponds to the Transport layer of the OSI model. See also *DoD networking model* and *Open Systems Interconnect*.

hot backup system   A complete duplicate of a set of computing services, stored in a server room. In the event of failure of the main system, the system can take over operation without any down time.

HTML   See *Hypertext Markup Language*.

HTTP   See *Hypertext Transfer Protocol*.

hub   A Physical-layer device that serves as a central connection point for several network devices. A hub repeats the signals that it receives on one port to all other ports.

Hypertext Markup Language (HTML)   A set of codes used to format text and graphics that will be displayed in a browser. The codes define how data will be displayed.

Hypertext Transfer Protocol (HTTP)   The protocol used for communication between a Web server and a Web browser.

IBM data connector   A connector used to connect IBM Token Ring stations with Type 1 STP cable. This connector is both male and female, so every IBM data connector can connect to any other IBM data connector. See also *shielded twisted-pair cable*.

ICMP   See *Internet Control Message Protocol*.

IEEE   See *Institute of Electrical and Electronics Engineers*.

IEEE 802.*x* standards   The IEEE standards for LAN and MAN networking.

IEEE 802.1 LAN/MAN Management A standard that specifies LAN/MAN network management and internetworking.

IEEE 802.2 Logical Link Control A standard that specifies the operation of the Logical Link Control (LLC) sublayer of the Data Link layer of the OSI model. The LLC sublayer provides an interface between the MAC sublayer and the network layer. See also *media-access control* and *Open Systems Interconnect*.

IEEE 802.3 CSMA/CD Networking A standard that specifies a network that uses a logical bus topology, baseband signaling, and a CSMA/CD network-access method. See also *Carrier Sense Multiple Access/Collision Detection*.

IEEE 802.4 Token Bus A standard that specifies a physical and logical bus topology that uses coaxial or fiber-optic cable and the token-passing media-access method.

IEEE 802.5 Token Ring A standard that specifies a logical ring, physical star, and token-passing media-access method based on IBM's Token Ring.

IEEE 802.6 Distributed Queue Dual Bus (DQDB) Metropolitan Area Network A standard that provides a definition and criteria for a DQDB metropolitan area network (MAN). See also *metropolitan area network*.

IEEE 802.7 Broadband Local Area Networks A standard for broadband cabling technology.

IEEE 802.8 Fiber-Optic LANs and MANs A standard containing guidelines for the use of fiber optics on networks, including FDDI and Ethernet over fiber-optic cable. See also *Fiber Distributed Data Interface* and *Ethernet*.

IEEE 802.9 Integrated Services (IS) LAN Interface A standard containing guidelines for the integration of voice and data over the same cable.

IEEE 802.10 LAN/MAN Security A series of guidelines dealing with various aspects of network security.

IEEE 802.11 Wireless LAN A standard for implementing wireless technologies such as infrared and spread-spectrum radio.

IEEE 802.12 Demand Priority Access Method   A standard that combines the concepts of Ethernet and ATM. See also *Asynchronous Transfer Mode* and *Ethernet*.

IETF   See *Internet Engineering Task Force*.

incremental backup   A backup method that copies only data that has changed since the last full or incremental backup.

Institute of Electrical and Electronics Engineers (IEEE)   An international organization that sets standards for various electrical and electronics issues.

Integrated Services Digital Network (ISDN)   A telecommunications standard for digital transmission of voice, data, and video signals over the same lines.

Intel 386 (I386) architecture   A platform that includes the 386, 486, Pentium, Pentium Pro, Pentium II, and Pentium III processors.

International Organization for Standardization (ISO)   The standards organization that developed the OSI model. This model provides a guideline for communications between computers.

Internet   A global network made up of a large number of individual networks connected through public telephone lines and TCP/IP protocols. See also *Transmission Control Protocol/Internet Protocol*.

Internet Architecture Board (IAB)   The committee that oversees management of the Internet. The IAB is made up of two subcommittees: the Internet Engineering Task Force (IETF) and the Internet Research Task Force (IRTF). See also *Internet Engineering Task Force* and *Internet Research Task Force*.

Internet Control Message Protocol (ICMP)   A message and management protocol for TCP/IP. The Ping utility uses ICMP. See also *Ping* and *Transmission Control Protocol/Internet Protocol*.

Internet Engineering Task Force (IETF)   An international organization that works under the Internet Architecture Board to establish standards and protocols relating to the Internet. See also *Internet Architecture Board*.

Internet layer   Layer of the DoD networking model that corresponds to the Network layer of the OSI model. See also *Open Systems Interconnect*.

Internet Protocol (IP)   The protocol in the TCP/IP protocol suite that is responsible for network addressing and routing. See also *Transmission Control Protocol/Internet Protocol*.

Internet Research Task Force   An international organization that works under the Internet Architecture Board to research new Internet technologies. See also *Internet Architecture Board*.

Internet Service Provider (ISP)   A company that provides direct access to the Internet for home and business computer users.

Internetwork Packet Exchange (IPX)   A connectionless, routable network protocol based on the Xerox XNS architecture. IPX is the default protocol for versions of NetWare earlier than NetWare 5. IPX operates at the Network layer of the OSI model and is responsible for addressing and routing packets to workstations or servers on other networks. See also *Open Systems Interconnect*.

IP   See *Internet Protocol*.

IP address   An address used by the Internet Protocol that identifies the device's location on the network.

IP proxy   A network device that makes all communications look as though they originated from a proxy server, because the IP address of the user who makes a request is hidden. IP proxy is also known as network-address translation (NAT).

IP spoofing   A situation in which a hacker tries to gain access to a network by pretending that his machine has the same network address as the internal network.

ipconfig   A Windows NT utility used to display that machine's current configuration.

IPX   See *Internetwork Packet Exchange*.

IPX network address   A number that represents an entire network. All servers on the network must use the same external network number.

ISDN See *Integrated Services Digital Network.*

ISDN terminal adapter The device used on ISDN networks to connect a local network (or single machine) to an ISDN network. The device provides power to the line and translates data from the LAN or individual computer for transmission on the ISDN line. See also *Integrated Services Digital Network.*

ISP See *Internet Service Provider.*

Java A programming language, developed by Sun Microsystems, that is used to write programs that will run on any platform that has a Java Virtual Machine installed.

Java Virtual Machine (JVM) Software, developed by Sun Microsystems, that creates a virtual Java computer on which Java programs can run. A programmer writes a program once, without having to recompile or rewrite the program for all platforms.

jumper A small connector (cap or plug) that connects pins, creating a circuit that indicates a setting to a device.

JVM See *Java Virtual Machine.*

kernel The central component of any operating system, managing all resources (memory, disk space, communications, and so on) for the operating system.

LAN See *local area network.*

LAN driver The interface between the NetWare kernel and the NIC installed in the server; also, a general category of drivers used to enable communications between an operating system and an NIC. See also *network interface card* and *kernel.*

Large Internet Packet (LIP) A technology used by the IPX protocol so that IPX can use the largest possible packet size during a transmission. See also *Internetwork Packet Exchange.*

laser printer A printer that uses a laser to form an image on a photosensitive drum. The image is then developed with toner and transferred to paper. Finally, a heated drum fuses toner particles onto the paper.

Layer 2 switch A switching hub that operates at the Data Link layer and builds a table of the MAC addresses of all the connected stations. See also *media-access control*.

Layer 3 switch Functioning at the Network layer, a switch that performs the multiport, virtual-LAN, data-pipelining functions of a standard Layer 2 switch, but that can perform basic routing functions between virtual LANs.

LCP See *Link Control Protocol*.

line conditioner A device used for protection against power surges and spikes. Line conditioners use several electronic methods to clean all power that comes out of the line conditioner.

Link Control Protocol (LCP) The protocol used to establish, configure, and test the link between a client and PPP host. See also *Point-to-Point Protocol*.

link light A small light-emitting diode (LED) located on both the NIC and the hub. The light usually is green and labeled Link (or something similar). A link light indicates that the NIC and the hub are making a Data Link layer connection. See also *hub* and *network interface card*.

link-state route discovery A route-discovery method that transmits special packets (Link State Packets, or LSPs) that contain information about the networks to which the router is connected.

link-state routing A type of routing that broadcasts its entire routing tables only at startup and possibly at infrequently scheduled intervals. Apart from those times, the router sends messages to other routers only when changes are made in the router's routing table.

Link Support Layer (LSL) Part of the Novell client software that acts as a sort of switchboard between the Open Datalink Interface (ODI) LAN drivers and the various transport protocols.

Linux A version of Unix developed by Linus Torvalds. Linux runs on Intel-based PCs and generally is free. See also *Unix*.

LIP See *Large Internet Packet*.

local area network (LAN)   A network that is restricted to a single building, group of buildings, or even a single room. A LAN can have one or more servers.

local groups   Groups created on individual servers. Rights can be assigned only to local resources.

locus destination   In NetWare, an indicator of which component system is affected by an error message.

log file   A file that keeps a running list of all errors and notices, the times and dates when they occurred, and any other pertinent information.

logical bus topology   A type of topology in which the signal travels the distance of the cable and is received by all stations on the backbone. See also *backbone*.

logical link control (LLC)   A sublayer of the Data Link layer that provides an interface between the MAC sublayer and the Network layer. See also *media-access control* and *topology*.

logical network addressing   The addressing scheme used by protocols at the Network layer.

logical parallel port   The port used by the CAPTURE command to redirect a workstation printer port to a network print queue. The logical port has no relation to the port to which the printer is actually attached (the physical port). See also *physical parallel port*.

logical port address   A value that is used at the Transport layer to differentiate among the upper-layer services.

logical ring topology   A network topology in which all network signals travel from one station to another in a ring configuration, being read and forwarded by each station.

logical topology   A description of the way that information flows on a network. The types of logical topologies are the same as the physical topologies, except that the information flow specifies the type of topology.

LSL   See *Link Support Layer*.

MAC See *media-access control*.

macro A script of commands that can be invoked with a single keystroke.

mail server A server that hosts and delivers e-mail.

MAN See *metropolitan area network*.

manufacturer's readme file A file that the manufacturer includes with software to give the installer information that does not appear in the software manuals. The file usually is a last-minute addition that includes tips on installing the software, possible incompatibilities, and any known installation problems that were discovered just before the product was shipped.

MAU See *Multistation Access Unit*.

media access The process of vying for transmission time on the network medium.

media-access control (MAC) A sublayer of the Data Link layer that controls the way that multiple devices use the same media channel. MAC controls which devices can transmit and when they can transmit.

member server A computer that has Windows NT Server installed but doesn't have a copy of the SAM database. See also *Security Accounts Manager*.

metropolitan area network (MAN) A network that encompasses an entire city or metropolitan area.

mirrored hard drive Two drives to which the same information is written. Therefore, if one of the drives fails, the information can be retrieved from the other drive. A single drive controller controls both drives. A mirrored hard drive is used for disk fault tolerance in a server.

multiple server backup A system in which multiple servers run continuously, each providing backup and production services at the same time. In this type of system, if a server fails, another takes over, without any interruption of service.

Multistation Access Unit (MAU) The central device in Token Ring networks that acts as the connection point for all stations and that facilitates the formation of the logical ring.

name resolution The process of translating (resolving) logical host names into network addresses.

name-space NLM A software component of the NetWare architecture that allows different file types to be stored and accessed on NetWare servers.

naming-conventions document A type of SOP that specifies how network entities are named. Some common items that have entries in the naming-convention document are servers, printers, user accounts, and test accounts. See also *standard operating procedures*.

NAT Acronym for network-address translation. See *IP proxy*.

National Computing Security Center (NCSC) The agency that developed the Trusted Computer System Evaluation Criteria (TCSEC) and the Trusted Network Interpretation Environmental Guideline (TNIEG).

NBTSTAT (NetBIOS over TCP/IP Statistics) The Windows TCP/IP utility that displays NetBIOS-over-TCP/IP statistics. See also *Network Basic Input/Output System* and *Transmission Control Protocol/Internet Protocol*.

NCP See *NetWare Core Protocol*.

NCSC See *National Computing Security Center*.

NDPS See *Novell Distributed Print Services*.

NDS See *Novell Directory Services*.

NDS tree A logical representation of a network's resources. Resources are represented by objects in the tree. The tree is often patterned on a company's functional structure. Objects can represent organizations, departments, users, servers, printers, and other resources. See also *Novell Directory Services*.

NetBEUI A transport protocol, based on the NetBIOS protocol, that has datagram support and support for connectionless transmissions. See also *Network Basic Input/Output System*.

NetBIOS See *Network Basic Input/Output System*.

NETSTAT A utility that determines which TCP/IP connections, inbound and outbound, the computer has. NETSTAT also allows the user to view packet statistics, such as how many have been sent and received. See also *Transmission Control Protocol/Internet Protocol*.

NetWare The network operating system made by Novell.

NetWare 3.*x* The version series of NetWare that supports multiple cross-platform clients with fairly minimal hardware requirements. The software uses a database called the bindery to keep track of users and groups, and is administrated with several DOS menu-based utilities (such as SYSCON, PCONSOLE, and FILER).

NetWare 4.*x* The version series of NetWare that includes NDS. See also *Novell Directory Services*.

NetWare 5.*x* The version series of NetWare that includes a multiprocessing kernel. The software also includes a five-user version of Oracle 8, a relational database, and the capability to use TCP/IP in its pure form.

NetWare Administrator The utility used to administer NetWare versions 4.*x* and later by making changes in the NDS directory. This utility is the only administrative utility needed to modify NDS objects and their properties. See also *Novell Directory Services*.

NetWare Core Protocol (NCP) The upper-layer NetWare protocol that functions on top of IPX and provides NetWare-resource access to workstations. See also *Internetwork Packet Exchange*.

NetWare Link State Protocol (NLSP) A protocol that gathers routing information based on the link-state routing method. The precursor of NLSP is Routing Information Protocol (RIP). NLSP is a more efficient routing protocol than RIP. See also *link-state routing*.

NetWare Loadable Module (NLM) A component used to give a NetWare server additional services and functionality. Unneeded services can be unloaded, thus conserving memory.

network-address translation (NAT) See *IP proxy*.

Network Basic Input/Output System (NetBIOS) A Session-layer protocol that opens communication sessions for applications that want to communicate on a network.

network-centric A term for network operating systems that use directory services that maintain information about the entire network.

Network File System (NFS) A protocol that enables users to access files on remote computers as though the files were local.

network interface card (NIC) A physical device that connects computers and other network equipment to the transmission medium.

Network layer Layer three of the OSI model, which is responsible for logical addressing and translating logical names into physical addresses. This layer also controls the routing of data from source to destination, as well as for the building and dismantling of packets. See also *Open Systems Interconnect*.

network media The physical cables that link computers in a network; also known as *physical media*.

network operating system (NOS) The software that runs on a network server, offering file, print, application, and other services to clients.

Network Support Encyclopedia (NSEPro) See *Novell Support Connection*.

NFS See *Network File System*.

NIC See *network interface card*.

NIC diagnostics Software utilities that verify that the NIC is functioning correctly and that test every aspect of NIC operation. See also *network interface card*.

NIC driver See *LAN driver*.

NLM See *NetWare Loadable Module*.

NLSP See *NetWare Link State Protocol*.

nonunicast packet A packet that is not sent directly from one workstation to another.

NOS See *network operating system*.

Novell Directory Services (NDS) A NetWare service that provides access to a global, hierarchical directory database of network entities that can be centrally managed.

Novell Distributed Print Services (NDPS)   A printing system, designed by Novell, that uses NDS to install and manage printers. NDPS supports automatic network-printer installation, automatic distribution of client printer drivers, and centralized printer management without the use of print queues.

Novell Support Connection   Novell's database of technical-information documents, files, patches, fixes, NetWare Application Notes, Novell lab bulletins, Novell professional-developer bulletins, answers to frequently asked questions, and other information. The database is available from Novell and is updated quarterly.

NT Directory Services (NTDS)   A system of domains and trusts for a Windows NT Server network.

NTDS   See *NT Directory Services*.

ODI   See *Open Datalink Interface*.

on-access scan   An antivirus scan that is run in the background as a file or a program is opened.

on-demand scan   An antivirus scan that a network administrator or user schedules manually or automatically.

Open Datalink Interface (ODI)   A driver specification, developed by Novell, that enables a single workstation to communicate transparently with several protocol stacks, using a single NIC and a single NIC driver.

OpenLinux   A version of the Linux network operating system developed by Caldera.

Open Systems Interconnect (OSI) model   A model defined by the ISO to categorize the process of communication between computers in terms of seven layers. See also *International Organization for Standardization*.

Oracle 8   Oracle's leading relational database software. A five-user copy is included with NetWare 5.*x*.

Orange Book   General term for the TCSEC. See also *Trusted Computer System Evaluation Criteria*.

OSI model   See *Open Systems Interconnect model*.

OS/2 Applications (OS/2 Subsystem)   A Windows NT feature that can run OS/2 applications, although the applications must use only the pure OS/2 development tools and run only in character mode. OS/2 graphical applications are not supported.

oversampling   A method of synchronous bit synchronization in which the receiver samples the signal at a much faster rate than the data rate. This method permits the use of an encoding method that does not add clocking transitions.

overvoltage threshold   The level of overvoltage that trips the circuit breaker in a surge protector.

packet   The basic division of data sent over a network.

packet switching   The process of breaking messages into packets at the sending router for easier transmission over a WAN.

passive detection   A type of intruder detection that logs all network events to a file for an administrator to view later.

patch   Software that fixes a problem with an existing program or operating system.

patch cable   Any cable that connects one network device to the main cable run or to a patch panel that in turn connects to the main cable run.

patch panel   A central wiring point for multiple devices on a UTP network. See also *unshielded twisted-pair cable*.

PDC   See *Primary Domain Controller*.

peer-to-peer network   Computers hooked together that have no centralized authority. Each computer is equal and can act as both a server and a workstation.

Permanent Virtual Circuit (PVC)   A technology used by frame relay that allows virtual data communications (circuits) to be set up between sender and receiver over a packet-switched network.

PGP   See *Pretty Good Privacy*.

physical bus topology A network that uses one network cable that runs from one end of the network to the other. Workstations connect at various points along this cable.

Physical layer Layer one of the OSI model, controlling the functional interface. See also *Open Systems Interconnect*.

physical media See *network media*.

physical mesh topology A network configuration that specifies a link between all devices on the network.

physical parallel port A port on the back of a computer that allows a printer to be connected with a parallel cable.

physical port An opening on a network device that allows a cable of some kind to be connected. Ports allow devices to be connected with cables.

physical ring topology A network topology that is set up in a circular fashion. Data travels around the ring in one direction, and each device on the ring acts as a repeater to keep the signal strong as it travels. Each device incorporates a receiver for the incoming signal and a transmitter to send the data on to the next device in the ring. The network depends on the signal's capability to travel around the ring.

physical star topology A network topology in which a cable runs from each network entity to a central device called a hub. The hub allows all devices to communicate as though they were directly connected. See also *hub*.

physical topology The physical layout of a network, such as bus, star, ring, or mesh.

Ping A TCP/IP utility that tests whether another host is reachable. An ICMP request is sent to the host, which responds if it is reachable. The request times out if the host is not reachable. See also *ICMP*.

Ping of Death A large ICMP packet sent to overflow the remote host's buffer, usually causing the remote host to reboot or hang. See also *ICMP*.

Plain Old Telephone Service (POTS) Another name for Public Switched Telephone Network (PSTN). See *Public Switched Telephone Network*.

plenum-rated coating Coaxial cable coating that does not produce toxic gas when burned.

point-to-point Network communication in which two devices have exclusive access to a network medium. A printer connected to only one workstation would be using a point-to-point connection.

Point-to Point Protocol (PPP) The protocol used with dial-up connections to the Internet. The protocol's functions include error control, security, dynamic IP addressing, and support for multiple protocols.

Point-to-Point Tunneling Protocol (PPTP) A protocol that allows the creation of Virtual Private Networks (VPNs), which allow users to access a server on a corporate network over a secure, direct connection via the Internet. See also *Virtual Private Network*.

polling A media-access-control method that uses a central device called a controller, which polls each device and asks whether it has data to transmit.

POP3 See *Post Office Protocol*.

port An opening that allows network data to pass through. See also *logical port* and *physical port*.

Post Office Protocol (POP3) The protocol used to download e-mail from an e-mail server to a network client. See also *Simple Mail Transfer Protocol*.

POTS Acronym for Plain Old Telephone Service. See *Public Switched Telephone Network*.

power blackout A total loss of power that may last for a few seconds or several hours.

power brownout A condition in which power drops below normal levels for several seconds or longer.

power overage A condition in which too much power is coming into the computer. See also *power spike* and *power surge*.

power sag A condition in which the power level drops below normal and rises to normal in less than a second.

power spike A condition in which the power level rises above normal and drops back to normal for less than a second.

power surge A condition in which the power level rises above normal and stays there for longer than a second.

power underage A situation in which the power level drops below the standard level. See also *power sag*.

PPP See *Point-to-Point Protocol*.

PPTP See *Point-to-Point Tunneling Protocol*.

Presentation layer Layer six of the OSI model, responsible for formatting data exchanges, such as graphic commands and conversion of character sets. This layer is also responsible for data compression, data encryption, and data-stream redirection. See also *Open Systems Interconnect*.

Pretty Good Privacy (PGP) A shareware implementation of RSA encryption. See also *RSA Data Security, Inc.*

Primary Domain Controller (PDC) A Windows NT server that contains a master copy of the SAM database. This database contains all usernames, passwords, and Access Control Lists for a Windows NT domain. See also *Security Accounts Manager*.

print server A centralized device that controls and manages all network printers. The print server can be hardware, software, or a combination of both. Some print servers are built into network-printer NICs. See also *network interface card*.

print services The network services that manage and control printing on a network, allowing multiple and simultaneous access to printers.

private key A technology in which both the sender and the receiver have the same key. A single key is used to encrypt and decrypt all messages. See also *public key*.

proactive defense A type of intruder defense that allows a person to ensure that the network is invulnerable to attack.

profile   A network-management concept used in Windows NT to define the user's environment. A user's Desktop colors and icons, program groups, Start-menu settings, and network connections are retained in a profile.

protocol   A predefined set of rules that dictate how computers or devices communicate and exchange data on the network.

protocol analyzer   A software-and-hardware troubleshooting tool that decodes protocol information to determine the source of a network problem and to establish baselines.

proxy   A type of firewall that prevents direct communication between a client and a host by acting as an intermediary. See also *firewall*.

proxy cache server   An implementation of a Web proxy. The server receives an HTTP request from a Web browser and makes the request on behalf of the sending workstation. When the response comes, the proxy cache server caches a copy of the response locally. The next time someone makes a request for the same Web page or Internet information, the proxy cache server can fulfill the request out of the cache instead of retrieving the resource from the Web.

proxy server   A type of server that makes a single Internet connection and services requests on behalf of many users.

PSTN   See *Public Switched Telephone Network*.

public key   A technology that uses two keys to facilitate communication: a public key and a private key. The public key is used to encrypt a message sent to a receiver. See also *private key*.

Public Switched Telephone Network (PSTN)   The U.S. public telephone network, also called Plain Old Telephone Service (POTS).

PVC   See *Permanent Virtual Circuit*.

QoS   See *Quality of Service*.

Quality of Service (QoS)   Data prioritization at the Network layer of the OSI model. QoS results in guaranteed throughput rates. See also *Open Systems Interconnect*.

radio-frequency interference (RFI) Interference on copper cabling systems caused by radio signals.

RAID See *redundant array of independent (or inexpensive) disks*.

Red Book General term for the TNIEG. See also *Trusted Network Interpretation Environments Guideline*.

reduced-instruction-set computing (RISC) A computer architecture in which the computer executes small, general-purpose instructions very rapidly.

redundant array of independent (or inexpensive) disks (RAID) A configuration of multiple hard drives used to provide fault tolerance should a drive fail. Different levels of RAID exist, depending on the amount and type of fault tolerance provided.

regeneration Process in which signals are read, amplified, and repeated on the network to reduce signal degradation, resulting in longer possible length of the network.

remote-access server A computer that has one or more modems installed to enable remote connections to the network.

repeater A Physical-layer device that amplifies and regenerates the signals that it receives on one port and resends or repeats them on another port. A repeater is used to extend the maximum length of a network segment.

RFI See *radio-frequency interference*.

RG-58 The type designation for the coaxial cable used in thin Ethernet (10Base2). RG-58 has a 50-ohm impedance rating and uses BNC connectors.

RG-62 The type designation for the coaxial cable used in ARCNet networks. RG-62 has a 93-ohm impedance rating and uses BNC connectors.

RIP See *Router Information Protocol*.

RISC See *reduced-instruction-set computing*.

RJ connector A modular connection mechanism that allows for as many as eight copper wires (four pairs), commonly used in phone (RJ-11) or 10BaseT (RJ-45) connections.

roaming profiles   Profiles downloaded from a server at each login. When a user logs out at the end of the session, changes are made and remembered for use the next time that the user logs in.

router   A device that connects two networks and allows packets to be transmitted and received between them. A router determines the best path for data packets from source to destination.

Router Information Protocol (RIP)   A distance-vector route-discovery protocol used by IP or IPX. RIP uses hops and ticks to determine the cost of a particular route. Although both IP and IPX use RIP, the versions of each protocol are protocol-dependent. See also *Internetwork Packet Exchange* and *IP*.

routing   A function of the Network layer that involves moving data throughout a network. Data passes through several network segments, using routers that can select the path that the data takes. See also *router*.

routing information table   A table that contains information about the location of other routers on the network and their distances from the current router.

RSA Data Security, Inc.   A commercial company that produces encryption software. *RSA* stands for Rivest, Shamir, Adleman, the founders of the company.

SAM   See *Security Accounts Manager*.

Secure Hypertext Transfer Protocol (S-HTTP)   A protocol used for secure communications between a Web server and a Web browser.

Security Accounts Manager (SAM)   A database in Windows NT that contains information about all the users and groups, and their associated rights and settings within a Windows NT domain.

Security log   A log file used in Windows NT to keep track of security events specified by the domain's audit policy.

segment   A unit of data smaller than a packet; also, a portion of a larger network. (A network can consist of multiple network segments.)

Sequenced Packet Exchange (SPX)   A connection-oriented protocol that is part of the IPX protocol suite. SPX operates at the Transport layer of the OSI model. The protocol initiates the connection between the sender and receiver, transmits the data, and then terminates the connection. See also *Internetwork Packet Exchange* and *Open Systems Interconnect*.

Serial Line Internet Protocol (SLIP)   A protocol that permits the transmission of IP packets over a serial connection.

server   A computer that provides resources to its clients on the network.

server configuration documents   General network documentation that includes information such as the current hardware configuration, currently installed software packages, and any installed patches.

server log file   A log file that lists errors that occur on the server.

Services for Macintosh (SFM)   Software that must be installed and configured before a Macintosh can access a Windows NT server.

Session layer   Layer five of the OSI model, which determines how two computers establish, use, and end a session. Security authentication and network naming functions required for applications occur at this layer. The Session layer establishes, maintains, and breaks dialogues between two stations. See also *Open Systems Interconnect*.

SFM   See *Services for Macintosh*.

Share-level security   A network security model in which instead of assigning rights for network resources to users, the administrator assigns passwords to individual files or other network resources (such as printers) and then gives these passwords to all users who need access to these resources. All resources are visible from anywhere on the network, and any user who knows the password for a particular network resource can make changes in it.

shielded twisted-pair cable   A type of cabling that includes pairs of copper conductors, twisted around each other, inside a metal or foil shield. This medium can support faster speeds than nonshielded wiring.

S-HTTP   See *Secure Hypertext Transfer Protocol*.

signal encoding The process whereby a protocol at the Physical layer receives information from the upper layers and translates all the data into signals that can be transmitted on a transmission medium.

signaling The process of transmitting data across the medium. Two types of signaling are digital and analog.

Simple Mail Transfer Protocol (SMTP) A program that looks for mail on SMTP servers and sends it along the network to its destination at another SMTP server.

Simple Network Management Protocol (SNMP) The management protocol created for sending information about the health of the network to network-management consoles.

Skipjack An encryption algorithm developed as a possible replacement for Data Encryption Standard (DES); classified by the National Security Agency (NSA). Not much is known about this encryption algorithm, except that it uses an 80-bit key.

SLIP See *Serial Line Internet Protocol*.

SMTP See *Simple Mail Transfer Protocol*.

SNMP See *Simple Network Management Protocol*.

Solaris An operating system based on Unix that adds the following capabilities: multithreading, symmetric multiprocessing, and real-time processing. Solaris can mount remote files automatically and includes utilities for configuring networks and installing software.

SOP See *standard operating procedures*.

source address The address of the station that sent a packet, usually located in the source area of a packet header.

SPS See *Standby Power Supply*.

SPX See *Sequenced Packet Exchange*.

standard operating procedures (SOP) The policies and guidelines outlining company standards and procedures; usually located in a company manual.

Standby Power Supply (SPS) A power-backup device that sends power directly to the protected equipment. A sensor monitors the power. When a loss is detected, the computer is switched over to the battery. Thus, a loss of power might occur (typically, for less than a second).

static entry An entry that is added to a TCP/IP ARP table manually. See also *Address Resolution Protocol.*

static routing A process in which the network administrator manually programs the router's routing table.

subdomains A logical grouping of domains into zones.

subnet mask A group of selected bits that identify a subnetwork within a TCP/IP network. See also *Transmission Control Protocol/Internet Protocol.*

subnetwork A network that is part of another network. The connection is made through a gateway, switch, or router.

surge protector A device that contains a special electronic circuit that monitors the incoming voltage level and then trips a circuit breaker when an overvoltage reaches a certain level. See also *overvoltage threshold.*

SYN flood A Denial of Service attack in which the hacker sends a barrage of SYN packets. The receiving station tries to respond to each SYN request for a connection, thereby tying up all the receiving station's resources. All incoming connections are rejected until all current connections can be established.

SYSCON The DOS menu-based utility used to administrate NetWare 3.*x*.

System log The Windows NT log file that keeps track of system-related events that occur on a computer.

TCP See *Transmission Control Protocol.*

TCP/IP See *Transmission Control Protocol/Internet Protocol.*

TCSEC See *Trusted Computer System Evaluation Criteria.*

TDMA See *Time Division Multiple Access.*

TDR See *time-domain reflectometer.*

telephony server   A computer that functions as a "smart" answering machine for the network. The server can also perform call-center and call-routing functions.

Telnet   A protocol that functions at the Application layer of the OSI model, providing terminal-emulation capabilities. See also *Open Systems Interconnect*.

template   A set of guidelines that can be applied to every new user account.

terminal emulator   A program that allows a PC to act as a terminal for a mainframe or a Unix system.

terminator   A device that prevents a signal from bouncing off the end of the network cable, which would cause interference with other signals.

test account   An account set up by an administrator to confirm the basic functionality of a newly installed application, for example. The test account has equal rights to accounts that will use the new functionality.

TFTP   See *Trivial File Transfer Protocol*.

Time Division Multiple Access (TDMA)   A method of dividing individual channels in broadband communications into separate time slots, allowing more data to be carried at the same time. TDMA also can be used in baseband communications.

time-domain reflectometer (TDR)   A tool, also called a *cable tester*, that sends out a signal and measures how much time the signal takes to return. The device is used to find short or open circuits.

time to live (TTL)   A field in IP packets that indicates how many routers the packet can cross (hops it can make) before it is discarded. TTL is also used in ARP tables to indicate how long an entry should remain in the table. See also *Address Resolution Protocol*.

TNIEG   See *Trusted Network Interpretation Environmental Guideline*.

token passing   A media-access method in which a token (data packet) is passed around the ring in an orderly fashion from one device to the next. A station can transmit only when it has the token. If it doesn't have the token, it can't transmit. The token continues around the network until the original sender receives the token again. If the token has more data to send, the process repeats. If not, the original sender modifies the token to indicate that the token is free for any other device to use.

Token Ring network A network based on a physical star, logical ring topology, in which data is passed along the ring until it finds its intended receiver. Only one data packet can be passed along the ring at a time. If the data packet goes around the ring without being claimed, it is returned to the sender.

tone generator A small electronic device, used with a tone locator to test network cables for breaks and other problems. The device sends an electronic signal down one set of UTP wires. See also *tone locator* and *unshielded twisted-pair cable*.

tone locator A device used with a tone generator to test network cables for breaks and other problems. The device senses the signal sent by the tone generator and emits a tone when the signal is detected in a particular set of wires. See also *tone generator*.

topology The physical and/or logical layout of the transmission media specified in the physical and logical layers of the OSI model. See also *Open Systems Interconnect*.

tracert The TCP/IP trace-route command-line utility that shows the user every router interface that a TCP/IP packet passes through on its way to a destination. See also *Transmission Control Protocol/Internet Protocol*.

trailer A section of a data packet that contains error-checking information.

transceivers The part of any network interface that transmits and receives network signals.

transient A high-voltage burst of current.

Transmission Control Protocol (TCP) The protocol located at the Host-to-Host layer of the DoD networking model. This protocol breaks data packets into segments, numbers them, and sends them in random order. The receiving computer reassembles the data so that the user can read the information. In the process, the sender and the receiver confirm that all data has been received; if not, the data is resent. TCP is a connection-oriented protocol.

Transmission Control Protocol/Internet Protocol (TCP/IP) The protocol suite developed by the U.S. Department of Defense in conjunction with the Internet. TCP/IP was designed as an internetworking protocol suite that could route information around network failures. Today, the protocol is the de-facto standard for communications on the Internet.

transmission media Physical cables and/or wireless technology across which computers communicate.

Transport layer Layer four of the OSI model, responsible for ensuring that the data packet created in the Session layer was received error-free. If necessary, the Transport layer also changes the length of messages for transport up or down the remaining layers. See also *Open Systems Interconnect.*

Trivial File Transfer Protocol (TFTP) A protocol similar to FTP that does not provide the security features of FTP. See also *File Transfer Protocol.*

Trusted Computer System Evaluation Criteria (TCSEC) Evaluation criteria released by the NCSC in 1983. TCSEC defines the standard parameters of a trusted computer in several classes, ranked by letter and number. TCSEC is referred to as the Orange Book. See also *National Computing Security Center.*

Trusted Network Interpretation Environmental Guideline (TNIEG) Evaluation criteria released by the NCSC that defines the certification criteria for trusted networks. TNIEG is referred to as the Red Book. See also *National Computer Security Center.*

T-series connections A series of digital connections leased from the telephone company. Each T-series connection is rated with a number based on speed. T-1 and T-3 are the most popular.

TTL See *time to live.*

twisted-pair cable A type of network transmission medium that contains pairs of color-coded, insulated copper wires that are twisted around each other. A twisted-pair cable consists of one or more twisted pairs in a common jacket.

UDP See *User Datagram Protocol.*

Uniform Resource Locator (URL) One way of identifying a document on the Internet. A URL consists of the protocol that is used to access the document and the domain name or IP address of the host that holds the document (http://www.sybex.com, for example).

uninterruptible power supply (UPS) A natural line conditioner that uses a battery and power inverter to run the computer equipment that plugs into it. The battery charger continuously charges the battery. The battery charger is the only thing that runs off line voltage. During a power problem, the battery charger stops operating, and the equipment continues to run off the battery.

Unix A 32-bit, multitasking operating system developed in the 1960s for use on mainframes and minicomputers.

unshielded twisted-pair cable Twisted-pair cable that consists of twisted pairs of copper wire with a simple plastic casing. Because no shielding is used in this cable, it is very susceptible to EMI, RFI, and other types of interference. See also *electromagnetic interference* and *radio-frequency interference*.

UPS See *uninterruptible power supply*.

URL See *Uniform Resource Locator*.

User Datagram Protocol (UDP) A protocol at the Host-to-Host layer of the DoD networking model, which corresponds to the Transport layer of the OSI model. Packets are divided into segments, given numbers, sent randomly, and put back together at the receiving end. UDP is a connectionless protocol. See also *connectionless protocol* and *Open Systems Interconnect*.

user-level security A type of network in which user accounts can read, write, change, and take ownership of files. Rights are assigned to user accounts, and each user knows only his or her own username and password, making this method the preferred method of securing files.

User Manager for Domains The Windows NT utility that manages all user accounts, groups, and policies for a Windows NT domain.

Utility NLM An NLM that is not a LAN driver, disk driver, name-space module, or platform-support module (for example, MONITOR.NLM or INSTALL.NLM). See also *NetWare Loadable Module*.

version conflict   The result of new software or patches that conflict with other installed products.

Virtual Private Network (VPN)   A network technology that uses the public Internet as a backbone for a private interconnection (network) between locations.

virus   A program intended to damage a computer system. Sophisticated viruses encrypt and hide in a computer, and may not appear until the user performs a certain action or until a certain date arrives. See also *antivirus*.

virus engine   The core program that runs the virus-scanning process.

volume   A logical way of organizing disk space into usable sections.

VPN   See *Virtual Private Network*.

WAN   See *wide area network*.

warm site backup   An offsite backup system that has the same systems as the primary system, but not the most current data. The system is offsite to reduce the chance that both the primary and backup systems will go down or be destroyed at the same time.

Web server   A server that holds and delivers Web pages and other Web content, using the HTTP protocol. See also *Hypertext Transfer Protocol*.

wide area network (WAN)   A network that crosses local, regional, and international boundaries.

Win16 Application (Win16 Subsystem)   A feature of Windows NT that can run almost any 16-bit Windows application, provided that the application conforms to the Microsoft standards for writing Windows 3.*x* applications.

Win32 Application (Win32 Subsystem)   A feature of Windows NT that can run 32-bit applications designed for Windows 95/98 and Windows NT.

Windows Internet Name Service (WINS)   A Windows NT service that dynamically associates the NetBIOS name of a host with a TCP/IP address. See also *Network Basic Input/Output System*.

Windows NT A 32-bit network operating system, developed by Microsoft, that uses centralized security, server networking services, and a broad range of utilities. See also *Windows NT 3.51* and *Windows NT 4*.

Windows NT 3.51 The version of Windows NT based on the "look and feel" of Windows 3.*x*. See also *Windows NT*.

Windows NT 4 The version of Windows NT based on the "look and feel" of Windows 95/98. See also *Windows NT*.

Windows NT Service A type of Windows program (a file with either an .EXE or a .DLL extension) that is loaded automatically by the server or manually by the administrator.

winipcfg The IP configuration utility for Windows 95/98 that displays the current TCP/IP configuration of a workstation.

WinNuke A Windows-based attack that affects only computers running Windows NT 3.51 or 4. WinNuke is caused by the way that the Windows NT TCP/IP stack handles bad data in the TCP header. Instead of returning an error code or rejecting the bad data, it sends Windows NT to the Blue Screen of Death (BSOD). Figuratively speaking, the attack "nukes" the computer.

WINS See *Windows Internet Name Service*.

workgroup A specific group of users or network devices, organized by job function or proximity to share resources.

World Wide Web (WWW) A collection of HTTP servers running on the Internet. The Web supports the use of documents formatted with HTML. See also *Hypertext Markup Language* and *Hypertext Transfer Protocol*.

worms A type of network attack that is similar to a virus. Worms, however, propagate themselves over a network. See also *virus*.

X Window A graphical user interface (GUI) developed for use with the various flavors of Unix.

Z.E.N.works Workstation-management software for NetWare. A light (scaled-down) version is included in NetWare 5.*x*.

Index

Note to the Reader: In this index, **boldfaced** page numbers refer to primary discussions of the topic; *italics* page numbers refer to figures.

Symbols & Numbers

(pound sign), for hosts file comments, 295
5-4-3 rule, 56
10Base2 cable, specifications, 25
10Base5 cable, specifications, 25
10BaseT cable, *297*
    crossover cable, *298*
    and RJ-45 connector, 198
    specifications, 25
68-pin SCSI connector, *192*, 192
100Base T4 cable, specifications, 25
100BaseFX cable, specifications, 26
100BaseTX cable, specifications, 26
100BaseVG cable, specifications, 26
802.2 standard, **70**
802.3 standard, **70–71**
802.4 standard, **71**
802.5 standard, **71**

A

ABEND.LOG file, 289
Access Control List (ACL), 174
accounts, for network access, **185–186**
acknowledgment of packet transmission, 91
ACL (Access Control List), 174
active hubs, **55–56**
administration. *See* change-control system
administrative accounts, **185–186**
administrative utilities, **231**
air quality, as environmental factor, 189
analog connections, 156, 197, *197*
antivirus procedures, 256
apparent network problem, 267
    study questions, 270–271
application filtering, by firewall, 175
Application layer (OSI), 21
    FTP in, 135–136
    Telnet in, 139
application log, 289
applications
    failures, 285

    patches, fixes, and upgrades, 250
    removing unnecessary components, **221–222**
    virus-protection, 256
applications, testing functionality, 229
archive attribute, 253
ARP (Address Resolution Protocol), **133**, *134*
    study questions, 140
automatic mode for DHCP servers, 105

B

backbone, **9**, *9*
backups
    multigeneration tape rotations, **220–221**, *221*
    of network, **251–256**
    on tape, **17–18**
    of workstation, **216–221**
        folder replication, **219–221**
        magnetic disks, **218**
        optical discs and CD-ROMs, **218**
        removable hard drives, **219**
        study questions, 234–235
        on tape, **217**
bandwidth, **30–31**
baseband, **30**
Basic Rate Interface (BRI), 154
Bearer (B) channel, 154
BGP (Border Gateway Protocol), 83
black box, 174
BNC connector, 22, **27**, *27*
Border Gateway Protocol (BGP), 83
bounded medium, **21–24**
    distance limitations, 24, *25*
    study questions, 38–39
    UTP as preferred, 23
BRI (Basic Rate Interface), 154
bridges, *69*, **69–70**
    study questions, 73
bridging routers, **81–82**
broadband, **31**
broadcast, of routing table, 84
brouters, **81–82**, 196
bus topology, *7*, 7

C

cable, 30
    coaxial, **21–22**, *22*
    distance limitations, 24, *25*
    installation issues, **196–199**

analog/digital signaling, **197**, *197*
patch cables and cable length, **198–199**
RJ-45 connectors, **198**
study questions, 203
study questions, 38–39
UTP as preferred, 23
CAPTURE command (NetWare), 227
Carrier Sense Multiple Access with Collision Detection (CSMA/CD), 70
CD-ROMs
for backup, **218**
vendor support, **291–292**
Centronics-50 SCSI connector, *192*, 192
Challenge-Handshake Authentication Protocol (CHAP), 151
change-control system
drive mapping, **224–226**
local changes with adverse network effects, **222–224**
network administration concepts, **230–232**
permissions, **229–230**
printer port capture, **226–228**
removing unnecessary software components, **221–222**
sample test, 240–245
study questions, 233–239
system return to original state, **215–216**
test objectives, 210–211
verifying equipment functionality, **229**
verifying functionality, **228–229**
workstation backups, **216–221**
workstation baseline documentation, 214
CHAP (Challenge-Handshake Authentication Protocol), 151
circuit filtering, by firewall, 175
class of IP address, 110, 111
cleaning tapes, 256
client reservation, 105
client-server network, 29
user-level security for, 172
clients, 29. *See also* workstation
for NetWare, 10
coaxial cable, **21–22**, 22
collision, 70
color, of UTP cable wires, 198
com domain, 108
COM port
IRQ and I/O address, 53
for modem, **159–160**
computers
placement of, 190
roles in networks, **28–31**
conflicts
avoiding when installing network interface card, 53
in MAC addresses, 72

connection-oriented transmissions, **91–92**
connectionless transmissions, 92
connections, 30
connectors, **24**, **26–27**
CONSOLE.LOG file, 289
copying files, FTP for, **135–136**
critical errors, 269
crossover cable, **297–298**
crosstalk, 22
CSMA/CD (Carrier Sense Multiple Access with Collision Detection), 70

D

Data (D) channel, 154
Data Link layer (OSI), 20
ARP (Address Resolution Protocol) and, 133
bridges, *69*, **69–70**
MAC addresses, 72
Point to Point Protocol (PPP) and, 151
sample test, 75–77
SLIP (Serial Line Internet Protocol) and, 152
study questions, 73–74
test objectives, 68
data transmission, encryption before, **173–174**
DB ports, 191
default gateways, **84**
study questions, 85
and TCP/IP, **104**, **114–115**
default ports for TCP/IP, 112
Device Manager (Windows), to check modem configuration, 158
DHCP (Dynamic Host Configuration Protocol), **104–105**
configuration, 116
diagnostics
for network interface card, **53–54**
running, 296
dial-up networking, **157–160**
study questions, 162–163
dictionaries, and password selection, 173
differential backup, 18, 253, *254*
digital signal, 197, *197*
DIP switches, for modem configuration, 158
disabled user accounts, 296
disaster recovery, 13, 251
tape backup for, **17–18**
disk drives, mapping, **224–226**
DMA (Direct Memory Access) channel, Plug and Play assignment for network interface card, 52

DNS (Domain Name System), 93, **105**
   problem solving, **294**
   workstation configuration for, **114**
documentation
   support, 249–250
      study questions, 258
   of workstation baseline, **214**
Domain Name System (DNS), 93, **105**
   problem solving, **294**
   workstation configuration for, **114**
down status, 293
drive mapping
   NetWare (Novell), **225–226**
   study questions, 236–237
   Unix, **226**
   Windows (Microsoft), **224–225**
drivers, removing unneeded, 222
dumb hub, 55
dumping image to workstation, 215
duplex communications, **28**
duplexing, **16–17**, *17*
dust, 189
dynamic assignment of TCP/IP addressing information, 105
Dynamic Host Configuration Protocol (DHCP), **104–105**
   configuration, **116**
dynamic protocols, used by routers, 83
dynamic route selection, 83

E

echo program, for network interface card diagnostics, 54
echoes, 54
edu domain, 108
EEPROM (Electronically Erasable Programmable Read-Only Memory), **52**
EGP (Exterior Gateway Protocol), 83
EIA/TIA standards, 198
electric power, UPS (Uninterruptible Power Supply) to manage, 193–194
electromagnetic interference (EMI), 22
   device location and, 190
Electronic Industries Association, 198
Electronically Erasable Programmable Read-Only Memory (EEPROM), **52**
electrostatic discharge (ESD), 292–293
   humidity and, 189
EMI (electromagnetic interference), 22
   device location and, 190
   STP (shielded twisted-pair cable) and, 23

encryption, **173–174**
   study questions, 177
environmental factors
   and network equipment, 189
   and problem determination, **292–293**
   study questions, 201
error logs, **289–290**
ESD (electrostatic discharge), 292–293
   humidity and, 189
Ethernet, 70
   10BaseT cable, *297*
      crossover cable, *298*
expiration of passwords, 173, 296
Explorer (Windows)
   to map network drives, 225
   for printer port capture, 227
Exterior Gateway Protocol (EGP), 83
external diagnostics, for network interface card, 54
external modem
   COM port settings, 160
   and UART chips, 159
external SCSI connectors, **192**, *192*

F

fault tolerance, **13–18**
   duplexing, **16–17**, *17*
   mirroring, **14**, *14*
   striping, **14–16**, *15*
   study questions, 35–36
Federal Communications Commission (FCC), 156
feedback, **287**
fiber-optic cable, **22**, *23*, 199
File Transfer Protocol (FTP), **107**, **135–136**
   default port, 112
   study questions, 141
firewalls, **174–175**
   study questions, 177–178
fixes
   to network, **256**
   to software, **250**
floppy disks, for backup, 218
fluorescent lights, EMI (electromagnetic interference) from, 190
folder replication, **219–221**
fox, 299
FTP (File Transfer Protocol), **107**, **135–136**
   default port, 112
   study questions, 141

G

gateways, **31**
 default, **84**
  study questions, 85
 and TCP/IP, **104**, **114–115**
geographical domains, 108–109
Ghost, 215
gov domain, 108
grandfather, father and son method of tape rotation, 220–221, *221*

H

half duplexing, 28
handholding, 268
hard drives, removable, **219**
hardware failures, 285
hardware loopback, *298*, **298–299**
heat, as environmental factor, 189
high availability, 13
 study questions, 35–36
 volumes and, **18**, *19*
high-level fault tolerance, from switching hubs, 56
host, 30
 remote connectivity requirements, 157
host files, **106**
host name, configuration, 116
hosts file, 106
 problem solving, **295**
hot-pluggable drives, 219
hound, 299
HTML (Hypertext Markup Language), 107
HTTP (Hypertext Transfer Protocol), **107**
 default port, 112
hubs, **55**, **55–56**, **194–195**
 link lights on, 288
 maximum distance of workstations to, 198
 placement of, 190
 in star topology, 7
humidity, 189
Hypertext Markup Language (HTML), 107
Hypertext Transfer Protocol (HTTP), 107
 default port, 112

I

I/O address
 Plug and Play assignment for network interface card, 52
 for ports, 53
ICMP (Internet Control Message Protocol), 136
IEEE (Institute for Electrical and Electronics Engineers)
 standards, **70–71**
  study questions, 73–74
image of workstation, 215
incremental backup, **18**, **253–254**, *255*
information transfer, 268
installing internal modem, 157–158
installing network
 cabling, **196–199**
 environmental factors, **188–191**
  computer equipment, 190
  device location, 190
  room conditions, **188–189**
 error messages, 191
 network elements, **191–196**
  brouters, **196**
  external SCSI connectors, **192**, *192*
  hubs, **194–195**
  media filters, **194**
  NIC (network interface card), 194
  patch panels, **194**
  peripheral ports, 191
  peripherals, **193**
  print servers, **193**
  routers, **195**, *195*, **196**
  switches, **194–195**, *195*
  UPS (Uninterruptible Power Supply), **193–194**
 preinstallation, **185–188**
  accounts, **185–186**
  IP address, 187
  IP configuration, 187
  passwords, 186
  protocols, 188
  standard operating procedures, 187
 sample test, 204–208
 study questions, 200–203
 test objectives, 184
Institute for Electrical and Electronics Engineers (IEEE)
 standards, **70–71**
  study questions, 73–74
int domain, 108
Integrated IS-IS (Integrated Intermediate System to Intermediate System), 83

Integrated Services Digital Network (ISDN), **154–155**
intelligent hubs, **56**
internal diagnostics, for network interface card, 53–54
internal modem, COM port settings, 160
Internet Control Message Protocol (ICMP), 136
Internet Domain Name, configuration, **116**
Internet domains, hierarchy, **108–109**
Internet Engineering Task Force, 111
Internet Protocol (IP), 108
Internet, TCP/IP and, 12, 103
Internetwork Packet Exchange/Sequenced Packet Exchange) protocol stack (IPX/SPX), **12**
internetworks, moving data between, 81
IP address, 110
    mapping to MAC address, 133
    when installing network, **187**
    for workstation, **113–114**
IP (Internet Protocol), 108
IP proxy, **113**
    configuration, **115**
ipconfig/winipcfg, **137**, *138*
    study questions, 142
IPX protocol, 12
IPX/SPX (Internetwork Packet Exchange/Sequenced Packet Exchange)
    packet transfer across TCP/IP WAN, 153
    protocol stack, **12**, 82
Irix, 11
IRQ
    for COM ports, 160
    Plug and Play assignment for network interface card, 52
    for ports, 53
ISDN (Integrated Services Digital Network), **154–155**

J

Jaz drives, 218
jumpers
    for modem configuration, 158
    for network interface card configuration, 53

K

key for encryption, 173
knowledge bases, **291**

L

LAN (local area network), **28**
    infrastructure troubleshooting, 54
    IP proxy to translate between Internet and, 113
    problem identification, 282–283
leasing addresses to client computer, 105
link lights, **288**
Linus, 11
LLC bridge, **70**
lmhosts file, 105–106
local resources, impact of use on network, **224**
location when installing network device, **190**
logical trouble indicators, 287–290
login accounts, **231**
logon, problems with, **296**
loopback plug, 54
lpr command (Unix), **228**
LPT port, IRQ and I/O address, 53
LS-120 drives, 218

M

MAC addresses, **72**
    for Dynamic Host Configuration Protocol, 105
    mapping TCP/IP addresses to, 133
    study questions, 74
MAC bridge, 70
Macintosh computers, DB-25 SCSI connector for, *192*, 192
magnetic disks, for backup, **218**
maintenance. *See* network maintenance
maintenance accounts, 185
MAN (metropolitan area network), **28**
manufacturers, MAC address assignment by, 72
Manufacturing Automation Protocol (MAP), 71
MAP command (NetWare), **224**
MAP (Manufacturing Automation Protocol), 71
mapping. *See* drive mapping
MAUs (multistation access units), 23, **57**
maximum port speed, **159**
media filters, **194**
mesh topology, **8**, *8*
metropolitan area network (MAN), 28
Microsoft. *See also* Windows (Microsoft); Windows NT
    TechNet CD, 292
mil domain, 108
modem, **157–160**, *158*
    COM port settings, **159–160**
    maximum port speed and, **159**

MONITOR.NLM, 290
monitors, 193
mount command (Unix), 226
moving files, FTP for, **135–136**
Multistation Access Unit (MAU), 23, **57**
multitasking, in Windows NT, 11

N

name resolution, **92–93**
    DNS (Domain Name System) for, 93
    host files for, **106**
    study questions, 95
    WINS (Windows Internet Name Service) for, **105–106**
NBTSTAT (NetBIOS-TCP/IP Statistics), **134**, *134*
    study questions, 140–141
NDS (Network Directory Service), 10, 93
net domain, 108
net use command, 225, 227
NetBEUI (NetBIOS Extended User Interface) protocol, **13**
    packet transfer across TCP/IP WAN, 153
NetBIOS computer names, 105
NetBIOS Extended User Interface protocol (NetBEUI), **13**
    packet transfer across TCP/IP WAN, 153
NETSTAT, **135**, *135*
NetWare Administrator, 231
NetWare Loadable Modules (NLMs), 10
NetWare (Novell), **10**
    administration rights, 230
    administrative accounts, 186
    drive mapping, **225–226**
    error logs, 289
    MONITOR.NLM, 290
    printer port capture in, **227**
    user-level security for, 172
network
    administration. *See* change-control system
    basic structure, **5–10**
        hierarchy, **9–10**
        physical topology, **5–8**, *6*
        sample test, 41–47
        study questions, 32–33
    categories, **28**
    computer roles in, **28–31**
    local changes with adverse effects, **222–224**
        study questions, 235–236
network address translation, 113
Network control panel (Windows), 114
Network Directory Service (NDS), 10

network elements, **27–31**
    study questions, 39–40
    testing functionality, 228–229
network interface card (NIC), 30, 194
    configuration, **51–53**
        EEPROM, **52**
        jumpers, **53**
        Plug and Play (PNP), **51–52**
    crossover cable to connect, 297
    default setting adjustments, **53**
    diagnostics, **53–54**
    for firewall, 174
    hardware loopback to test, **298–299**
    link lights on, 288
Network layer (OSI), 20
    routing, **81–84**
    sample test, 86–88
    study questions, 85
    test objectives, 80
network maintenance, 249
    antivirus procedures, **256–257**
    backups of network, **251–256**
        media storage practices, **255–256**
    patches and fixes, **256**
    sample test, 260–263
    support documentation, **249–250**
    test objectives, 248
Network Neighborhood
    to map network drives, 225
    for printer port capture, 227
network portion of IP address, 110
    classes for, **110–111**
network profile, 232
network redirection, 224
network tools
    crossover cable, **297–298**
    hardware loopback, *298*, **298–299**
    selecting, **300**
    study questions, 307–308
    tone generator and tone locator, **299**, *300*
New Technology directory Services (NTDS), 11
New Technology File System (NTFS), 11
NIC (network interface card), 30, 194. *See also* network interface card (NIC)
NLMs (NetWare Loadable Modules), 10
node in network, 7
node portion of IP address, 110
noise, active hubs and, 56
noncritical errrors, 269
nonparity striping, 14

Novell NetWare, 10. *See also* NetWare (Novell)
Novell, Support Connection CD, 292
NTDS (New Technology directory Services), 11
NTFS (New Technology File System), 11
NTTP, default port, 112

O

octet, 110
Open Shortest Path First (OSPF), 83
Open System Interconnection (OSI) model, **19–21**
    layers, functions and protocols, 20–21
    study questions, 36–38
operating systems, **10–11**
    administrative accounts, 230
    compatibility with TCP/IP, 103
    Novell NetWare, **10**
    study questions, 33
    Unix, **11**
    Windows NT, **10–11**
optical discs, for backup, **218**
org domain, 108
organizational domain, 108
OSI (Open System Interconnection) model, **19–21**
    layers functions and protocols, 20–21
    study questions, 36–38
OSPF (Open Shortest Path First), 83

P

packet filtering, by firewall, 174
PAP (Password Authentication Protocol), 151
parity striping, 14, 15, *16*
passive hubs, **55**
Password Authentication Protocol (PAP), 151
passwords, **172–173**
    expired, 296
    policy, 173
    for shared resources, 172
    study questions, 176–177
    when installing network, **186**
patch cables
    and cable length, **198–199**
    faults, **293**
patch panels, **194**
patches
    to network, **256**
    to software, **250**

peer-to-peer network, 29
    server changes on, 222–224
    share-level security for, 172
per-port management, by switching hubs, 56
per-port switching, 56
performance monitors, **290**
peripheral ports, **191**
peripherals, **193**
permissions for administration, 229–230
    study questions, 238
phone connector (RJ-11), 26
physical address, 72. *See also* MAC addresses
Physical layer (OSI), 20, **51–54**
    network interface card (NIC), configuration, 51–53
    networking components, 54–57
    sample test, 62–65
    SLIP (Serial Line Internet Protocol) and, 152
    study questions, 58–60
    test objectives, 50
physical network topology, **5–8**, *6*
physical trouble indicators, 287–290
    study questions, 303–304
Ping (Packet Internet Groper), **136**, *137*
    study questions, 141
Plug and Play (PNP), **51–52**
    and modem install, 158
Point to Point Protocol (PPP), **151**
Point to Point Tunneling Protocol (PPTP), *153*, *153*, *154*
policies, **232**
pool of TCP/IP addresses, 105
POP3 (Post Office Protocol 3), **107**
    default port, 112
port address, 110
port numbering, for TCP/IP, **111–112**
ports. *See also* printer port capture
    peripheral, **191**
Post Office Protocol 3 (POP3), **107**
    default port, 112
power lights, **288**
PPP (Point to Point Protocol), **151**
PPTP (Point to Point Tunneling Protocol), *153*, *153*, *154*
Presentation layer (OSI), 21
    FTP in, 135–136
    Telnet in, 139
Primary Rate Interface (PRI), 154
print servers, **193**
printer port capture, **226–228**
    in NetWare, **227**
    study questions, 237
    in Unix, **228**
    in Windows, **227**

prioritizing multiple problems, **269**
    study questions, 271–272
problem solving. *See also* troubleshooting network
    determining nature of problem, 267–269
    handholding, 268
    information transfer in, 268
    prioritizing multiple problems, 269
    sample test, 273–276
    study questions, 270–272
    technical service, **269**
    test objectives, 266
procedures, **232**
profiles, **232**
protocol analyzers, 296
protocols, **12–13**
    diagnosing which are running, 135
    removing unneeded, 222
    routable, **82–83**
    study questions, 3431
    when installing network, **188**
Public Switched Telephone Network (PSTN), **156**

Q

queues, 193

R

radio-frequency interference (RFI), device location and, 190
RAID (Redundant Array of Inexpensive Drives), 13, 14, 15
remote connectivity. *See also* dial-up networking
    ISDN (Integrated Services Digital Network), **154–155**
    PPP (Point to Point Protocol), **151**
    PPTP (Point to Point Tunneling Protocol), **153**, *153*, *154*
    PSTN (Public Switched Telephone Network), **156**
    requirements, **157**
    sample test, 164–167
    SLIP (Serial Line Internet Protocol), **152**
    study questions, 161–162
    test objectives, 150
removable hard drives, **219**
repeaters, 57
replication of folders, **219–221**
resistor, in bus topology, 7
restoring backup files after failure
    from differential backup, 253
    from incremental backup, 254
RFI (radio-frequency interference), device location and, 190
rights, 229, **232**

ring topology, **5–6**, *6*
RIP (Routing Information Protocol), 83
RJ-11 connector, 26
RJ-45 connector, 24, **26**, *26*, **198**
rotating backup tapes, 217
    multigeneration, **220–221**, *221*
routable protocols, **82–83**
routers, 30, **81**, *82*, **195**, *195*, *196*
    dynamic route selection, **83**
    as gateways, 84
    placement of, 190
    in star topology, 7
    static route selection, **84**
routing, **81–84**
    study questions, 85
    tracert to track, **138**, *139*
Routing Information Protocol (RIP), 83
routing table, 81
    for route selection, 83
    updating for static route selection, 84
Routing Table Maintenance (RTMP), 83

S

sample test, 143–147, 320–340
    change-control system, 240–245
    Data Link layer (OSI), 75–77
    network basic structure, 41–47
    Network layer (OSI), 86–88
    network maintenance, 260–263
    Physical layer (OSI), **62–65**
    security, 179–181
    TCP/IP (Transmission Control Protocol/Internet Protocol), 123–129
    TCP/IP utilities, 143–147
    Transport layer (OSI), 96–99
    troubleshooting network, 309–317
SAP (Service Advertisement Protocol), 93
scanning, for viruses, **256**
SCSI connectors, external, **192**, *192*
security
    encryption, **173–174**
    firewalls, **174–175**
    network models, **171–172**
    passwords, **172–173**
    sample test, 179–181
    study questions, 176–178
    test objectives, 170
security log, 289

segments in network, 9, **10**
semipermanent mode, 105
Sequenced Packet Exchange (SPX), 12
Serial Line Internet Protocol (SLIP), 151, **152**
serial ports, maximum port speed, **159**
server, **29**
    and backup strategy, 216
    status check, 293–294
Service Advertisement Protocol (SAP), 93
service-provider-initiated name resolution, **93**
service-requester-initiated name resolution, **93**
Session layer (OSI), 21
    FTP in, 135
    Telnet in, 139
share-level security, **172**
shared files, 222–223
    overwritten, **223–224**
shares, 224
shielded twisted-pair cable (STP), 23, *24*
Shortest Path First (SPF), 83
signal, active hubs to boost, 55
Simple Mail Transfer Protocol (SMTP), **107**
    default port, 112
Simple Network Management Protocol (SNMP), **107**
    active hubs and, 55
SLIP (Serial Line Internet Protocol), 151, **152**
SMTP (Simple Mail Transfer Protocol), **107**
    default port, 112
SNMP (Simple Network Management Protocol), **107**
    active hubs and, 55
software
    failures, 285
    patches, fixes, and upgrades, **250**
    removing unnecessary components, **221–222**
    testing functionality, 229
    virus-protection, 256
Software Pursuits, SureSync, 219
Solaris, 11
SOPs (standard operating procedures), **187**
SPF (Shortest Path First), 83
spoolers, 193
SPX (Sequenced Packet Exchange), 12
standard backup procedures, **251–252**
standard operating procedures (SOPs), **187**
star topology, 7, *8*
static assignment of TCP/IP addressing information, 104–105
static route selection, **84**
STP (shielded twisted-pair cable), 23, *24*
study questions, 140–142
    change-control system, 233–239
    Data Link layer (OSI), **73–74**

dial-up networking, 162–163
environmental factors, 201
installing network, 200–203
network maintenance, 258–259
Physical layer (OSI), 58–60
problem solving, 270–272
remote connectivity, 161–162
routing, 85
security, 176–178
TCP/IP (Transmission Control Protocol/Internet Protocol), 117–122
TCP/IP utilities, 140–142
Transport layer (OSI), 94–95
troubleshooting network, 301–308
subnet mask, 110–111
    DHCP for automatic assignment, 104
    for workstation, **113–114**
subnetworks, **84**
support documentation, **249–250**
    study questions, 258
SureSync, 219
switches, **194–195**, *195*
    in star topology, 7
switching hubs, **56**
synchronization, in folder replication, 220
SYSCON, 231
SYS$LOG.ERR file, 289
system log, 289

T

tape backup, **17–18**
    storage practices, **255–256**
tape drives, cleaning, 256
TCP/IP Protocol Properties dialog box (Windows), 114
TCP/IP (Transmission Control Protocol/Internet Protocol), 12, 82
    addressing, **110–112**
        network classes, 110–111
        port numbering, **111–112**
    configuration, **112–116**
        IP proxy, **113**
        workstation parameters, **113–116**
    domain server hierarchies, **108–109**
    fundamentals, **103–109**
    individual protocols, **106–108**
    sample test, 123–129
    study questions, 117–122
    test objectives, 102

TCP/IP utilities
    ARP (Address Resolution Protocol), **133**, *134*
    FTP (File Transfer Protocol), **135–136**
    ipconfig/winipcfg, **137**, *138*
    NBTSTAT (NetBIOS-TCP/IP Statistics), **134**, *134*
    NETSTAT, **135**, *135*
    Ping (Packet Internet Groper), **136**, *137*
    sample test, 143–147
    study questions, 140–142
    Telnet, **139**
    test objectives, 132
    tracert (trace route) utility, **138**, *139*
TCP (Transmission Control Protocol), 91, 106
technical support, by telephone, **291**
Telecommunications Industries Association, 198
telephone network, 156
telephone technical support, **291**
Telnet, **139**
    default port, 112
    study questions, 142
terminal adapter for ISDN, 155
terminal emulation, 139
terminator, in bus topology, 7
test accounts, **186**
test objectives, 132
    basics, 2–3
    change-control system, 210–211
    Data Link layer (OSI), 68
    installing network, 184
    Network layer (OSI), 80
    network maintenance, 248
    Physical layer (OSI), 50
    problem solving, 266
    remote connectivity, 150
    security, 170
    TCP/IP (Transmission Control Protocol/Internet Protocol), 102
    TCP/IP utilities, 132
    Transport layer (OSI), 90
    troubleshooting network, 278–280
testing. *See also* sample test
token passing, 71
Token Ring networking technology, 71
tone generator, **299**, *300*
    warning, 300
tone locator, **299**, *300*
topology of network, 5–8, 6
tracert (trace route) utility, **138**, *139*
    study questions, 142
training users, **268**

transceivers, 57
Transmission Control Protocol/Internet Protocol (TCP/IP), **12**
Transmission Control Protocol (TCP), 106
Transport layer (OSI), 20
    connection-oriented transmissions, **91–92**
    connectionless transmissions, **92**
    name resolution, **92–93**
    sample test, 96–99
    study questions, 94–95
    test objectives, 90
troubleshooting network
    common resources, 290–292
        telephone technical support, **291**
        vendor support CDs, **291–292**
        World Wide Web, **291**
    physical and logical trouble indicators, **287–290**
    Ping to test for host connection, 136
    problem determination, 292–296
        abnormal physical conditions, **292–293**
        configuration, **294–295**
        patch cable faults, **293**
        running diagnostics, **296**
        server status check, **293–294**
        user accounts validation, **296**
        virus check, **295**
    problem identification, **281–283**
    sample test, 309–317
    standard methods, 282
    study questions, 301–308
    systematic process, 283–287
        documentation of solution, **286**
        feedback, **287**
        formulating correction, **285**
        implementing correction, **286**
        isolating cause, **285**
        issue identification, 284
        problem re-creation, 284
        testing solution, **286**
    test objectives, 278–280
    user problems vs. system problem, **287**
twisted-pair cable, **23–24**, *24*

U

UART (Universal Asynchronous Receiver/Transmitter) chips, 159
UDP (User Datagram Protocol), 92, **107**
UNC (Universal Naming Convention), 224–225

Uninterruptible Power Supply (UPS), **193–194**
Universal Asynchronous Receiver/Transmitter (UART) chips, 159
Universal Naming Convention (UNC), **224–225**
Unix, **11**
    administrative accounts, 186
    drive mapping, **226**
    printer port capture, **228**
unshielded twisted-pair cable (UTP), 23, *25*, **196–199**
    points of failure on network using, 54
up status, 293
updating virus lists, 256
upgrades to software, **250**
upgrading workstation, returning to original state after, 215
UPS (Uninterruptible Power Supply), **193–194**
user accounts, 231
    to test network, 186
    validation, **296**
User Datagram Protocol (UDP), 92, **107**
user-level security, **172**
User Manager (Windows NT), 231
user training, **268**
username, 231
UTP (unshielded twisted-pair cable), 23, *25*, **196–199**

V

VBRUNxxx.DLL, 223
vendor support CDs, **291–292**
version conflicts, impact on network, **222–223**
virus, 256, **295**
virus lists, 256
Visual Basic Runtime library, 223
volumes, high availability and, *19*

W

WAN (wide area network), **28**, *29*
    problem identification, **282–283**
Windows DLLs, 222
    overwritten, **223–224**
Windows Internet Name Service (WINS), **105–106**
    problem solving, **294–295**
Windows (Microsoft)
    drive mapping, **224–225**
    printer port capture, **227**
    server changes on peer-to-peer networks, **222–224**
    TCP/IP concepts for, **104–106**
Windows NT, **10–11**

administration rights, 230
administrative accounts, 186
drive mapping, **224–225**
error logs, 289
folder replication, 219
Performance Monitor, 290
printer port capture, **227**
server changes on peer-to-peer networks, 222–224
user-level security for, 172
WINS (Windows Internet Name Service), 93, **105–106**
    configuration, **115**
    problem solving, **294–295**
workgroup hub, 55
workgroup, problem identification, **282–283**
workstation, **29**
    backups, **216–221**
        folder replication, **219–221**
        magnetic disks, **218**
        optical discs and CD-ROMs, **218**
        removable hard drives, **219**
        study questions, 234–235
        on tape, **217**
    baseline documentation, **214**
    displaying current connections, 135
    image of, 215
    maximum distance to hub, 198
    problem identification, **282–283**
    remote connectivity requirements, **157**
    removing unnecessary software components, **221–222**
    returning to original state after upgrade, 215
    TCP/IP configuration parameters, **113–116**
World Wide Web, 107
    resources for troubleshooting, **291**

Z

Zip drives, 218

MCSE CORE REQUIREMENT STUDY GUIDES FROM NETWORK PRESS

Sybex's Network Press presents updated and expanded second editions of the definitive study guides for MCSE candidates.

MCSE: NETWORKING ESSENTIALS Study Guide, Second Edition
EXAM 70-058
James Chellis, Charles Perkins, Matthew Strebe
ISBN: 0-7821-2220-5
704pp; 7½" x 9"; Hardcover
$49.99

MCSE: NT WORKSTATION 4 Study Guide, Second Edition
EXAM 70-073
Charles Perkins, Matthew Strebe and James Chellis
ISBN: 0-7821-2223-X
784pp; 7½" x 9"; Hardcover
$49.99

MCSE: NT SERVER 4 Study Guide, Second Edition
EXAM 70-067
Matthew Strebe, Charles Perkins with James Chellis
ISBN: 0-7821-2222-1
832pp; 7½" x 9"; Hardcover
$49.99

MCSE: NT SERVER 4 IN THE ENTERPRISE Study Guide, Second Edition
EXAM 70-068
Lisa Donald with James Chellis
ISBN: 0-7821-2221-3
704pp; 7½" x 9"; Hardcover
$49.99

MCSE: WINDOWS 98 Study Guide
EXAM 70-098
Lance Mortensen, Rick Sawtell
ISBN: 0-7821-2373-2
800pp; 7½" x 9"; Hardcover
$49.99

A $50.00 SAVINGS!

MCSE Core Requirements Box Set
ISBN: 0-7821-2245-0
4 hardcover books;
3,024pp total; $149.96

Microsoft Certified Professional Approved Study Guide

NETWORK PRESS — SYBEX

STUDY GUIDES FOR THE MICROSOFT CERTIFIED SYSTEMS ENGINEER EXAMS

NETWARE® 5 CNE®
STUDY GUIDES FROM
NETWORK PRESS®

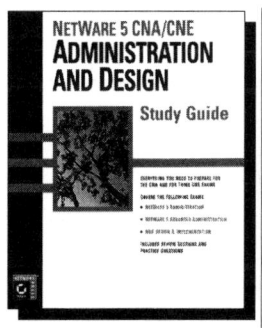

NetWare® 5 CNA℠/CNE®: Administration and Design Study Guide
ISBN: 0-7821-2387-2
864 pp.; 7½" X 9"
$44.99, Hardcover

Covers:

NetWare® 5 Administration (the CNA test)

NetWare® 5 Advanced Administration

NDS Design & Implementation

NetWare® 5 CNE®: Core Technologies Study Guide
ISBN: 0-7821-2389-9
512 pp.; 7½" X 9"
$44.99, Hardcover

Covers:

Networking Technologies

Service & Support

NetWare® 5 CNE®: Integrating Windows NT® Study Guide
ISBN: 0-7821-2388-0
448 pp.; 7½" X 9"
$39.99, Hardcover

Covers:

Integrating Windows® NT®

NetWare® 5 CNE®: Update to NetWare® 5 Study Guide
ISBN: 0-7821-2390-2
432 pp.; 7½" X 9"
$39.99, Hardcover

Covers:

NetWare® 4.11 to NetWare® 5 Update

www.sybex.com

Network+ Exam Objectives

Objective	% of Exam
Basic Knowledge	**16%**
Demonstrate understanding of basic network structure	
Identify the major network operating systems, the clients that best serve specific network operating systems, and the directory services	
Associate IPX, IP, and NetBEUI with their functions	
Define and explain terms related to fault tolerance and high availability	
Define the layers of the OSI model	
Describe the characteristics of networking media and connectors	
Identify the basic attributes, purpose, and function of network elements	
Physical Layer	**6%**
Given a scenario, select an appropriate course of action if a client workstation does not connect to the network after installing or replacing a network interface card	
Identify network components and the differences between them	
Data Link Layer	**5%**
Describe Data Link-layer concepts	
Network Layer	**5%**
Explain routing and Network-layer concepts	
Transport Layer	**4%**
Explain Transport-layer concepts	
TCP/IP Fundamentals	**12%**
Demonstrate knowledge of TCP/IP fundamentals	
Demonstrate knowledge of the fundamental concepts of TCP/IP addressing	
Demonstrate knowledge of TCP/IP configuration concepts	
TCP/IP Suite: Utilities	**8%**
Explain how and when to use TCP/IP utilities to test, validate, and troubleshoot IP connectivity	
Remote Connectivity	**5%**
Explain remote-connectivity concepts	
Specify elements of dial-up networking	
Security	**6%**
Identify good practices to ensure network security	
Implementing the Installation of the Network	**6%**
Demonstrate awareness that administrative and test accounts, passwords, IP addresses, IP configurations, relevant SOPs, etc., must be obtained prior to network implementation	

Exam objectives are subject to change at any time without notice and at CompTIA's sole discretion. Please visit CompTIA's Web site (www.comptia.org) for the most current exam-objectives listing.